MYTHS OF
RICH OF
& POOR

In Memory of
Robert F. Baker, Jr.

MYTHS OF RICH & POOR

Why We're Better Off Than We Think

W. Michael Cox

Richard Alm

BASIC
BOOKS

A Member of the Perseus Books Group

The informtion in Figure 1.3 and elsewhere regarding features found in automobiles is courtesy of *Ward's Automotive Reports*.

The views expressed with this book are those of the authors and should not be attributed to the Federal Reserve System or the Federal Reserve Bank of Dallas.

Published by Basic Books,
A Member of the Perseus Books Group

FIRST EDITION

Designed by Rachel Hegarty

A CIP catalog record for this book is available from the Library of Congress.
ISBN 0-465-04784-X

99 00 01 02 03 ❖/RRD 10 9 8 7 6 5 4 3 2 1

Contents

List of Tables and Figures　　　　　　　　　vi
Acknowledgments　　　　　　　　　　　　ix
Preface　　　　　　　　　　　　　　　　xi

Part One
**Myths About Income
and Living Standards**

1　Waking Up to Good Times　　　　　　3

2　New and Improved!　　　　　　　　23

3　Time for Symphonies and Softball　　53

4　By Our Own Bootstraps　　　　　　69

5　Still on Top of the World　　　　　　91

Part Two
Myths About Jobs

6　The Upside of Downsizing　　　　　111

7　Somebody Always Flipped Hamburgers　139

8　The Economy at Light Speed　　　　157

9　The Great American Growth Machine　179

Epilogue　　　　　　　　　　　　　　197
Notes　　　　　　　　　　　　　　　　203
Index　　　　　　　　　　　　　　　　249

List of Tables and Figures

Chapter 1
Waking Up to Good Times

Figure 1.1	Average Hourly Wages	5
Table 1.1	The World Through Rip's Eyes	7
Figure 1.2	New Homes: Bigger and Better	9
Figure 1.3	Better Equipped on the Highway	11
Table 1.2	Even the Poor Have More	15
Table 1.3	How People Spend Their Money	17
Figure 1.4	A Second Look at What We Earn: Per Capita Income, Total Compensation, and Hourly Wages, 1953–97	19
Table 1.4	Estimates of the Bias in Consumer Price Index Inflation	21

Chapter 2
New and Improved!

Table 2.1	The Modern Age's Bounty	26
Figure 2.1	Working Less for Our Daily Bread	41
Table 2.2	Time Is on Our Side: Work Time Required to Buy Various Products and Services	43

Chapter 3
Time for Symphonies and Softball

| Table 3.1 | Work Time | 55 |
| Table 3.2 | Less Work, More Leisure | 57 |

Chapter 4
By Our Own Bootstraps

Figure 4.1   Slicing Up the American Pie   70
Figure 4.2   A Caste Society?   71
Table 4.1   Moving On Up   73
Table 4.2   The Poor Are Getting Richer Faster   74
Figure 4.3   Income Mobility by Education:
                 Even Dropouts Earn More   75
Table 4.3   Living Standards on the Rise   76
Figure 4.4   A Second Opinion from the Treasury   77
Figure 4.5   The Steepening of Lifetime Earnings   84

Chapter 5
Still on Top of the World

Table 5.1   Per Capita Income,
                 Job Creation Among Nations   94
Table 5.2   Americans' Living Standards
                 Still Stand Out   97–98
Table 5.3   Balance of Payments,
                 by the Numbers   101
Figure 5.1   As Nations Grow Richer,
                 Economic Performance Converges   108

Chapter 6
The Upside of Downsizing

Table 6.1   Job Creation and Destruction, 1985–96   114
Table 6.2   Job Creation by Firm Size   115
Table 6.3   America's Top 30 Jobs Since 1900   118–119
Table 6.4   The Churn: Jobs Then, Jobs Now   120
Table 6.5   New Companies Rising to the Top   122
Figure 6.1   Railway Employment   125
Table 6.6   Technological Unemployment   127
Table 6.7   Dialing for Pennies   129
Table 6.8   More Output, Fewer Workers   130
Table 6.9   Less Equals More   131
Figure 6.2   Save Jobs on the Canals   134

Chapter 7
Somebody Always Flipped Hamburgers

Figure 7.1	America's Jobs (A) and Output (B) Move to Services	142
Table 7.1	A Snapshot of Where Americans Work	144
Figure 7.2	Growth Lies in Services	145
Figure 7.3	Hourly Earnings in Manufacturing and Services	147
Figure 7.4a	Higher Spending, More Services: Household Spending on Goods vs. Services, 1997	150
Figure 7.4b	Higher Spending, More Services: Per Capita Spending on Goods vs. Services, 1947–97	150
Figure 7.4c	Higher Spending, More Services: Per Capita Spending on Goods vs. Services, 1987	151
Figure 7.5	Relative Prices: Services vs. Goods	152
Figure 7.6	Higher-Paid Service Jobs Lead the Way	155

Chapter 8
The Economy at Light Speed

Table 8.1	Top 10 Inventions and Discoveries Since the Civil War	160
Figure 8.1	Spread of Products into American Households	162
Table 8.2a	Tools of the Ages	172
Table 8.2b	What's a Person to Do?	173
Table 8.3	It's Not the Industry, It's the Education	176–177

Chapter 9
The Great American Growth Machine

Figure 9.1	Maslow's Hierarchy of Needs	182
Figure 9.2	How Progress Happens	188

Acknowledgments

Writing a good-news book takes courage. Cutting through the dense thicket of economic cynicism, one is bound to encounter more than a few contentious creatures. That's why it helps to get support from talented and insightful people. We've received encouragement over the past five years from a variety of sources, most generously from Leo Linbeck, former Chairman of the Board of the Federal Reserve Bank of Dallas, and Robert McTeer, the Bank's President. At the outset and throughout the book's journey, Leo and Bob provided both inspiration and insight. We first presented our analysis of the U.S. economy in essays printed in the Dallas Fed's annual reports from 1992 to 1997. We're grateful for the bank's support on those projects.

Nick Gillespie, Robert Poole, and Virginia Postrel of the Reason Foundation helped us spread the optimistic message of this book. Our efforts were also helped by David Boaz, Edward Crane, and Stephen Moore of the Cato Foundation; John Goodman, Dorman Cordell, and Merrill Mathews at the National Center for Policy Analysis; editor Karl Zinsmeister with the American Enterprise Institute for Public Policy Research; and Greg Rehmke and Winston Elliott with the Free Enterprise Institute. Many others gave us reason to believe that what we had to say was important—through informal discussion or through an encouraging e-mail. The list includes economists Alan Meltzer of Carnegie Mellon University, Dwight Lee of the University of Georgia, Richard McKenzie of the University of California at Irvine, and Ed Rubenstein of The Hudson Institute; economists Larry Kudlow of American Skandia, John Rutledge of Rutledge and Co., and Steve Hanke of Johns Hopkins University; as well as author George Gilder and author and columnist Marilyn vos Savant.

Our work wouldn't have reached as many eyes and ears without the help and attention of the media. We owe a debt of gratitude to the newspapers, magazines, and broadcasters that delivered our message to all parts of the nation. You know who you are and we're extremely grateful. Always on hand for cogent consideration of this

Acknowledgments

book's issues were the staff members of the Dallas Fed, most notably Harvey Rosenblum, Mark Wynne, and Meredith Walker. Academic colleagues who were generous with their time include Roy Ruffin of the University of Houston and Nathan Balke and Gregg Huffman of Southern Methodist University. As first-time authors, new to this business, we also owe much to those who guided us through the process of writing a book—in particular, our literary agent Lynn Chu, who saw the virtue in a well-reasoned exposition on America's long economic triumph. At Basic Books, William Frucht helped organize and edit our arguments, and Richard Fumosa diligently helped present our evidence.

Preface

Pessimism or Prosperity?

Over the past quarter century, it's become fashionable to portray the United States as a society in economic decline. Time and time again, Americans hear that they live in a nation where incomes are falling, jobs are disappearing, inequality is increasing, and daily life keeps getting harder. The gloomy outlook rests on a few hand-picked statistics. These numbers point to sagging wages, lackluster economic growth, less-than-stellar productivity gains, ballooning trade deficits, lost manufacturing jobs, a widening income gap between rich and poor, and America's failure to keep pace with the growth rates of other nations.

Pessimism about the economy wouldn't be bothersome if it were merely a matter of a few discouraging data points. Bigger issues are at stake. When the shortcomings are piled atop one another, they suggest that the American Dream is becoming an illusion, that progress can no longer be taken for granted, that future generations will swallow the bitter pill of downward mobility.

In books, articles, scholarly reports, and sound bites, spreading the bad news has become a cottage industry. Just the titles on the bookshelves are enough to send an optimistic reader into a funk: *A Future of Lousy Jobs?* (Gary Burtless), *Silent Depression: The Fate of the American Dream* (Wallace C. Peterson), *Declining Fortunes: The Withering of the American Dream* (Katherine S. Newman), *The Overworked American: The Unexpected Decline of Leisure* and *The Overspent American: Upscaling, Downshifting, and the New Consumer* (Juliet B. Schor), *The Great U-Turn: Corporate Restructuring and the Polarizing of America* (Bennett Harrison and Barry Bluestone), *The End of Affluence* (Jeffrey Madrick), *The Politics of Rich and Poor* (Kevin Phillips), *The Great Depression of 1990* (Raveendra Batra), *The Judas Economy: The Triumph of Capital and the Betrayal of Work* (William Wolman and Anne Colamosca).

The pessimism arises from a variety of sources—left and right, academics and activists, corporations and Congress. Yet the overall message is unmistakable: The U.S. economy has failed in almost every important way. The main points of the critique:

1. Americans' living standards have been falling since the early 1970s.
2. The rich are getting richer and the poor are getting poorer. Most of us are getting nowhere.
3. Life is getting harder: We're working more, and there's never enough time to enjoy life.
4. Both adults have to work these days to maintain a family's standard of living.
5. Because Americans' incomes are falling, the United States is no longer the Land of Opportunity, particularly for the less educated.
6. Despite decades of affirmative action and moral suasion, women and minorities are falling further behind.
7. The United States, once the world's undisputed leader, is falling behind in the race for economic supremacy, passed up by the world's fast-growing nations.
8. Employment prospects are bleak because good jobs are being destroyed as companies lay off workers to boost profits and splurge on executive pay.
9. American workers are no longer as productive as they once were.
10. As companies ship our high-paying manufacturing jobs overseas, the United States is left with inferior service jobs, condemning the country to become "a nation of hamburger flippers."
11. The current generation of children may be the first in history not to live as well as their parents.
12. America's economic fortunes will erode further because the country isn't fit to compete in the high-technology world of the future.

These statements of America's economic failure are not just wrong but, in each and every instance, spectacularly wrong. When it comes to economic analysis, they're the myths of our times: the myths of rich and poor. They ignore an abundance of facts that show that the U.S. free-enterprise system continues to deliver prosperity. Living standards are steadily improving for all segments of society. Upward mobility remains within the grasp of a large majority of Americans. Plenty of good jobs are being created. All told, economic progress still thrives in the United States. We are better off than in the past, and the next generation of Americans will be even better off than the current one.

*   *   *

Amid the profusion of intellectual fads, spins, and machinations, it's hard for most Americans to get a handle on our economy, a complex, $8.5 trillion behemoth employing 130 million workers. Few of us have ready access to the myriad statistics needed for an accurate assessment of U.S. economic performance. That's the reason for this book: To set forth the truth about the U.S. economy. It will provide an antidote to the prevailing pessimism. The chapters that follow offer a fresh look at the country's economic performance, concentrating on the past quarter century—the era bemoaned by those who see the economy spiraling into decline.

There will be no hocus-pocus on any page of this book. Every proposition will rest firmly on facts and figures, nearly all of them available from government agencies and in publications found in most good-sized libraries, including the *Statistical Abstract of the United States.* Although simple numbers often speak eloquently, they can't always make the case without explanation and interpretation. It's important to appreciate how the economy works, to see where it's been and where it's going, and to understand what we can expect from it. This book will provide all that, too, without resorting to mumbo-jumbo. Every conclusion is spelled out as clearly as possible.

Although what's written stands on its own merit, it's a good idea to state at the outset what this book doesn't say. It doesn't say everything is hunky-dory. Proving the naysayers wrong about overall performance of the economy doesn't imply that the country has no problems. No survey of American society can avoid uncovering adversity and inequity—and our survey is no exception. We concede that the economy could have performed even better. In fact, we agree with many pessimists that the United States would be well served by improved education, less heavy-handed regulation, more stable families, and greater personal discipline. We don't deny that blemishes exist. We don't catalogue society's difficulties for the simple reason that those ills have already received plenty of ink. Placing too great an emphasis on problems is no more justifiable than ignoring them. To make points about larger issues, however, we don't for the most part, focus on the stresses and strains that come with progress. The central purpose of this book is to demonstrate that a pervasively negative view of the economy doesn't square with reality. We acknowledge at the outset the economy's blemishes, but we don't see poverty, inequality, or other deficiencies as the defining characteristics of our times.

In this book we do not say that this nation has succeeded in making *everyone* better off in *every* way. The impoverished, the unemployed, the underclass, and the downwardly mobile have hardly disappeared. Even in boom times, some of us face bleak and precarious lives, but these personal hardships aren't representative of what's happening to the great majority of Americans. Instead of generalizing from a few dramatic statistics or anecdotes, this book's focus will stay, first and foremost, on the great center of society. Wherever possible, we rely on the numbers that define broad trends—averages, medians, per capita figures, and rates of change. These statistics don't represent any single individual's experience, but they're the best guide to what's going on in the nation as a whole.

This book doesn't say anything explicitly about whether Americans are happy. We focus on the American economy and the billions of data points that define it. The statistical mills churn out reams of numbers on income, earnings, consumption, prices, working conditions, fringe benefits, and other matters. We know of no objective measure of happiness, especially for the nation as a whole. Happiness is as individual as a fingerprint, and bigger houses and ever more ingenious gadgets may make some of us happier. For others, this may not do the trick. Many will argue that material abundance doesn't create happiness. We are economic researchers, not philosophers or psychologists. We don't know whether economic progress brings happiness, but we strongly suspect that the absence of it yields misery.

Finally, this is a book about economic forces at work. It will occasionally wander into other aspects of society—the changing roles of women, the evolving family structure, trends in education. We venture into these subjects with some trepidation, usually for the sake of examining economic trends, not to draw inferences on larger issues. The great migration of women from the home into the workplace, for example, affects patterns of employment, income, and consumer demand. Do working women raise happy, healthy children? It's an interesting question but, like the subject of happiness, beyond the scope of a book about the economy.

* * *

The scenario of despair and decline conjures up a future in which most of us are poorer, cowering at the prospect of a pink slip, envying those lucky few who strike it rich in a *Wheel of Fortune* economy. It's not hard to understand why these prospects would anguish so many Americans. Our traditional attitudes and our heritage are charged with optimism. Immigrants by the millions came to these shores in search of a better life. The Founding Fathers created a society on a belief in freedom and prosperity. The concept of a Land of Opportunity isn't just cultural baggage, easily discarded. It has been the American experience for generations. During most of this nation's 200 years, its citizens could take economic progress as a birthright—or at least that's the way it comes down to us, the beneficiaries of our forebears' hard work and sacrifice. Economic failure, if it came to pass, would profoundly affect what we are as a nation and how we think about our own futures.

We borrow Mark Twain's observation: "It isn't what we don't know that kills us, it's everything we know that ain't so." Incorrect and ill-informed views of reality can distort choices about working, investing, voting, and national affairs. That's why this book is so important, especially now, when the United States faces the challenge of remaking itself for the post-industrial, post–Cold War era. Confidence in our economic system will help us face the challenges of the future. Once Americans understand that the economy has been working better than ever, they stand a better chance of making the right decisions for themselves and their families—as workers, investors, consumers, and citizens.

The notion of America as economic failure can't go unchallenged. This book will debunk the case for America's economic decline—specifically, those 12 propositions listed a few pages ago. Part One examines myths about income and living standards. Are living standards really falling? Will our children fail to live as well their parents? Are we having to work harder? Does it take two incomes to maintain our living standards? Does an expanding gap between low- and high-income workers amount to an increase in inequality and signal an end to upward mobility? Is America falling behind other countries in standards of living?

Part Two examines myths about jobs. Is the United States being ravaged by downsizing? What determines the creation and destruction of jobs? Are good jobs disappearing from the United States? Are we becoming "a nation of hamburger flippers"? Will there be economic growth and good jobs in the future?

Chapter 9 sums up the book's message for Americans as consumers, workers, and investors. We show how what we call the Great American Growth Machine continues to deliver what we want. We warn that many of the suggested remedies to problems that don't exist will leave us worse off. In the epilogue, we consider a compelling question: If the economy is doing so well, why do so many of us feel so bad?

In the second half of the 1990s, America's economy has been on a roll, with expanding employment, rising incomes, low inflation, and soaring stock prices. The "misery index"—the sum of the inflation and unemployment rates—fell to its lowest point in more than a generation. Consumer confidence rose to levels not seen since the late 1960s. Good times don't mute the message of this book. Capitalism's critics aren't as vocal or as visible as they were in times of economic turmoil, but they'll be back with a vengeance at the next downturn in the business cycle. In the late summer of 1998, a decline in the stock market and troubles in Asia and Latin America had already filled the air with gloom—even though the U.S. economy was still healthy.

Just as important, Americans won't maintain a robust, enduring faith in their nation's economic future until they've broken the pessimists' spell. If Main Street America can appreciate the benefits as well as the downside of economic change, it may diminish anxiety and restore faith in the future. Perhaps most important of all, a constant dirge of economic failure, if left unanswered, threatens to undermine the free-enterprise system. Our market-based economy, where individuals rather than governments make most of the choices about work, spending, and investment, has delivered to the United States the world's highest standards of living. Those who harp on a vision of the country's decline are, whether by design or not, attacking the source of our prosperity. Understanding how free enterprise works can only help us avoid making foolish mistakes that might jeopardize our economic future.

PART ONE

Myths About Income and Living Standards

1 WAKING UP
TO GOOD TIMES

IN THE AMERICA OF THE 1990S, hard-luck stories weren't hard to find. Just look on the front page of the *New York Times*. James Sharlow, a 51-year-old Los Angeles resident with two grown daughters, lost a $130,000-a-year job with Eastman Kodak in January 1993. He spent more than two years searching in vain for work, all the while depleting the family's savings. In Baltimore, job instability had gnawed away at Rene Brown's paychecks since the early 1980s, when she earned $8.50 an hour at a meat-packing plant. After that, she worked for $7.25 an hour in a bank's mail room, $4.75 an hour loading newspapers, and $4.25 an hour cleaning office buildings. Connecticut's 51-year-old Steven Holthausen, his marriage a casualty of the family's faltering finances, found work dispensing tourist information for the state at $12,000 a year, barely a quarter of what he once made as a loan officer.

In less turbulent times, Americans could shrug off the occasional glitches of the capitalist system as something that happened to someone else. We might listen to stories of economic misfortune with sympathy for laid-off, downsized, and marginalized workers, but with little sense of foreboding. Not today. Almost without exception, the steady drumbeat of stories about downward mobility and dead-end jobs are offered up as cautionary tales: *There but for the grace of God . . .*

The experiences of Sharlow, Brown, and Holthausen, when amplified by the stories of thousands caught in similar misfortunes, leave the impression of a nation going downhill, its economy failing in ominous ways. Do these discouraging snapshots of American life indicate what's in store for the rest of us? Are ordinary Americans trapped in a system incapable of raising living standards? Anecdotes can only illustrate, not prove. In good times and bad, workers and their families move up and down in society's pecking order. Individual fortunes can vary year in and year out, reflecting new jobs, promotions, layoffs, retirement, the rise of one industry, and the fall of another. One person's hardship may be offset by others' successes, all with a randomness that doesn't tell us much about how well the overall economy is working.

Making an argument for declining American living standards cries out for more broad-based evidence. More often than not, the argument rests on falling real wages. At first glance, the trend appears decidedly grim: After adjusting for inflation, average hourly wages rose at an annual rate of 2 percent from 1953 to 1973. Then they stagnated for five years before beginning a long slide, falling at an average annual rate of 0.7 percent through 1996. The total decline over two decades exceeded 15 percent (see Figure 1.1). If Americans earn less, it stands to reason they can't muster the financial wherewithal to maintain their standards of living. Case closed.

Not quite. At best, real wages are an indirect barometer of how well we're doing. If we want to know about living standards, it's better to use direct indicators of what Americans own, what they buy, and how they live, not some proxy, whether it be earnings or income. Before accepting wholesale the verdict of the data on real wages, Americans should at least consider what's happening to *consumption*. If the data indicate that the average family doesn't have as much now as in the early 1970s, it will confirm the case for the country's economic decay. An America consuming more than ever, however, would go a long way toward refuting a pessimistic view that relies on anecdotes and the data on declining real wages.

Fortunately, there's plenty of hard evidence. Each year, government and private-sector number-crunchers collect boatloads of data on nearly every aspect of our lives. The diligent researcher can look up the size of our houses, the appliances we own, the cars we drive, the hours we work, the money we spend at restaurants, the trips we take, and much more. The numbers are plentiful, reliable, and readily available to anyone who spends a few hours in the library or on its electronic equivalent, the Internet.

The statistics on consumption—the most direct measure of Americans' well-being—point to a nation that's better off now than at any other time in its history. Yet they rarely find a place in discussions of the nation's living standards, a debate dominated by measures of income and earnings.

FIGURE 1.1   Average Hourly Wages

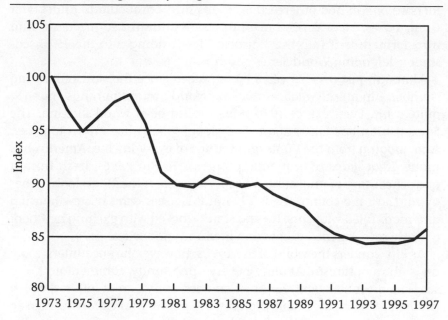

What We Had Then, What We've Got Now

In looking at what an average American consumes, comparisons to the early 1970s are what matters most. After all, few of us could possibly doubt that the country is much better off today than a century ago, when our great-grandfathers and great-grandmothers lived without electricity, telephones, refrigerators, indoor plumbing, and disease-fighting antibiotics. The past quarter century is the crux of the controversy: For those who perceive economic decay in America, the early 1970s were a turning point, when just about all the widely cited gauges on the economy started to slip, bringing to an end a golden era when growth was steady, paychecks were getting fatter, jobs were secure, and gasoline sold at the rock-bottom price of 35 cents a gallon.

Was the early 1970s the U.S. economy's great watershed? Finding out will require a fresh perspective. So imagine a modern-era Rip van Winkle, an economist this time, rather than the indolent farmer of Washington Irving's fable. He falls asleep in 1970 and reawakens on a bright spring day in the late 1990s, rubbing sleep from his eyes. Among his memories before dozing off: Watching George C. Scott portray Patton on the big screen, tuning in *Rowan & Martin's Laugh-*

In on television, and listening to the Beatles sing "Let It Be." President Richard Nixon had ordered U.S. troops into Cambodia to attack Viet Cong bases. New York's once-hapless National League team had transformed itself into the "Miracle Mets," going into the 1970 season as defending World Series champs.

Although just over 25 years have passed since the start of his long slumber, Rip quickly realizes that the world around him has changed quite a bit. Events since 1970 have indeed been world-shaking. The Soviet Union has fallen apart. The global village has grown together. And, judging from the sights and sounds of everyday life, America has made great leaps of economic progress. To Rip's eyes, fresh from a quarter century of undisturbed sleep, America in the 1990s looks richer by far than the country he left behind. He sees acres of new housing and roads filled with cars. He sees stores stocked with exciting new gadgets. He sees Americans enjoying life in myriad ways.

As Rip wanders the world of the 1990s, however, he encounters more angst than optimism. At almost every opportunity, commentators and scholars grumble about the American economy's great failures, which condemn the average family to growing poorer and expose workers to the ravages of downsizing. Bewildered by the hand-wringing, our Rip van Winkle sets out to discover the truth about the American economy. As a researcher, he knows where to find the right facts and figures. After poring over the data for the years of his slumber, Rip concludes he wasn't just daydreaming. Americans are indeed better off—on average, possessing more of just about everything (see Table 1.1).

A good place to start is where we live—home sweet home. The nation has continued to add to its housing stock: In the middle of the 1990s, home builders finished more than 1.1 million single-family residences a year, well above the annual average of 1970 to 1975, a time when the coming of age of the Baby Boomers flooded the market with new buyers. As building continued at a brisk pace, our houses have also gotten bigger. From 1970 to 1997, the typical new home increased in size by the equivalent of two 16-by-20-foot rooms. Homes aren't just larger. They're also much more likely to be equipped with central air conditioning, decks and patios, swimming pools, hot tubs, ceiling fans, and built-in kitchen appliances—all included in the purchase price. Fewer than half of the homes built in 1970 had two or more bathrooms; by 1997, 9 out of 10 did. In 1997, 87 percent of new homes included garages, up from 58 percent in 1970. The garages, moreover, had also gotten bigger: Three-quarters of new homes had space for two or more cars, compared with little

TABLE 1.1   The World Through Rip's Eyes

Item	1970	Mid-1990s*
Average size of new home (square feet)	1,500	2,150
Average household size (persons)	3.14	2.64
Average square feet per person in the household	478	814
New homes with central heat and air-conditioning	34%	81%
New homes with a garage	58%	87%
Housing units lacking complete plumbing[a]	6.9%	2.3%
Homes lacking a telephone[a]	13.0%	6.3%
Households with computer	0%	41%
Households with no vehicle[a]	20.4%	7.9%
Households with two or more vehicles[a]	29.3%	61.9%
Households with color TV	34.0%	97.9%
Households with cable TV	6.3%	63.4%
Households with two or more TV's	30.7%	72.8%
Households with videocassette recorder	0%	89%
Households with answering machine	0%	65%
Households with cordless phone	0%	66%
Households with computer printer	0%	38%
Households with camcorder	0%	26%
Households with cellular phone	0%	34%
Households with CD player	0%	49%
Households with clothes washer	62.1%	83.2%
Households with clothes dryer	44.6%	75.0%
Households with a microwave	<1%	89.5%
Households with coffeemaker	88.6%	99.9%
Households with dishwasher[b]	26.5%	54.6%
Households with vacuum cleaner	92.0%	99.9%
Households with frost-free refrigerator	<25%	86.8%
Households with outdoor gas grill[c]	<5%	28.5%
Mean household ownership of furniture[b]	$2,230	$3,756
Mean household ownership of appliances[b]	$943	$1,547
Mean household ownership of video and audio products[b]	$308	$2,671
Mean household ownership of jewelry and watches[b]	$728	$1,784
Mean household ownership of books and maps[b]	$731	$1,074
Mean household ownership of sports equipment[b]	$769	$1,895
Mean household net worth[a]	$86,095	$126,843
Median household net worth[a]	$27,938	$59,398
Vehicles per 100 persons aged 16 and older[a]	53	94
Work time to buy gas for a 100-mile trip	49 minutes	26 minutes
Annual visits to doctor[d]	4.6	6.1
Per capita consumption of bottled water (gallons)[b]	<1	11.1
Americans taking cruises	0.5 million	4.7 million
Air-travel miles per capita	646	>2,260
Per capita spending on sporting goods[b]	$60	$213
Recreational boats per 1000 households[a]	139	173
Manufacturers' shipments of recreational vehicles[a]	30,300	281,000

*Mid–1990s data are for 1997, except where indicated.
[a] Data for 1995. [b] Data for 1996. [c] Data for 1993. [d] Data for 1994.
All monetary figures are in constant (1997) dollars.

more than a third in the early 1970s (see Figure 1.2). Today's new homes also contain more energy-saving features, including thicker insulation and double-paned windows. These improvements are doing their job: In a new house, average energy consumption, measured in BTUs per square foot, fell by at least a third from the 1970s to the 1990s.

Why focus on just new homes? New, single-family dwellings that come on the market in any given year are just a small part of the housing market, but they are the best measure of what buyers *demand* and what they can *afford* at any time. Looking at the entire housing stock, including homes built a century or more ago, will tell us little about how housing has changed over a 25-year period. In effect, we'd be measuring what the economy of the past could provide.

Bigger, better-equipped homes would be a mirage if only a few well-heeled families could afford to own them. The rich do live in the fanciest houses, no doubt about it, but the average family hasn't been left out. Home prices are a lot higher than they used to be, of course. The median price of a new, single-family dwelling rose from $23,400 in 1970 to $145,500 in 1997, but the comparison tells us little about affordability. Families can pay more for today's homes because incomes are higher—four times greater than they were in the early 1970s. And mortgage rates are lower, a 30-year conventional loan having fallen from 8.6 percent to less than 7.0 percent. We shouldn't forget, moreover, that today's higher prices pay for added square footage and amenities. In the late 1990s, most of us can afford the essential part of the American dream—a home of our own. Proof comes in home-ownership rates: In the third quarter of 1997, 66 percent of households, a total of 68 million individuals and families, owned homes—an all-time record.

If housing is affordable, why don't even more American families own their own homes? Current rates of home ownership may match the nation's preference for buying versus renting. Today's economy provides a wealth of housing options, including apartments, lofts, condominiums, town homes, high-rises, and gated enclaves. Young Americans often prefer the flexibility and camaraderie of apartment living—and there's a place for them. Senior citizens might gladly dispense with the rigors of maintaining a home and yard—and there's a place for them. Longer-term trends add some perspective. Home ownership was quite low in the 1920s, less than 25 percent of the population. In the boom that came after World War II, the proportion quickly rose to about 60 percent; it has climbed only slightly

FIGURE 1.2   New Homes: Bigger and Better

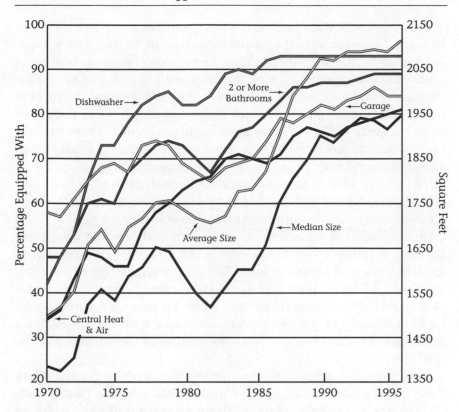

since then, to 66 percent. A fairly steady rate over several decades, in good times and bad, indicates that affordability isn't the primary reason more families don't own their own homes.

The average age at which Americans buy their first home has increased roughly four years, from 27.9 in 1970 to 32.4 in 1996. Pessimists might attribute the delay to deteriorating economic conditions: With paychecks pinched, young families must wait four extra years before they can afford a house. Jumping to that conclusion ignores lifestyle changes. The median age at the time of first marriage, an event that often precedes home buying, increased from 22 in 1970 to 26 in 1996—once again, four years. In the mid-1990s, an additional 8 percent of us decide never to marry, so even the financially well-off might delay house hunting for a few years. The number of children per household has declined from 1.3 in 1970 to 0.9 today, suggesting that more families don't include children. All these changes no doubt affect home-buying patterns, and they're most likely responsible for the extra time Americans take before settling down.

Rip's survey of then and now finds plenty of good news beyond housing. His research shows that Americans in the 1990s have stocked up on the amenities that make everyday life easier and more enjoyable. The percentage of families with dishwashers, clothes washers and dryers, blenders, toasters, vacuum cleaners, swimming pools, automatic sprinklers, and outdoor gas grills has increased since the early 1970s. In 1996, manufacturers turned out an incredible 100 million small appliances, from electric knives to waffle irons. The average number of televisions in a household rose from 1.4 in 1970 to 2.4 in 1997, a gain made all the more striking by the fact that each home, on average, had fewer people to watch them. In fact, televisions are rapidly approaching the level of one per person. More than 40 percent of American households owned personal computers in 1997, a product that didn't even exist in the 1970s. Comparing 1970 to 1996 and adjusting for inflation, the typical American family owned 8.7 times more audio and video equipment. It had 68 percent more furniture and 64 percent more kitchen appliances. Books and maps? They were up 47 percent. Even kids shared in the nation's prosperity: Per-child spending on toys, adjusted for inflation, quadrupled since 1970.

America's love affair with the automobile can't be denied. More than 9 of 10 households now own passenger vehicles. Nearly two-thirds have two or more. Among those 16 years and older, vehicles per 100 people rose from 53 to 94 in just 26 years. Within a few years, the country may become the first in history to have more passenger vehicles than people. Dozens of automotive innovations improve performance, safety, and comfort: antilock brakes, air bags that cushion occupants during a collision, turbochargers, cruise control, automated air conditioning and heating, sun roofs, adjustable steering wheels, and windshield-wiper delays. Today's cars are loaded with "power." They're more likely to have power steering, windows, seats, door locks, and rearview mirrors. They're also more likely to have radial tires and tinted glass (see Figure 1.3).

Americans are enjoying more luxuries, too. The average amount spent on jewelry and watches, after adjusting for higher prices, more than doubled from 1970 to 1996. A typical American drinks 11 gallons of bottled water, up from less than 1 in 1970. For fun and games, an average family possesses more than twice the gear for sports and hobbies. Per-household ownership of pleasure boats rose by 25 per-

FIGURE 1.3   Better Equipped on the Highway

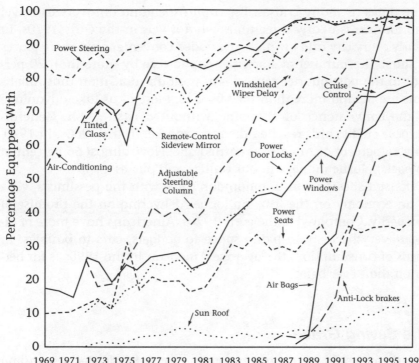

cent in the past two or three decades. Manufacturers' shipments of recreational vehicles are nine times what they were in the early 1970s. In the quarter century up to 1996, per-person annual outlays rose from $60 to $213 for sporting goods, including gains of 14 percent for bicycles and, just since 1980, 26 percent for snowmobiles. While American households consumed more, they had enough money left to dig deeper into their pockets for worthy causes: Per capita donations to charities, adjusted for inflation, rose from $402 a year in 1970 to $569 a year in 1996.

The average American's spending on services has risen 83 percent since the early 1970s. We're taking advantage of health clubs, financial advisers, landscapers, dating services, caterers, pest-control companies, dry cleaners, car-detailing shops, valet parking stands, and literally hundreds of other businesses that entertain us, pamper us, and save us time and effort. We eat out more often. After accounting for inflation and a growing population, spending on restaurant meals is up by 45 percent. We travel more often and to more exotic destinations. On a per capita basis, average annual miles flown on commercial flights more than tripled in the past 25 years. We take nine times as many cruises. Per capita spending on overseas travel and tourism is nearly three times what it was in the early 1970s. In nearly every city and town, there's added convenience in more places to shop. The number of stores per capita rose by more than 20 percent in the past quarter century—in itself an indication that Americans are buying more than they used to. More of us take advantage of the convenience of shopping without a cash stash. General-purpose credit cards reached the mass market in the 1960s. In 1970, only 16 percent of Americans carried one. Now, almost 66 percent of us pack "plastic money" in our wallets and purses.

The statistics on consumption don't jibe with the pessimists' view of an economy on the fritz, no longer delivering on the promise of prosperity. Compared to the early 1970s, Americans have more of almost everything, from living space to gadgets, cars to baubles. In terms of consumption, the average American in the 1990s is far better off than ever before.

The Saving Grace

Americans could, of course, be paying for a fin-de-siècle spending spree by depleting their assets. There's been plenty of hand-wringing over the country's low saving rate, compared with that of other nations, and persistent worry over rapidly rising consumer debt. It's probably wise to ask whether American families are trading their tomorrows for the instant gratification of today's consumption.

The answer can be found by looking at Americans' wealth. If the country were on a reckless spending spree, households would be running down their net worth, depleting tomorrow's nest eggs to keep up with the Joneses. It's just not so. Although many Americans may not be socking away enough money for rainy days and retirement, we're not, on average, squandering our assets. Including savings deposits, stocks, bonds, pension plans, certificates of deposit, real estate, and other tangible assets, U.S. households had an inflation-adjusted average net worth of $216,843 in 1995, compared with only $86,095 in 1970. It's certainly true that rich Americans are accumulating a lot of the wealth. Yet the gains didn't come solely at the top end of the income distribution. Half of American families had a net worth of at least $59,398 in 1995, more than double the median net worth of 1970.

Savings are fertilizer for economic growth. The United States might well be better off if Americans saved more of their income. For the individual, however, decisions on how much to spend and how much to save are really about lifetime consumption. In effect, we choose between spending now or later—perhaps much later when it comes to estates. Most people set aside money in their peak earning years, so they'll have it later in life, primarily for their children's college costs and for their own living expenses after age 65. As Baby Boomers move into their peak earning years and begin to contemplate retirement in the next century, they probably will funnel more money into savings. Indeed, there are signs Americans are becoming avid investors in this decade, particularly in stock and bond mutual funds. From 1990 through the end of 1997, at a time when they were buying bigger houses, fancier cars, and all those consumer goods, Americans poured more than $1.5 trillion into mutual funds. It paid off handsomely as financial-market indicators roared upward by more than 200 percent through the end of 1997, a big windfall for families with the foresight to invest. Counting just net financial holdings, a figure that doesn't include home equity and other real property, households averaged $211,923 in 1997, up from an inflation adjusted $118,488 in 1990, $64,847 in 1980, and $33,007 in 1970. A typical family's wealth is rising rapidly in the 1990s, so Americans now have the best of all worlds—more consumption and more savings.

Is consumer debt the Achilles heel of our consumption boom? There's no denying that Americans are deeper in hock than ever before. In 1997, the average household owed $12,514 in consumer debt, a figure that includes credit cards, retail-store accounts, automobile loans, and similar obligations but not mortgages. The consumer-debt burden has risen fivefold since the early 1970s. Debt, of course, becomes excessive only when it rises beyond the ability to pay. If Americans have higher incomes and more financial assets, they can carry more debt. Consumer credit as a percent of income is up, but only by about two weeks of annual earnings. In 1970, an average household would need 11 weeks' income to pay off its consumer debt. Now it would take about 13 weeks. As a proportion of net financial assets, average consumer debt in 1997 stood just about where it was in 1970, at roughly 5 percent, although the burden did creep up slightly, to almost 7 percent, in the late 1970s and early 1980s. The narrow range suggests American families stay in a comfort zone, willing to assume more debt when they're at 5 percent and cutting back as they approach 7 percent.

Some Americans no doubt get into trouble with easy credit, but there's no compelling evidence that the typical American family faces overwhelming debt. In fact, there may be a hidden message of hope in our willingness to borrow money. When consumers antici- pate hard times, they hunker down. They pay off existing obli- gations, and they're wary of taking on new ones. Perhaps the fact that millions of Americans feel optimistic enough to borrow suggests that most of us aren't convinced the economic future will be bleak.

Progress and Poverty

What about those at the bottom echelons of society? The nation could very well be consuming and saving more, with all the goodies going to the upper and middle classes and with the poor worse off, not just in relative terms but absolutely as well. At least one statistic seems to suggest that many low-income Americans aren't keeping up: The na- tion's poverty rate rose from 12.6 percent in 1970 to 13.3 percent in 1997—a widely cited blemish on our economic performance.

Although the country hasn't done as much to eradicate poverty as we might hope, the record isn't entirely bleak. Digging beneath the poverty rate uncovers data indicating that the poor are better off than they were a quarter century ago. Once again, it's important to look at consumption rather than income. The numbers show that America's poor—those with incomes of $13,220 or less for an aver- age-sized family in 1996—are living better than they used to. Home ownership among poor families rose from 37 percent in the early 1970s to 41 percent in the 1990s. In addition, today's poor house- holds are more likely than those of a decade ago to own appliances and motor vehicles. The percentage of poor households with washing machines rose from 58.2 percent in 1984 to 71.7 percent in 1994. Ownership of dryers rose from 35.6 percent to 50.2 percent. Three- fifths of poor families had microwave ovens in 1994, up from one- eighth a decade ago. Nine of 10 poor households had color televisions, and 6 of 10 could play movies on videocassette recorders. Almost three-quarters of the families owned at least one car (see Table 1.2).

Perhaps most astonishing of all, poor households of the 1990s in many cases compared favorably with an average family in the early 1970s in owning the trappings of middle-class life. For example, al- most half of the poor households had air conditioners in 1994, com-

TABLE 1.2   Even the Poor Have More

Percent of Households With:	Poor Households 1984	Poor Households 1994	All Households 1971
Washing machine	58.2	71.7	71.3
Clothes dryer	35.6	50.2	44.5
Dishwasher	13.6	19.6	18.8
Refrigerator	95.8	97.9	83.3
Freezer	29.2	28.6	32.2
Stove	95.2	97.7	87.0
Microwave	12.5	60.0	<1.0
Color television	70.3	92.5	43.3
Videocassette recorder	3.4	59.7	0
Personal computer	2.9	7.4	0
Telephone	71.0	76.7	93.0
Air-conditioner	42.5	49.6	31.8
One or more cars	64.1	71.8	79.5

pared to less than a third of the country as a whole in 1971. The pattern holds true for dryers, refrigerators, stoves, microwaves, and color televisions. What's more, today's poor are less likely to be excluded from the benefits of our consumer society. For example, they have greater access to credit. In 1970, only 2 percent of families in the bottom 9 percent of the income distribution had general-purpose credit cards. By the mid-1990s, the percentage had grown to 26.5. The logical conclusion: Being poor doesn't entail the same degree of deprivation it once did. In fact, by the standards of 1971, many of today's poor families might be considered members of the middle class.

At first blush, it's not apparent how the poor can increase their consumption yet still not escape from the poverty statistics. Part of the answer lies in spending patterns. Among households below the poverty line, outlays for food, clothing, and shelter were down to 37 percent of consumption in 1995, compared with 52 percent two decades earlier, 57 percent in 1950, and 75 percent in 1920. Over time, the prices of necessities have fallen relative to average hourly wages, so just getting by takes less effort. The smaller the share of income going to meet basic needs, the more money left over to purchase the goods and services that most poor households once had to do without.

Another part of the puzzle involves a widening gap between earning and spending for low-income households. The poverty rate tells us how many Americans are trying to scrape by on meager incomes.

It gives an incomplete accounting of the resources available to families on society's lowest rungs. Most households in the bottom fifth of the income distribution consume well beyond their current earnings. In 1995, an average low-income household made $6,305 a year before taxes. Consumption—what the poor spent, not what they earned—totaled $13,130 (see Table 1.3).

How can poor families consume more than they earn? Many supplement their income through unemployment benefits, Aid to Families with Dependent Children, Medicare, Medicaid, food stamps, school lunches, rent subsidies, and other programs. Moreover, many low-income households can tap into other resources. Workers temporarily laid off make little money, but they can usually fall back on their savings rather than reduce their standard of living. Although many retirees have low incomes, their houses, cars, and furnishings are in many cases paid for, and they've got a nest egg for spending on vacations and grandkids. In 1993, 302,000 families with incomes of less than $20,000 lived in homes valued at more than $300,000.

University of Texas economist Daniel Slesnick recalculated the poverty rate on the basis of inflation-adjusted expenditures rather than income. To remove the vagaries of inflation, he adapted the government's definition and put a household's poverty threshold at three times the annual cost of consuming a nutritionally adequate diet for all its members. Slesnick's results show that the proportion of poor in the United States, measured by consumption, fell steadily from 31 percent in 1949 to 13 percent in 1965 and to 2 percent at the end of the 1980s. If the problem of poverty is one of access to goods and services, then this lower rate might give a better indication than the official poverty figures of how well the American economy has done in lifting poor families over the past three decades.

Looking at consumption, moreover, shows an even greater leveling of society. At the bottom of the income distribution, households are smaller—an average of 1.8 persons, 0.6 of whom are working. Households in the top fifth of income averaged 3.1 persons, 2.1 of them holding jobs. Top-income households outearned bottom ones by a factor of 14 to 1. When it comes to consumption per person, the gap shrinks to only 2.3 to 1. What's more, poorer households work less, so they have more time to meet their needs through home production—such tasks as cooking, house cleaning, maintenance, child care, yard work, and laundry. Although these chores make families better off, they aren't included in statistics that measure consumption. Yet when high-income earners pay cooks, maids, nannies, gardeners,

TABLE 1.3   How People Spend Their Money

	Lowest Fifth	Middle Fifth	Highest Fifth
Household income (before taxes)	$6,305	$28,242	$89,011
Household consumption			
Food	$2,490	$4,270	$7,522
Clothing	$759	$1,502	$3,402
Shelter	$2,741	$4,423	$8,919
Telephone, utilities	$1,460	$2,122	$3,044
Transportation	$2,021	$5,745	$11,155
Health care	$1,099	$1,700	$2,417
Other	$2,560	$5,563	$15,747
Total consumption	$13,130	$25,325	$52,206
Average household size	1.8	2.6	3.1
Consumption per person	$7,294	$9,741	$16,841
Other uses of income			
Taxes	$1,004	$4,672	$16,643
Cash contributions	$284	$697	$1,914
Education	$308	$273	$1,172
Financial flows[a]	($8,421)	($2,725)	$17,076

[a] Insurance, pensions, investment expenses, and dissaving plus government transfers.
Data are current dollar figures for 1995.

and others to perform the same services, it gets captured in reports on consumption expenditures, making them appear to be better off.

Mathematics makes no compromises. It dictates that 20 percent of American households will lie at the tail end of the income distribution, always relatively "poor" by the standards of society, no matter how much they consume. No one wants to minimize the plight of the truly down-and-out. America's low-income families, however, are better off now than they were at any time in the past. The data on consumption lead to an unmistakable conclusion: The poor are not getting poorer.

Real-Wage Reality

Data on consumption and saving provide overwhelming support for the notion that American living standards are still improving, not just for the well-to-do but for low-income families as well. Yet all the numbers fail to dispel the nagging issue of declining real wages. How can Americans afford to increase their consumption when their earnings slipped by 15 percent in two decades? One possibility: The data on real wages, even if compiled accurately, aren't a good measure of Americans' economic fortunes over the past quarter century.

As it turns out, there are other ways of evaluating Americans' earning power. A straightforward alternative to real wages is inflation-adjusted per capita personal income. Its virtue is that it captures all sources of income—not just wages but interest, dividends, rent, and profits. A simple division of total output by the number of people, per capita income isn't skewed by changes in the way we work, the way we live, how we're paid, and what we produce. Trends in per capita income belie the downward mobility found in real wages. These statistics indicate that Americans grew consistently richer during the entire post–World War II era. The growth rate did slow down. Real per capita income has risen by an annual average of 1.6 percent since 1974, compared with 2.6 percent in the 1950s and 1960s (see Figure 1.4).

The statistics on real wages suffer from a glaring omission: fringe benefits. Over the past two decades, as tax rates grew steeper and incomes rose, the country witnessed a surge in nonwage benefits. Workers chose to take more of their compensation in the form of additional health care, contributions to retirement savings, or employee assistance programs. Compared with a generation ago, more employers are providing eye care, dental benefits, paid maternity leave, and stock-purchase plans. Today's most progressive companies are starting to offer day care, paternity leave, and spouse-relocation benefits— all virtually unheard of in the early 1970s. Overall, nonmonetary benefits as a percentage of wages have increased by a third since 1970. The extras cost money, and they're properly part of workers' earnings. When fringe benefits are included in measuring income, statisticians call it "total compensation." Like per capita income, total compensation shows slower growth in the past 20 years. Once again, though, the bottom line differs sharply from real wages: The average worker is better off than his or her counterpart in the early 1970s, with a cumulative gain in total compensation of more than 17 percent. Both per capita income and total compensation, by showing greater purchasing power, make it plausible that Americans would be able to increase consumption over the past quarter century.

Looking beyond real wages gives a truer picture of how we're doing, but even per capita income and total compensation have their flaws. Most important, they tend to shortchange our economic gains by using price indexes that overstate inflation. This glitch makes today's earnings seem punier than they really are when presented in "real" terms. The fault lies in the Consumer Price Index (CPI), duly reported each month in just about every newspaper in America. Statisticians can easily survey stores and markets, noting how prices

FIGURE 1.4   A Second Look at What We Earn: Per Capita Income, Total Compensation, and Hourly Wages, 1953–97

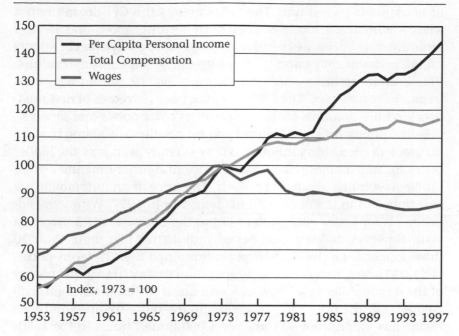

change on televisions, oranges, sporting goods, toothpaste, taxi fares, visits to the dentist, and nearly 90,000 other goods and services. What they fail to adequately capture, however, is the constant introduction of new products and the perpetual tweaking of product design. When prices rise, it sometimes means consumers pay extra for the same goods and services, so they're worse off. However, well-being doesn't fall as much when higher prices reflect better quality and new bells and whistles. Especially over long periods of time, the CPI captures both types of "inflation," and it can't adequately separate the two.

The CPI emerges from a slowly evolving "market basket" of goods and services put together from a detailed survey of 29,000 consumers. Devising a product list that captures the great diversity of American consumption is expensive and time-consuming, so the government has revised the basket only every decade or so. As a result, new goods and services usually enter the inflation index only after they've been on the market for several years. Pocket calculators showed up on desks and countertops in the early 1970s, but they didn't make the price index until 1978. The statistics ignored personal computers and videocassette recorders until 1987. Cellular telephones didn't show up in the CPI until 1998, when nearly 40 percent of households owned one. The delay means the CPI doesn't reflect what Americans actually buy. More important, goods and services typically start out very expensive, then go through a period of rapidly falling prices as they enter the mainstream of our consumer culture. Videocassette recorder prices, for example, fell 70 percent before entering the price index. The CPI misses the price decreases of new products but fully accounts for higher prices of older goods and services.

Better quality and new features present another stumbling block to accuracy in measuring inflation. We've already seen how the higher prices for new homes reflect added space and other amenities. It's a problem with just about all products. The price of an automobile tire rose from $13 in the mid-1930s to about $75 in 1997. With some adjustments for better quality, the CPI put the increase at 1.5 percent a year. However, today's steel-belted radial tires last more than 10 times longer than the old four-ply cotton-lined tires. In terms of cost per 1,000 miles, tires are now cheaper than at any time in the history of the automobile. Yale University economist William Nordhaus calculated that the price of light, including the bulb, fixtures, and electricity, has fallen from 40 cents per 1,000 lumen hours in the 1880s to a tenth of a cent today, a decline of 99 percent. By conventional measures of inflation, however, light bulbs and fixtures are up 180 percent since 1880.

The CPI covers a tremendous array of goods and services, and it would be an overwhelming task to decide how much of each month's price increase to allocate to higher quality. As America approaches the twenty-first century, new and better products are coming fast and furious, making it likely that the CPI is falling farther and farther behind the marketplace. Government statisticians are aware of the bias caused by new and improved products. To improve the quality of the data, they're likely to reduce the gap between revisions of the inflation index from 11 years to 4 or 5. Even with the change, the numbers will miss a lot of what's going on and will consistently overstate inflation and understate growth in wages, income, and productivity.

In the mid-1990s, scholars found that the CPI overstates inflation by a little more than 1 percentage point a year (see Table 1.4). The errors aren't just statistical aberrations of interest only to the cloistered fellows of academia. The mismeasured CPI affects the allocation of resources in the federal budget—particularly the more than 50 percent of it classified as "entitlements." It affects the wage and price calcula-

TABLE 1.4   Estimates of the Bias in Consumer Price Index Inflation

Authors	Percentage Points
Advisory Commission (1996)	1.1
Michael Boskin (1995)	1.5
Congressional Budget Office (1994)	0.5
Michael R. Darby (1995)	1.5
W. Erwin Diewert (1995)	1.5
Robert J. Gordon (1995)	1.7
Alan Greenspan (1995)	1.0
Zvi Griliches (1995)	1.0
Dale W. Jorgenson (1995)	1.0
Jim Klumpner (1996)	0.4
Lebow, Roberts, Stockton (1995)	1.0
Ariel Pakes (1995)	0.8
Shapiro and Wilcox (1996)	1.0
Wynne and Sigalla (1994)	1.0
Average	**1.1**

tions of private industry. Just as important, it can distort our view of the nation's economic performance. Inflation errors feed into many of the angst-inducing numbers on real wages, income, productivity, and growth. If we correct inflation by a little more than a percentage point a year over two decades, the decline in real wages vanishes, turning into a 12 percent increase since 1978. Per capita income no longer slows down. There's no ebbing of productivity growth, a measure of output per worker. If inflation were more accurately measured, growth rates would appear more robust, with a mediocre 2.4 percent transforming into 3.5 percent. Small statistical distortions might not seem worth worrying about, but they add up to significant long-term implications. Correcting a one-percentage-point error in the CPI over 25 years would increase our measures of real income per capita to $37,015 in 1997, a gain of $8,857 for every man, woman, and child. A mere percentage point of faster real growth cuts the time required to double living standards from 70 years to 34 years.

The pessimistic view of the economy begins to unravel once we look at how much more Americans consume today. The data speak loud and clear: Both average-income and low-income American households enjoy higher living standards than they did 25 years ago. The conclusion rests on direct measures of what everyday Americans actually possess. This material wealth cannot be simply ignored in favor of the worst-case scenario that emerges from trends in real wages and other statistics, especially with their faults. Once we correct the biases in our statistics and see that the free-enterprise system is still delivering higher pay and growth, we needn't scratch our heads over how the country has been able to afford a record-smashing consumption binge. Perhaps best of all, our Rip van Winkle hasn't yet exhausted the evidence of the country's continuing economic progress over the past quarter century.

2 NEW AND IMPROVED!

WOULD YOU RATHER BE an average American of the 1990s or a millionaire in the 1890s? At first blush, many of us might be tempted to grasp the apparent wealth. The Robber Barons and their families could splurge on mansions with plush furnishings, private railway cars, phalanxes of servants, clothing tailored from collars to cuffs, the finest food, silver and china, works of art, first-class accommodations, enough jewelry to bedeck a bevy of Liz Taylors. They could afford any ostentatious display money could buy. It was, without doubt, a life of luxury and privilege, far removed from the daily grind of the era's typical working stiff.

After more careful reflection, however, today's Americans might not forsake the creature comforts and conveniences of the modern age. A nineteenth-century millionaire couldn't grab a cold drink from the refrigerator. He couldn't hop into a smooth-riding automobile for a 70-mile-per-hour trip down an interstate highway to the mountains or seashore. He couldn't call up news, movies, music, and sporting events by simply touching the remote control's buttons. He couldn't jet north to Toronto, south to Cancun, east to Boston, or west to San Francisco in just a few hours. He couldn't transmit documents to Europe, Asia, or anyplace else in seconds. He couldn't run over to the mall to buy autofocus cameras, computer games, mountain bikes, or movies on videotape. He couldn't escape the summer heat into air-conditioned comfort. He couldn't check into a hospital for a coronary bypass to cure a failing heart, get a shot of penicillin to ward off infection, or even take an aspirin to relieve a headache.

None of these goods and services were available a century ago, not at any price. The refrigerator, introduced in the early 1900s, didn't become commonplace until the 1920s. Decades later, the same technology made air conditioning possible. The first transcontinental automobile trip required 51 exhausting days in 1903. The first television broadcast took place in 1926. Commercial air travel began in 1926. Fax transmissions and electronic mail became possible in the 1980s. Open-heart bypass surgery wasn't possible until the late 1960s. Penicillin was invented in 1928. Aspirin didn't reach the market until 1915.

Now, all these goods and services are the birthright of the American masses, and can be purchased for just a small portion of a typical worker's annual income. Trading places with an 1890s millionaire would mean giving up more than we gain. Over time, a well-functioning economy delivers progress in many forms. We've already seen that average Americans of the 1990s possess bigger, better-equipped houses, more cars, and growing stocks of every variety of consumer product. The economy's bounty doesn't end there. No catalogue of rising living standards would be complete without products that didn't exist for past generations, products that are vastly improved, products enhanced by greater variety, or products that deliver their services for less time and effort.

We all can remember the wonderful goods and services of days gone by—the rock-solid, always dependable rotary-dial telephone, or a doctor making a house call. Nostalgia buffs may regret the passing of the artifacts of earlier times, but the gains more than make up for the losses. Touch-tone telephones now offer call waiting, call forwarding, automatic dialing, answering machines, and advance notice of whether a friend or an insurance salesman is on the other end. Who would really want an old-style phone? A doctor climbing the staircase with his little black satchel is a comforting image, but he had relatively little to offer beyond his bedside manner. When illness or accident strikes, the chances of recovery are obviously greater with today's doctors—armed not with just a stethoscope and tongue depressor but with the past quarter century's medical advances.

Companies always tout what they sell as *new and improved!* It's not just hype. Although the words sound like a slogan from a toothpaste advertisement, much of what's available in today's marketplace really *is* new and improved.

What Money Can Now Buy

America entered the twentieth century as a primarily agrarian society but quickly transformed itself into an industrial one. Now it's tumbling headlong into the next phase of economic development—

the Information Age, an era in which brainpower will propel the economy forward. In just a few generations, the archetypal product of our economy changed from the steel plow to the automobile to the computer. If nothing else, this swift metamorphosis symbolizes the economy's proclivity for finding new ways to meet human needs.

In our fast-moving age, we've become so accustomed to change, so used to the rush of new gizmos and gadgets, that we take for granted the marvels arriving on store shelves. We often forget that frenetic innovation is a thoroughly modern phenomenon. It might well take Rip van Winkle, encountering our world after a 25-year sleep, to fully appreciate how far we've come in just a few decades. Our ever observant Rip could find an enormous number of new and better products that burst onto the market during a time when, pessimists say, Americans were becoming worse off. Just about every U.S. household owns dozens of goods and services that were, at best, available to only a handful of wealthy or resourceful consumers in the early 1970s (see Table 2.1).

In a typical middle-class household, Rip can find plenty of things he hadn't even imagined before dozing off. Americans cook meals in minutes using microwave ovens. We flick electronic devices on and off by remote control. We wake up with coffee already brewed by computerized appliances competing for countertop space with toasters, electric can openers, bread makers, and blenders. We quickly clean up small messes with hand-held vacuums. We simply dispose of dirty diapers. After taking snapshots, we dispose of our cameras as well. We keep our pets from wandering with invisible electronic fences. We figure checking-account balances and grocery-store bills on solar-powered calculators, some no bigger than credit cards. The tiny calculator is typical of many new products. It has become so ubiquitous, useful, and necessary that many of us assume that it's been around for generations. Not so. The first one, a Texas Instruments model, appeared on the market in 1972, replacing bulky adding machines, perplexing slide rules, and longhand ciphering.

Twenty-five years ago, only a few families could watch movies at home on videotape machines, clunky devices that sold for thousands of dollars. Even if they could afford the equipment, finding a place to rent a film might take some doing. Today, four out of five American households own videocassette recorders, and 64 million Americans are card-carrying customers of Blockbuster Entertainment Inc., the nation's largest video-rental company, with 4,438 stores and counting. Until enough Americans owned VCRs, Blockbuster had no rea-

TABLE 2.1   The Modern Age's Bounty

A Sampling of New or Greatly Improved Products Since 1970		A Sampling of Medical Advances
Microwave oven	Laser printer	Radial keratectomy
Camcorder	Cordless phone	CAT-scan
Voice mail	Hand-held calculator	Ultrasound
Disposable diapers	Personal computer	In vitro fertilization
Modem	CD-Rom drive	Organ transplants
Internet	Electronic mail	Liposuction
Overnight delivery	Automatic teller	Soft contact lenses
Virtual reality	Doppler radar	Home pregnancy tests
Anti-lock brakes	Satellite navigation	Anti-allergenics
Fiber-optic cables	Satellite dishes	Monoclonal antibodies
Radar detector	Auto-focus camera	Cornea transplants
Cellular phone	Answering machine	Non-aspirin painkillers
Home-security systems	Small-screen TVs	Recombinant DNA drugs
Speech synthesizers	Big-screen TVs	Retin-A (cosmetics)
Pagers	Remote controls	Anti-ulcer drugs
Quartz/digital watches	Home theaters	Artificial pancreas
Fax machine	Digital/LED displays	LASIK eye surgery
Coffee makers	Video games	Tissue regeneration
Electronic date books	Food processors	Gene therapy
Electric knives	Aspertame	Hair restoration
In-line skates	Interactive toys	Impotence treatment
CDs and CD players	Exercise equipment	3-D Neurosurgery
Automobile airbags	All-terrain vehicles	Telemedicine
Videocassette recorder	Video Phones	Cryopreservation

son to open so many neighborhood stores. Now a family can watch Oscar-winning movies in the comfort of the living room for $3 or less, just a fraction of what it costs for a ticket to the theater. Toss a 75-cent packet into the microwave, and a couple of minutes later fresh popcorn is ready. The VCR isn't just for Hollywood's big-budget creations. A quarter century ago, families juggled schedules to be home for *Marcus Welby, M.D.* or *All in the Family*. Nowadays, any household with a teenager clever enough to operate a VCR can videotape shows, providing the convenience of watching what we want when we want.

A generation ago, family vacations captured with the 8-mm movie camera weren't ready for guffaws and giggles until the film returned from the photo lab. Today, palm-held camcorders make instant home movies—with sound, no less—that can be easily edited. We Americans grab the video camera to film our children being born, playing soccer, graduating from high school, and getting married. The videotapes pop out of the camera and into the VCR, ready to view on the television set. It's the perfect product for a society grow-ing accustomed to instant gratification.

Every once in a while, the nation scratches its collective head as Americans lose their senses over the latest version of the pet rock. Fads will come and go, but for the most part new products won't find lasting places in our everyday lives unless they provide useful ser-vices, ones worth paying hard-earned money for. What doesn't fulfill customers' needs, wants, or desires falls by the wayside.

The personal computer, a compact descendant of the hulking ma-chines of a quarter century ago, may provide the modern age's best ex-ample of a useful new product. It's not just the machines, of course. It's also the increasingly imaginative software that we can use with them, making routine tasks easier. Over the past two decades, computers have swept into our workplaces, our homes, and our schools. More than 100 million Americans used computers in 1996, a statistic that no doubt became out-of-date before it was even published. The computer will loom even larger in the future, as machines get easier to use and as the next generation comes of age computer-savvy. Today's young people are growing up with computers. American schools had nearly 7 million of them at the start of the 1996–97 school year, 11 times what they had a decade earlier. The number of students per computer dropped from 62.7 in 1984–85 to 7.4 in 1996–97.

We use computers every day to keep track of household finances, run small businesses, work on home projects, rummage through the wealth of information on CD-ROMS and listen to radio programs from all over the world. Here's a statistic to impress computer geeks: In 1998, the number of software titles exceeded 250,000. For many Americans, the computer's greatest benefit may lie in access to the In-ternet, obscure to all but a few scientists before the 1990s. Getting even the most rudimentary information once required a trek to the library or a series of frustrating phone calls. Now a worldwide net-work of interconnected computers permits users to tap into millions of Web sites, some with entertainment, some with information, some with goods for sale. From the comfort of our offices or living rooms, we can make reservations for a flight to Paris, browse companies' help-wanted advertising, catch up on the news or the latest sports scores, see if everything's still up-to-date in Kansas City. We can track investments and trade stocks: In 1998, Americans had 3 million on-line investing accounts, and the number likely will hit 14.4 million by 2002, according to Forrester Research. Electronic mail offers al-most instant delivery anywhere in the world. On-line chat rooms create electronic versions of cocktail parties. They're global gab-fests that can inform, entertain, titillate, and infuriate. In 1997, Intel Corp., a leading American technology company, introduced a computer version of the videotelephone, which uses a monitor-mounted videocamera and the Internet to transmit the images of the callers at both ends. Other companies use the technology to provide parents with live hookups to children's day-care centers.

Nothing succeeds like success. In a fast-moving era, truly significant innovations touch off whole new waves of technologies, each one enhancing the usefulness of what preceded it. Peripherals make computers more valuable by adding to what they can do. The mouse and touch-sensitive screens and even pens are replacing typewriter keyboards for issuing commands to computers. With the invention of the modem, the telephone can link up two computers, allowing them to swap data through a cacophony of squeaks, squawks, and squeals. Laser printers have made typing-pools obsolete. At the touch of a button, ink-jet models produce documents in a rainbow of colors, making every desktop a potential publishing house. Scanners enter volumes of information in a few seconds. A device has even been invented specifically for entering business cards into an address book. Digital photography, including a new generation of filmless cameras, puts the family album onto the computer's hard disk, so images can be edited, stored, sent over the Internet, or incorporated into Christmas cards. Programmable CD-ROMS came onto the market in 1997, opening the possibility of a huge increase in the computer's capacity to store data.

Usefulness comes in many forms. For an on-the-go society, an increasingly important feature is portability. A generation ago, just about every appliance except the portable radio had to be plugged in. These days, many electronic gadgets are no longer tethered to the wall. Battery-powered laptop computers, many of them just as powerful as desktop machines, allow users to take their jobs or hobbies almost anywhere. Another innovation using computer technology is the pocket organizer, a wallet-sized gadget that stores schedules, telephone numbers, addresses, important dates, and lists of clothing sizes for every member of the family. Motorists wanting to make a call while on the road once spent a lot of time searching out a pay telephone. Now, cellular technology has put the phone in the front seat, ready for getting a shopping list from home or making emergency calls when stranded on the highway. Cellular-phone companies served more than 64 million subscribers in 1998, up from 91,600 in 1984. As models have gotten smaller, the cellular telephone has turned into a personal accessory that can be taken almost anywhere in a pocket or handbag.

It's been said thousands of times: We live in a shrinking world. The phrase means, of course, that communication is getting faster and more reliable. In-a-hurry Americans wanting to send documents to another city in the early 1970s had little choice but to rely on the U.S. Postal Service. Federal Express pioneered overnight delivery in 1973. These days, the next day isn't fast enough. Facsimile machines and electronic mail can send the printed word just about anyplace on Earth in a few seconds. Teleconferences, impossible before satellites and fiber-optic connections, bring busy people face to face in an instant, often eliminating the time and expense of a long journey across the country or abroad. Getting cash once meant a trip to the bank, open from 9 A.M. to 3 P.M. Monday through Friday, excepting holidays. Today, day or night, on Christmas Day or the Fourth of July, we can make deposits and withdrawals in just seconds from automatic-teller machines all over the world.

Talking to a tape recorder rather than a human being was annoying at first, but the answering machine has become commonplace in homes and offices. Dialing up from the road, we can find out who called when we're out of town. A pager may beep all too often in the middle of a movie theater, but it does help busy people stay in touch. Parents are even using them to keep tabs on their kids. When the answering machine and pager first came on the market, many of us pledged never to use them. Once we saw how these devices added flexibility and convenience to our everyday lives, we not only used them, we came to depend on them. How many of us now wonder how we ever made it through a day without answering machines and pagers?

As the country has grown wealthier, we've found more time and money for entertainment. It shouldn't be surprising, then, that many of the past quarter century's most successful new products were among the most fun. When Elvis was king of rock 'n' roll, vinyl records could be ruined by warps and scratches. Today's compact discs produce better-quality sound. And they're virtually in normal use. Satellite dishes, introduced in the 1980s, multiply what's on television even as they get smaller and smaller. Modern-day kids spend hours playing video games that offer sports, adventures in outer space, aerial dogfights at twice the speed of sound, and the eerie worlds of blood and gore. Paintball, a martial exercise that replaces bullets with harmless globs of paint, lets adults and teenagers play the kids' shoot-'em-up game with realism. Virtual-reality technology—simulating sights, sounds, and sensations via computers—is no longer just for training airline pilots. It makes for a new generation of increasingly sophisticated arcade games. Leading-edge companies are working on a fusion of computers, television, and telecommunications, opening the possibility of all sorts of interactive entertainment and information.

We're also finding new outlets for fitness and recreation. Home gyms, stationary bikes, rowing machines, stair-stepping devices, and abdominal crunchers give busy fitness buffs an option of exercising in the home. In-line skates, introduced in the 1980s, make exercise more fun. New heart-pounding outdoor activities include all-terrain vehicles, jet skis, snowboards, windsurfers, indoor rock-climbing walls, and bungee-cord jumps.

Medicine has moved forward by leaps and bounds. The past 25 years have brought myriad medical breakthroughs—new drugs, new treatments, and new diagnostic tools—to enhance and prolong our lives. The pharmaceutical industry's laboratories have synthesized new pills to treat cancers, heart disease, headaches, ulcers, obesity, arthritis, mental disorders, hair loss, and impotence. DNA research now produces drugs specially designed for each patient. Every year, progress is being made against AIDS. Three decades after the first heart transplant, doctors are routinely transplanting livers, kidneys, lungs, and other organs. The number of operations has risen steadily over the past quarter century. Heart transplants rose from less than 10 in 1970 to 2,352 in 1997. Procedures involving other organs went from a few hundred in the 1970s to 17,619 in 1997. In all organ transplants, the one-year survival rate now exceeds 75 percent. A generation ago, few procedures were successful. Advances in medical technology are providing tangible benefits. We've never been healthier. Average life expectancy at birth rose by five years in the past quarter century. In the first half of the 1990s, it increased by nearly a year. We're healthier, too. Surveys by the U.S. Department of Health and Human Services show a drop in the portion of Americans who rate their health as "fair or poor"—from 12.2 percent in 1975 to 9.6 percent in 1994. Infant mortality rates fell from 20 deaths per 1,000 live births in 1970 to 8 in 1994. The death rate from natural causes fell by 27 percent between 1970 and 1990, with most of the progress coming in combating diseases of the heart.

New medical devices touch our everyday lives. Easy-to-use home tests tell us about pregnancy and the AIDS virus. In vitro fertilization, artificial insemination, and fertility drugs help couples have children. Quick, painless laser procedures can correct some patients' blurry vision, freeing them from wearing glasses. For the headaches of the early 1970s there was aspirin. Today's throbbing isn't any less painful, but among the ever growing array of over-the-counter remedies consumers can choose from acetaminophen (in Tylenol), ibuprofen (in Advil, Motrin, and other brands), naproxen sodium (in Aleve), and ketoprofen (in Orudus KT and Actron). Americans bought antacids a quarter century ago, but such new over-the-counter drugs as Axid, Pepcid AC, Tagamet, and Zantac 75 prevent heartburn before it starts. In the early 1970s, doctors used X-rays to examine bones and teeth, but today they can use CAT scans and magnetic resonance machines to examine soft tissues. Sonograms help ensure that babies are born healthier. They can also tell parents whether to paint the nursery pink or blue. Although some may dismiss them as pure vanity, liposuction, cosmetic surgery, hair-replacement treatments, and contact lenses that turn brown eyes blue—improve our looks and self-esteem. The latest turn-back-the-clock technique involves removing wrinkles with injections of a patient's own cloned collagen. Computerized devices help paraplegics establish greater independence. The emerging practice of "telemedicine" uses video cameras, computers, and phone lines to allow doctors to treat patients from afar.

Not all the advances of the past quarter century are on store shelves. Even if consumers don't buy the innovations, they get the benefits. Doppler radar improves the accuracy of weather forecasting. At the supermarket, clerks ring up prices by swiping each item across a bar-code scanner, moving goods and people through the checkout line a little more quickly and helping stores keep track of inventory. Modern technology has seeped into the production process, making plants more productive and enhancing quality control. Robots build automobiles and sew blue jeans. Computers run entire factories. Fiber-optic cables half the width of a human hair deliver faster, clearer telephone calls. In cellular phones, microchips translate words into electronic pulses, reduce static, and store telephone numbers. Deliveries speed up because hand-held computers, some of which "read" handwriting, allow warehouse workers to process orders and keep track of inventory almost instantly. Software goes into thousands of behind-the-scenes applications, from managing air-traffic control systems to tracking packages in global transit to bringing to life the dinosaurs of *Jurassic Park*.

If Not New, At Least Better

Not everything was invented in the last generation, of course. A typical household contains plenty of products that have stood the test of time. Our Rip van Winkle might wonder what a beeper does or how a video-cassette recorder works, but he would certainly recognize telephones, televisions, refrigerators, stoves, and lawn mowers. In using them, however, he'd find that most are a lot better than they used to be.

Take the automobile. Although car buffs may still rave about the Corvettes and Mustangs of yesteryear, today's models offer more powerful engines and travel 60 percent farther on a gallon of gas. A quarter century ago, cars needed maintenance twice a year. Now they routinely travel up to 100,000 miles between tune-ups. A lot of it has to do with the microchip. The typical modern car has more than two dozen computers to regulate fuel mixture, timing, ignition, suspension, engine diagnostics, emissions, air bags, instrument panels, seat positions, and more. The cars that zoom down today's highways possess more computing power than the *Apollo 11* landing module that first put astronauts on the moon.

We've already seen that new cars have dozens of built-in improvements—from air bags and antilock brakes to power windows and door locks. That's not all. Tires fix their own flats. Sound systems, with quadraphonic speakers and compact-disc players, outperform most home stereos of 1970. At least 20 million drivers have installed radar detectors in their cars since Dale Smith, a victim of one speeding ticket too many, developed the Fuzzbuster. The latest accessory making its mark on our car-besotted culture is a navigating device that determines a car's precise location by fixing on global-positioning satellites. Once the tracking system becomes standard equipment, folding maps may become as distant a memory as walking across the room to change channels on the television. Consumers appreciate all the improvements in their vehicles: The J. D. Power survey for the 1997 model year found the overall quality of new cars and trucks to be the best ever.

DuPont's old slogan "Better living through chemistry" finds confirmation all around us. Treatments make modern fabrics last longer and require less care, adding to the value of clothing and linens. Plastics can be strong, flexible, and light enough to make grocery and garbage bags, or hard and clear enough for windows capable of stopping a bullet. Teflon keeps food from sticking to pots and pans and lubricates engine parts. Today's photographic film offers brighter, truer colors. New cleaning products reduce the need for scrubbing and kill germs with antibacterial agents. Charcoal ignites with the touch of a match. In toothpaste, fluoride is yesterday's news. The 1990s saw the introduction of formulas to fight tartar, a cause of tooth decay and gum diseases. The toothbrush of 25 years ago came in one basic design, with a flat, rectangular surface and straight edge. At least 25 models are on drug-store shelves today, and they've been enhanced with new shapes and rippled bristle designs, making it easier to clean between teeth and deep into the mouth. A change of bristle color reminds us when to replace the toothbrush.

An important way companies continuously improve products is by adding new features. Color televisions incorporate stereo sound, on-screen displays and picture-within-a-picture windows previewing second and third channels, all activated by remote control. Connecting the "surround sound" stereo system with the television creates a home theater for middle-class families. The standard 35-mm camera comes equipped with automatic focus, built-in flash, zoom lenses, and automatic settings to compensate for varying levels of light. Tape recorders fit in pockets and purses. Programmable memories, embedded in products' computer chips, make microwave ovens, videocassette recorders, televisions, cellular phones, and other devices more user-friendly. Digital video and still cameras come equipped with small screens that show what finished pictures will look like. Pagers now deliver not only phone numbers but text and voice messages as well. The office copier isn't just faster. It can also reproduce color, handle up to five sizes of paper, change the size of the image, and even collate, punch holes, and staple.

Practically all new refrigerators are now frost-free, and many feature ice-makers and through-the-door water dispensers. Ovens clean themselves. Yesterday's blender has now become a food processor, with attachments for slicing, dicing, mincing, pureeing, juicing, and more. Lawn mowers incorporate electric starters to eliminate the tug-of-war with the engine and solid-state ignitions to reduce the need for tune-ups. Rear-bagging attachments make mowers more maneuverable. Some models mulch grass clippings to nourish the lawn and relieve our backs of the strain of raking.

Computers improve by leaps and bounds. At the start of the 1990s, the fastest microprocessor could handle 27 million instructions per second. The latest generation, out in 1998, ramped up to a phenomenal 2 billion instructions per second. Indeed, nothing exemplifies the speed of today's technology better than Moore's law, formulated by Intel's Gordon Moore in the 1960s. He observed that the power of the microchip would double every 18 months. With the advances of the 1990s, the interval for each milestone in computer performance has shrunk to nine months. More powerful computers can run more sophisticated programs. Spreadsheets capable of juggling thousands of numbers allow small businesses to control their entire finances from a single desktop model.

Greater power is just an appetizer on the menu of computer advances. Hard drives can store as much data as a good-sized library. Eye-pleasing color monitors replaced the green-tinted ones of the early 1980s. Sound cards have given computers the ability to beep, chirp, bark, talk, and play music. The common telephone-line modem picks up speed year by year: America entered the 1990s using modems with a top speed of 9.6 kilobytes per second. By 1997, the fastest telephone modem had reached 56 kilobytes per second. Intel, Microsoft Corp., and Compaq Computer Corp. joined with several telephone companies to promise modems 30 times faster at the end of 1998. Power and speed aren't the only constants in computer technology. Another perpetual theme is smaller and smaller. The latest palm-sized models weigh less than a pound, but they can run full-scale computer programs, with some even providing fax programs and Internet connections.

Since the introduction of solid-state electronics, televisions, radios, stereos, and other appliances don't go dead with blown vacuum tubes. Are appliances more reliable? Here's one piece of empirical evidence: While the number of household television sets jumped from 81 million in 1970 to 217 million in 1995, the number of radio and television repair shops fell from 7,953 to 5,351. The decrease from 10 to only 2.5 shops per 100,000 televisions indicates that fixing televisions isn't a growth industry. Modern appliances are far more energy-efficient, too. Since 1972, electricity usage fell 62 percent for refrigerators, 50 percent for dishwashers, 42 percent for clothes washers, and 36 percent for air conditioners. Greater reliability and efficiency aren't just characteristics of major appliances: Light bulbs also last longer and use less electricity.

We may not be better athletes, but improvements in sports equipment probably allow us to play better. Few products have come as far as the humble sneaker. Wilt Chamberlain wannabes of the early 1970s took to the court in canvas-topped Converse All-Stars, with unpadded, flat rubber bottoms. Aspiring Michael Jordans of the 1990s lace up leather-upper models cushioned with pneumatic pumps, air pockets, or gels. Nike, Reebok, and other manufacturers spend millions of dollars a year on research and development to find ways to add support, absorb shocks, improve traction, and extend durability. The benefit for athletes, whether National Basketball Association stars or weekend warriors, is better performance and fewer injuries. Oversized golf clubs, now made with graphite and titanium, hit balls farther with fewer errant shots into the rough. The wood and steel tennis rackets of the 1970s became obsolete with the introduction of models crafted of graphite, ceramics, and Kevlar, all of which provide greater control and power. The "sweet spot" grew bigger, while the grips became better cushioned to absorb the shock of overhead slams. Bicycles lost their banana seats, but they're now made of lighter-weight metals and ease the strain of hill climbing with up to 21 gears. New styles with wide tires and sturdy frames created a whole new sport of off-road biking.

Critics of American materialism might call many of these consumer products trivial, mere toys for a spiritually bankrupt lifestyle. That's a value judgment that can be neither verified nor refuted. One person's nuisance might be another's blessing. Try telling an opera buff that the clarity of sound on a compact disc isn't a great boon to mankind. Try telling a motorist stranded on a lonely highway that a cellular telephone isn't a godsend. Many of us no doubt question the social value of video games and liposuction, but on the whole, technology has made life more pleasurable and less burdensome. We shouldn't forget, moreover, that the list of commonplace advances made over the past 25 years includes robots that allow doctors to operate without slicing into patients, computers that increase productivity, lifesaving air bags in automobiles, and a host of other inventions.

We ought to marvel at this. Just walk from room to room and count the number of things that even the richest Americans could only have dreamed of owning a mere 25 years ago. The bounty is far from finished. Some Cadillac models in the year 2000 will offer night-vision technology, borrowed from the military's early 1990s Desert Storm exercise in the Middle East, to allow drivers to see cars, pedestrians, and animals in the dark or fog. In the next few years, American consumers are likely to get the chance to buy Dick Tracy–like wristwatch phones, hand-held translators for the spoken word, the crystal-clear images of high-definition televisions, flat television screens that hang on the wall like pictures, electric cars, robotic vacuum cleaners, synthetic skin to repair burn victims' disfigurement, cloned organs, and much more.

Variety Spices Up the Economy

New and improved products are only one way the American economy is enriching consumers. Further evidence of rising living standards comes from the modern marketplace's profusion of models, colors, flavors, styles, sizes, shapes, and speeds. There's been an explosion of variety in nearly every product category. A cynic might brush it all off as frivolous duplication, but variety allows each of us to select more of the characteristics we value. Black telephones work just fine, but some people simply prefer red, white, or baby-blue ones. In a world of black shoes, a woman might not go barefoot, but she'll enjoy an evening out more if she wears shoes that match her dress. Vanilla ice cream is good. The choice of 31 flavors is better, especially if your taste buds are all set for mocha chocolate almond.

It might be cheaper to standardize consumer products. In fact, that was the very inclination of the now-defunct communist states, where bureaucrats dictated that one or two models of cars and a few types of shoes would be enough. Even in the United States, variety wasn't always an important selling point. The best the technology of the early industrial era could do was stamp out endless undifferentiated copies. Thus, Henry Ford offered the Model T in one color—black. Today's production methods offer greater flexibility. Mass production is giving way to mass customization. Here's a device that captures the concept perfectly: CD World, a New York company, formed a joint venture with Sprint, the long-distance telephone company, to create Music Point kiosks, which allow customers to create their own compact discs from an inventory of 50,000 songs.

As with so many other aspects of a free-enterprise economy, variety is simply a matter of giving consumers what they want. The market delivers a multiplicity of styles, brands, models, and colors in tacit recognition of the fact that tastes and preferences aren't homogeneous. It does so from a motive no more sublime than the self-interest of companies looking to make money. Variety increases value to consumers, so producers who indulge our tastes for it increase their sales. We have more diversity because there's a market for it, one built on rising incomes. Poor societies have few choices. Variety is a luxury available to wealthy nations.

As one looks back over the past quarter century, examples of the increasing variety are as easy to find as new products. Our choice of restaurants has expanded to include Ethiopian, Korean, Egyptian, Vietnamese, and dozens of other types of cuisine. A big-city Yellow

Pages lists restaurants that specialize in the food of more than 40 countries. We have Coke, Diet Coke, and two types of caffeine-free Coke—and those are just the offerings of one flavor by one company. All told, nationally distributed brands of types of carbonated soft drinks grew from 20 in 1970 to 87 in 1995. In fact, the number of diet colas today exceeds the total number of brands on the market in 1970. Commonly available fruit juices once could be counted on the fingers of both hands. Today's supermarkets stock 30 or more, including such blends as guava-orange and cranberry-grape. The number of brands of breakfast cereals jumped from 160 in 1980 to 340 in the mid-1990s.

Snack foods cater to almost every taste, from the traditional potato chips and pretzels to Fritos Chili Cheese–Flavored Corn Chips and Rold Gold Honey Mustard–Flavored Sourdough Pretzel Bits. Frito-Lay Co., the nation's snack-food leader since the 1960s, offered 10 varieties of potato chips, corn chips, cheese snacks, onion rings, and pretzels in 1970. By 1996, the company offered 78 different flavors of these and similar products, not including cookies and dips. Beer connoisseurs lament the passing of regional breweries, but the marketplace has responded with an array of widely distributed beers, with some outlets carrying nearly 400. In addition, an explosion of microbreweries is reviving the tradition of locally produced beer fresh from the tap.

Although such automakers as Renault and Citroen have left the highly competitive U.S. automobile market since the early 1970s, today's consumers can now choose from nearly twice as many producers, both domestic and foreign, whose assembly lines turn out more makes with more options than ever before. All told, a car shopper dedicated to exploring all possibilities would have to sift though 1,200 different styles of vehicles. The sport-utility vehicle (SUV), a hot-selling cross between the van and the station wagon, didn't reach showrooms until the 1980s. Now, the SUV inventory stretches to nearly 40 models, from 20 manufacturers.

Televisions in 1972 came in five screen sizes—10 inches to 24 inches. Now, manufacturers customize televisions for dozens of uses, ranging from 3-inch hand-held models to 11-footers too big for our living rooms. What we watch on our television sets provides further testimony to increasing variety. A generation ago, most people tuned in what the three networks served up, with perhaps an independent station or two. Now, cable television offers access to dozens of stations—news, sports, educational programs, movies, MTV, and, for those who still wish to return to the 1950s, seemingly endless reruns of *I Love Lucy*. In 1996, 3 of 10 American households paid for cable service, up from a negligible amount in 1975. The next wave of television began arriving in the 1990s: satellite-based digital-TV systems. Using dishes no larger than a pepperoni pizza to receive signals from space, they expand household viewing options beyond even cable. DirectTV, one of the leading brands, offers more than 175 channels, including 32 for sports and 14 for movies. Pay-per-view features eliminate the drive to the Blockbuster store. Satellite systems fully enfranchise viewers in remote areas that have few over-the-air stations or limited access to cable. Radio is no longer local, either. Via the Internet, listeners can now tune in to hundreds of radio stations from every part of the world.

Despite oft-heard laments that Americans no longer have time to read, magazines crowd the newsstands in unprecedented numbers. General-interest publications aren't the only source of growth. New magazines cater to ever narrower interests. On a windy day, try *American Kite*. A doll collector surely won't want to miss an issue of *Barbie Bazaar*. Those on the go might stop long enough to pick up *Trailer Life*. For devotees of photography, the offerings run the gamut from *Aperture* to *Zoom*. Even all these magazines haven't quenched our thirst for the written word. The number of new books and editions coming from U.S. publishers rose from 36,071 in 1972 to 62,039 in 1995.

American ingenuity isn't limited to high technology. Retailers too are always trying out new ideas for reaching customers, remaking their industry with one innovation after another. As far back as the 1940s, stores started following their customers to the suburbs, giving rise to highway-hugging malls that just grew bigger and bigger. The newest ones are offering as much entertainment as shopping. In the past two decades, Wal-Mart, Target, and other discounters arrived to challenge traditional department stores. Hundreds of specialty stores increased the variety of goods available in the marketplace. In 1996, the United States has an estimated 20 square feet of retail space for every man, woman, and child, up from 14.7 in 1986. Great Britain, second in the world, has only 2 square feet per person. General merchandising catalogues such as Sears, Roebuck and Montgomery Ward lost favor over the years, but L.L. Bean, Victoria's Secret, and others created their own niches in the mail-order sector. The growth of cable television made possible the Home Shopping Network and other video retailers. Virtual storefronts, the latest wrinkle in reaching customers, are now popping up by the thousands on the Internet.

Just as in the evolution of any technology, each new idea in retailing created winners and losers among companies and reshuffled jobs. The ultimate beneficiaries, of course, have been consumers, who've gotten added convenience, a wider selection, and lower prices.

Within the confines of a few pages, it's impossible to catalogue every new product and every new wrinkle of the past 25 years. A shopping trip almost anywhere in America will provide ample proof of the astonishing array of goods and services on sale. A few numbers provide a good summary. In 1996 alone, 8,594 consumer products entered the U.S. market. The survey includes only packaged goods at grocery and drug stores, so it misses big chunks of innovation, including the proliferation of electronic marvels. To fit all the new and improved merchandise, retail space had to triple over the past 25 years. The lament of modern consumers isn't that there's too little to buy but that there are *too many* choices.

Decisions, decisions.

The Price Isn't Always Right

Those who yearn for the good old days wax nostalgic about the prices of everyday goods and services. At the start of the 1970s, Americans paid $4,287 for a new Ford Galaxie 500. It took just 20 cents to buy a hamburger at McDonald's, then still at work selling its first billion. The prices of yesteryear certainly look like bargains when measured against what today's Americans pay—$17,995 for a 1997 Ford Taurus and $1.89 for a Big Mac.

Everything does seem to cost more than it used to. The Consumer Price Index, the government's main gauge of inflation, shows that a bundle of goods that cost $100 in 1970 now goes for nearly $400. It's enough to make us anguish about inflation eating away at our living standards. Even when prices are going up at a moderate rate, it's easy to get the impression we're running in place, our paychecks always a few steps behind what we pay for food, gasoline, utilities, and household goods.

The prices we pay, however, aren't an accurate guide to the real cost of goods and services, especially over long periods of time. The discrepancy lies in the fact that money doesn't retain a constant value. Over time, prices go up. The value of money goes down. Dollar-and-cents prices give the impression that what we buy is getting more expensive year by year. We shouldn't forget, though, that wages and incomes go up at the same time. The best way to get around the inflation in money prices lies in figuring what goods and services cost in terms of a standard that doesn't change—hours and minutes of work. Time is money. We've all heard that. For the vast majority of American workers, it's literally true. The real price of whatever we buy is how long we have to work to earn the money for it. Henry David Thoreau noted this in *Walden:* "The cost of a thing is the amount of what I will call life which is required to be exchanged for it, immediately and in the long run."

The rate of exchange between time and money is a function of productivity, the value of a typical worker's output in an hour. Our productivity determines the value of our time—that is, our wages. As each generation of companies and workers has grown more productive, wages have risen faster than prices. To put it another way, the cost of just about everything we consume, expressed in the currency of time, has been going down. In fact, there's a regular pattern to *real* prices in our dynamic economy. Soon after products come onto the market, their wage-adjusted prices fall quickly. Once goods and services become commonplace, prices usually continue to fall, but at a slower rate. This tendency shows up in such everyday purchases as housing, food, clothing, gasoline, electricity, and long-distance telephone rates. It applies to manufactured goods, including automobiles, home appliances, and the modern age's myriad electronic marvels. Year after year, it takes less of our work time to buy entertainment and services—movies, pizza, airline tickets, dry cleaning, and the like. The real cost of living in America keeps going *down.*

We can see it first thing in the morning. In terms of work time, the price of bacon and eggs has fallen 40 percent since 1970. Coffee requires the same work effort as it did a quarter century ago, although the supermarket price has risen by a factor of four. The cost of a half gallon of milk fell from 10 minutes in 1970 to 7 minutes in 1997. A pound of ground beef declined by more than 5 minutes. The labor cost of a three-pound chicken fryer has dropped more than 9 minutes. A dozen oranges is worth 10 minutes' work, cheaper by 6 minutes since 1970. A sample of 12 food staples—a market basket varied enough to provide three square meals—shows that what required 2 hours, 22 minutes of work time to buy in 1970 now takes only 1 hour, 45 minutes. The supermarket receipt for these groceries would have read $7.93 in 1970 and $23.06 in 1997, an increase of 191 percent. After adjusting for higher wages, the market basket was actually 26 percent cheaper (see Figure 2.1).

FIGURE 2.1 Working Less for Our Daily Bread

FOOD BASKET		
Tomatoes, 3 lb.	Oranges, 1 dozen	Lettuce, 1 lb.
Eggs, 1 dozen	Coffee, 1 lb.	Beans, 1 lb.
Sugar, 5 lb.	Milk, half gallon	Bread, 1 lb.
Bacon, 1 lb.	Ground beef, 1 lb.	Onions, 1 lb.

Saving the equivalent of 37 minutes of work per week isn't inconsequential for living standards. The consumers' gain on just these 12 supermarket items, bought once a week, adds up to 32 hours a year, enough to purchase ticket packages for a family of four to Disney's Magic Kingdom, Epcot, and MGM Studios in Orlando, Florida.

In 1997, a new, single-family home cost six times what it did in the early 1970s—in dollar terms. After adjusting for the increase in the size of new homes and higher pay, however, most of the inflation disappears. A 1,975-square-foot, median-priced new home cost 9,961 hours in 1970 and 11,039 hours in 1997, or 1,078 additional hours. Over 27 years, then, the average work time required to buy a new home rose only 10 percent, or the equivalent of six months. Mortgage rates are a percentage point lower than they were in the early 1970s. On a house with a 5 percent down payment, the break in interest payments will trim the work cost of a new house over a 30-year purchase by 1,561 hours, a reduction of nine months on the job needed to pay for the house.

Another consideration involves a decrease in household size during the past quarter century. Each residence today houses, on average, fewer people than it did in 1970, so in buying a median-sized home each person is getting more square feet. If we take into account shrinking household size, then an individual's living space is actually 6 percent cheaper than it was in 1970. The adjustments show that housing is more affordable, but they still haven't captured all of the added value in most of the homes coming onto the market. As we've already shown, new homes are more likely to contain central heating, air conditioning, kitchen appliances, extra bathrooms, garages, better insulation, and many other extras. Prices of new homes include these amenities, so an accounting of what's happened to the real cost of housing remains elusive.

What's inside our homes is getting cheaper, too. Over the past quarter century, consumers benefited from declines in the work-time cost of at least 80 percent for kitchen stoves, 60 percent for dishwashers, 64 percent for clothes washers, 56 percent for vacuum cleaners, 54 percent for clothes dryers, 40 percent for refrigerators, and 39 percent for lawn mowers. A mattress and box spring slipped from 84 hours in 1970 to 61 hours in 1997. Room air conditioners now cost 23 hours of work for a 5,000-BTU unit, down from 45 in 1970. A portable radio declined from more than 13 hours to less than 1 hour. One hundred kilowatt hours of electricity is cheaper than at any time since 1974 (see Table 2.2).

If any invention has put a mark on American culture, it's the car. We take it as our birthright to own one—often, two or three. Higher sticker prices don't seem to cool the nation's ardor for the automobile. No wonder. When the appropriate adjustments are made, many models are more affordable than their counterparts of a generation ago. The 1970 Ford Galaxie 500, a mid-size family sedan, cost 1,400 hours of work when equipped with just a few of the options that are standard on today's automobiles. The 1997 Ford Taurus, a top-selling mid-size car, took 1,365 hours—roughly a week less. As a bonus, the Taurus's price covered features unavailable on the Galaxie—dual air bags, power windows and doors, adjustable steering wheel, cassette deck, and other goodies. That's not the end of the road for American drivers. A gallon of gasoline required just 5.7 minutes of work in 1997, compared with 6.4 minutes in 1970, three years *before* oil prices

TABLE 2.2 Time Is on Our Side: Work Time Required to Buy Various Products and Services

Product	1900	1910	1920	1930	1940	1950	1960	1970	1980	1990	Latest
Minutes:											
Half-gallon of milk	56	49	37	31	21	16	13	10	8.7	8	7
One-pound loaf of bread	*	16	13	10	7	6	5.4	4	4	4	3.5
One dozen oranges	*	*	69	63	27	21	20	15	11	11	9
Hershey chocolate bar	20	16	6	6	5	2	1.3	1.8	2	2.2	2.1
Gallon of gasoline	*	*	32	22	17	11	8.3	6.4	10	6.5	5.7
Movie ticket	*	*	17	17	16	18	17	28	22	23	19
Hours and Minutes:											
Three-minute coast-to-coast call	*	90 hrs. 40 min.	30 hrs. 3 min.	16 hrs. 29 min.	6 hrs. 7 min.	1 hr. 44 min.	1 hr.	24 min.	11 min.	4 min.	2 min.
Pair of Levis	9 hrs. 42 min.	9 hrs. 30 min.	10 hrs. 36 min.	5 hrs. 18 min.	4 hrs. 30 min.	4 hrs.	2 hrs.	2 hrs.	2 hrs.	2 hrs.	3 hrs.
Three-pound chicken	2 hrs. 40 min.	3 hrs. 5 min.	2 hrs. 27 min.	2 hrs. 1 min.	1 hr. 24 min.	1 hr. 11 min.	33 min.	22 min.	18 min.	14 min.	14 min.
100 kilowatt hrs. of electricity	107 hrs. 17 min.	49 hrs. 48 min.	13 hrs. 36 min.	11 hrs. 3 min.	5 hrs. 52 min.	2 hrs. 0 min.	1 hr. 9 min.	39 min.	45 min.	43 min.	38 min.
Computing power of 1 MIPS	*	*	*	*	*	515,000 lifetimes	na	1.2 lifetimes	41 wks.	13 hrs.	9 min.
McDonald's Big Mac	*	*	*	*	*	*	*	10 min.	9 min.	9.5 min.	8 min.
100 miles of air travel	*	*	*	12 hrs. 46 min.	8 hrs. 14 min.	4 hrs. 7 min.	2 hrs. 43 min.	1 hr. 42 min.	1 hr. 27 min.	1 hr. 11 min.	1 hr. 2 min.

surged. If we consider the 60 percent increase in average miles per gallon that cars get now, the work time to drive a typical car 100 miles has been nearly halved over the past quarter century—from 49 minutes in 1970 to 28 minutes today. Time spent on the job to rent a car fell 37 percent. Judged by the cost per mile, modern tires cost half what they used to. Batteries requiring constant maintenance once went dead every few years. Now, they don't need servicing at all, and they're guaranteed for a car's life, reducing the cost of just cranking up the engine.

Americans possess more free time than ever. So it's not surprising that our consumption centers on leisure-time activities. What helps make good times good is the declining real costs of everyday pleasures. The price of a movie fell from 28 minutes in 1970 to 19 minutes in 1997. Compared to a generation ago, each 100 miles of air travel now requires 40 minutes less work, a boon to vacationing families. A seven-day Caribbean cruise declined from 51 hours in 1972 to 45 hours in 1997. It's even getting cheaper to look good: The price of dry cleaning a dress dropped by 3 percent. A men's suit from Hart, Shaffner & Marx sells for $525, or 40 hours of work time. In 1970, it was $165—or 49 hours. Soft contact lenses plummeted from 95 hours, 14 minutes in 1971 to 3 hours, 48 minutes in 1997—and the latest versions are more comfortable and can be worn longer.

We're a nation of junk-food junkies, a fact that outrages nutritionists and gourmets alike. Our health and palates aside, Americans may be eating more of these foods because they're getting cheaper. A large pepperoni pizza cost 1 hour, 11 minutes in 1970. Now, it's down to 50 minutes. A 6.5-ounce serving of Coca-Cola declined from 3.5 minutes in 1970 to 1.5 minutes today. A 1-ounce bag of Lay's potato chips dropped by a third in the past 25 years. A McDonald's hamburger now costs 20 percent less in minutes of work than it did in 1970. The Big Mac fell 13 percent. The world-famous double-decker hamburger also captures what we as consumers do as we get wealthier—move up to higher quality. It's true for houses and cars. Nostalgists often ignore improvements in goods and services, yet remember fondly the prices they paid long ago for the cheapest versions of products.

When we talk about prices, it's usually because they're going up. For many products, however, they go down, not just in work hours but in straight dollars and cents. A hand-held calculator too bulky to fit easily into a pocket or purse sold for $120 in 1972. A mere quarter century later, a true *pocket* calculator sells for $9.99—cheaper even than a slide rule was in 1952. A 19-inch color television with remote control sold for as little as $299 in 1997, compared with $620 in 1971 and more than $1,000 when color came on the market in the mid-1950s. In 1997, a family could buy a 25-inch model for less than the 19-inch set cost in 1971. Videocassette recorders entered the mainstream consumer market at $985 in 1978. Twenty years later, models offering more precise picture tracking, on-screen programming, and other features cost less than $200. Cellular telephones sold for $4,200 in 1984; they're down to less than $100 today. Some deals are even sweeter: The telephones themselves are often free to customers who sign on with a service provider. On top of that, the monthly fees are about half what they were a decade ago. Camcorders, now smaller and with added features, cost less than half of the $1,500 they did in 1987. These aren't isolated examples. During the past generation, money prices fell for microwave ovens, pagers, generic drugs, long-distance telephone calls, and computer peripherals.

Falling prices and rising wages make a powerful combination for consumer welfare. After money prices are converted into hours and minutes of work, many of the modern age's signature products become even better bargains. The calculator's price plummeted from 31 hours in 1972 to 45 minutes, less time than it takes for lunch. A color television that required one month's work to buy in 1971 is now just three days' work. Videocassette recorders sell for 15 hours—90 percent less than they did in 1970. Over the past 25 years, work time required to buy a cellular telephone declined 97 percent. It took an average worker more than 97 hours on the job to buy a microwave oven in 1975. Now, it's down to 15 hours. In 1977, video cameras arrived on the consumer market at a cost 62 hours of work. Two decades later, the camcorder's cost is down to 42 hours.

Computing power provides perhaps the most startling example of something getting cheaper as it becomes an everyday product. An IBM mainframe circa 1970, capable of 12.5 million calculations per second (MIPS), sold for almost $4.7 million. Today, we may easily pay less than $1,000 for a personal computer capable of operating 20 times faster. In average work time, the cost of computing is down to 19 minutes for each 1 million calculations per second, a price likely to continue falling. And what about the IBM mainframe of the mid-1970s? Owning enough computing power to plow through 1 million calculations per second would have taken 1.25 lifetimes of work.

The Internet provides a stunning example of how computers are reducing costs. Once a researcher buys his machine and signs up with a service provider, the marginal cost of information, in money terms at least, falls to zero. In cyberspace, he can travel in seconds from libraries in the Ukraine to the United Kingdom, a trip that would cost thousands of dollars via conventional transport. For the typical family, an Internet connection promises to reduce the time, effort, and money spent on everyday tasks. Comparing the prices and features of new cars used to take days of trudging from one dealer to another. Now, it can be done in a few hours by visiting Web sites.

Whether it's calculators or computers, Americans are getting the best of all worlds—improved products for less effort. This isn't new. While the gains in work-time costs over the past quarter century are matters of minutes, a longer-term view shows spectacular decreases in the work time required to buy many products. Three pounds of chicken took 2 hours, 40 minutes of toil in 1919. Today it is 14 minutes. The price of a kilowatt of electricity converted into 11 work hours in 1930—but today it is 38 minutes. As late as 1950, a three-minute telephone call required more than two and a half hours' work. Today it requires just 2 minutes.

Today's commonplace consumer goods aren't likely to post spectacular price declines in the future, but the future will bring a new generation of products that will repeat the pattern of falling prices. In the late 1990s, electronics manufacturers will begin offering high-definition television (HDTV), a technology that promises to deliver crystal-clear images into American living rooms. When HDTV sets hit the market toward the end of 1998, they cost as much as a used car, about $8,000 and up. Within a few years, they no doubt will sell for a quarter or even a tenth of their original price. If the past counts for anything, the hours of work required to own one of the sets will fall even faster than the dollars-and-cents price.

That so many products have become more and more affordable isn't simply dumb luck. Just about all goods and services go through a cycle of falling prices and improving quality as companies ratchet up to large-scale production, as markets expand, as competition arrives in the marketplace, and as goods and services evolve from luxuries to everyday conveniences. The falling real cost of living shows up in such everyday necessities as housing, food, gasoline, and electricity. It also applies to manufactured goods—clothing, home appliances, and the modern age's myriad electronic marvels. Year after year, it takes less work time to afford entertainment and services—movies, haircuts, airline tickets, dry cleaning, and the like.

What were once luxuries become everyday necessities—and whole industries are born, creating jobs for many workers. Many of the growth industries of the future will be those cutting-edge products that have small markets today. By looking back, we can see this clearly. An American living in 1900, with enough foresight, could have anticipated the coming of some of the great industries and technologies of the twentieth-century: electricity, automobiles, telephones, radios, cameras, recorded music. A small segment of society already enjoyed these products, but in the coming decades they would blossom into mass-market phenomena. Thirty years later, with the country in the depths of the Depression, a perceptive American might have seen the next generation of new industries ready to come of age—for example, passenger air travel and television. In the first two decades after World War II, jet aircraft became available for civilian use, and the transistor revolutionized electronics. Consumption became more democratic. Up-and-coming industries included housing, fast food, travel and tourism, leisure pursuits, and all kinds of prepared foods. Minute Rice came on the market in 1951. The TV frozen dinner arrived in 1954, and sugar-free soft drinks arrived in 1962. Conveniences introduced in the 1950s and 1960s included solar batteries, Pampers, electric typewriters, stereo records, felt-tip pens, credit cards, touch-tone phones, and cassette tape recorders. At home, families splurged on appliances, from clothes dryers and air conditioners to dishwashers and vacuum cleaners. Fast-forward one more time. So many of the new products from the 1970s and 1980s are already fixtures in our lives: cable television, cellular telephones, computers, calculators, facsimile machines, videocassette recorders, camcorders, compact discs, and dozens of chip-based electronic gadgets.

The story of how the automobile came to be the signature product of America's consumer culture illustrates how economic forces work to consumers' benefit. Henry Ford's critics dismissed the automobile, selling for the equivalent of two years' factory wages in 1908, as a "rich man's toy," beyond the means of the workers who built it. Early automakers built each vehicle to order, an expensive, time-consuming enterprise. Ford revolutionized the industry with the assembly line, the key to efficient mass production. He standardized parts and developed networks of suppliers. By doing this, Ford took advantage of the gains from specialization, which increases efficiency by allowing workers and companies to do what they do best. Over the years, the automobile industry expanded, spreading overhead costs over longer production runs. Just as important, it continually invested in new technology. The development of plastics after World War II, for example, led to lighter, less expensive parts. By the 1990s, robots had taken over the routine jobs on the assembly line. Computers are lead-ing the latest assaults on production costs in the automobile indus-try. A frontal crash test, which in 1985 cost $60,000 to perform, can now be simulated in cyberspace for $200. A three-dimensional object printer cut the cost of prototype parts from $20,000 to $20.

Companies don't make consumers better off out of civic duty. The spur is competition—and it was fierce in the early years of the auto-mobile industry. The United States had more than 360 car manufac-turers in 1920, all sensing a fast-growing industry, all vying in a race that had no clear-cut winners. The companies that emerged from the fracas were those offering consumers the highest quality at the low-est price. Hundreds dropped out of the market, but their efforts didn't go to waste. Good ideas—the automatic transmission, for example—were embodied in the products of industry survivors. Now, as the market becomes increasingly global, automakers are still vying for customers, a fact documented by the proliferation of new features and improved quality in recent decades.

The automobile industry hasn't been alone in adopting modern technology and production methods. Increased productivity has spread across the economy, from agriculture and services to mining and manufacturing. If anything, competition in most industries is growing more relentless, in both price and quality. The benefits flow to consumers in the form of greater value—more for our money and more money for our time.

The rigorous application of industrial technologies increased pro-ductivity, which means more output from each worker. Productivity is the vital element in more affordable products. As each worker's output rises, the cost of production falls. Output per hour of work in the U.S. economy increased by almost a third between 1973 and 1997. In manufacturing, it nearly doubled. Greater productivity pushed wages up, decade by decade, for most American workers, a big part of the explanation of how we as a society can afford more of just about everything.

Falling real prices points us toward the role of the well-to-do in dri-ving progress forward. New products are usually *very* expensive, well beyond the budgets of all but a few wealthy families or big corpora-tions. A relatively small number of consumers—for the most part, the wealthy—are the first to acquire new products. They're in a position to create new markets simply because they've got money to buy, even at what for most of us would be prohibitive prices. Even so, few en-trepreneurs ever got rich selling to the rich. The real money lies in bringing products within the reach of the masses. Ford knew that. So does Bill Gates. Over time, wealthy Americans' free spending spurs a great democracy of consumption because it starts the process of lowering prices. It's as if we're all standing in line, joining in the consumption of goods and services as they come within our budget. Many of us have to wait for what we want, but the compensation lies in getting what's better for less.

The economics of it is straightforward. Virtually every new product requires an up-front investment, often sizable, to cover the cost of getting started. Whether innovation springs from business start-ups or established companies, it requires money for research and development as well as the physical plant, machinery, equipment, and labor needed to launch production. Soon enough, there will be bills for advertising and marketing. The cost of reaching the first customer ranges from a few thousand dollars for a mom-and-pop enterprise to billions of dollars for *Fortune* 500 companies. Producers, armed with an exclusive niche in the marketplace and eager to recoup their initial investment, charge high prices at first, usually knowing full well that only a few consumers will have the wherewithal to afford. Over time, as fixed costs are spread over more and more sales, prices come down. The economist Joseph Schumpeter took note of this facet of free enterprise decades ago: "Queen Elizabeth owned silk stockings. The capitalist achievement does not typically consist in providing more silk stockings for queens but in bringing them within the reach of factory girls in return for steadily decreasing amounts of effort."

In nurturing infant industries and product lines, the rich pay most of the new industries' early fixed costs—including research, plant and equipment, and market development. A three-minute phone call from New York to San Francisco, for example, cost $20.70 when first available in 1915. Earning an average hourly wage of less than 23 cents, the working stiff of the day would have had to labor more than 90 hours to afford a call. Yet long-distance telephone service did take root in the marketplace. *Somebody* had to pay the high price. Who was it? The rich, of course. In doing so they paid the fixed cost of bringing long-distance service to the masses in America. Today, nearly all of us can afford long-distance calls. A three-minute coast-to-coast connection cost less than 50 cents in 1997, or a scant two minutes of work.

Without the rich, fewer new goods and services would find their way to the rest of us. Over the years, wealthy Americans financed the emergence of the automobile, airplane travel, color televisions, computers, and many other products, all now readily available to the masses in America. As goods and services filter down to the rest of us, prices more nearly reflect companies' variable cost, including labor and raw materials. The ratio of the fixed to variable costs differs from one product to another. The dichotomy helps explain why some goods and services show quick, steep price reductions, while others go through the process more gradually. Big declines usually occur where fixed costs are high—computers, electronics, or pharmaceuticals, for example. Where fixed costs aren't overwhelming, companies start out charging prices closer to variable cost. The low-fixed-cost pattern fits food and personal services: For example, the rock-bottom "capital" required to cut hair is a pair of scissors. Long-distance telephone services, on the other hand, can't exist without miles of wires, switches, and microwave towers.

Capitalism's critics, especially those who value equality above all else, fret that the economy works to the benefit of the wealthy at the expense of the poor. Nothing could be more wrong. Economic progress actually emerges from a system of price discrimination— against the wealthy, not against the working classes. In most economic systems, the rich take advantage of the masses. Under capitalism, it's the masses who benefit at the expense of the rich. By harnessing the power of unequal income distribution, free markets have routinely brought the great mass of Americans products once beyond the reach even of kings. It's a very effective redistribution mechanism that uses the wealthy to pull the rest of us along.

As we're getting and spending, many of us see only a world of rising prices. We fail to appreciate how much further each hour of our work goes. Finding the real cost of our consumption strips away our money illusions. A clearer perspective carries important implications for the intellectual tug-of-war over our market economy and its future. The fact that so much of what we consume takes smaller pieces of our paychecks provides us with a powerful rebuttal for those who argue that the American economy is in decline. Having to work less to buy many of today's goods and services helps explain why we can afford to consume so much more than Americans of a quarter century ago.

Today's Americans do, of course, work harder than previous generations for some goods and services, but many price increases, when converted into work time, amount to little more than a few blinks of an eye. The cost of a Hershey's chocolate bar rose from 10 cents to 45 cents over 25 years. In the currency of work time, it now costs just 18 seconds more than it used to. Although a five-stick pack of Wrigley's chewing gum jumped from a nickel to a quarter, it costs a mere six seconds more in work time. Cost increases for other goods and services aren't as benign. In 1998, it takes an hour more of work to buy a pair of Levi's jeans than it did in 1970. In terms of work time, tuition and fees at public colleges have jumped from 133 hours to 260 hours since the mid-1960s. Prices have gone up even faster in America's private institutions. In 1966, average annual tuition and fees at private colleges required 537 hours or work. Thirty years later, it was up to 1,295 hours.

When we're paying more, most of the time were getting more. Levi's jeans, for example, now arrive on store shelves after a "stone washing" process that makes them more comfortable. While the notion that college might actually be getting better may raise some eyebrows, one thing we can objectively measure is the dollar value of a sheepskin. If we compare the earnings of college graduates with those of high-school graduates, the increase in annual earnings of those with a bachelor's degree increased by two thirds in the past quarter century. Doctor bills are getting more expensive, too, but few of us doubt that medical care is better than it used to be. The past quarter century brought organ transplants, CAT scans, and other diagnostic tools and new drugs to treat cancer, depression, heartburn, and other ailments. Working harder for better goods and services isn't quite as good as getting more for less, but it's still a way of achieving higher living standards.

3 TIME FOR SYMPHONIES AND SOFTBALL

THE ABUNDANCE OF GOODS AND SERVICES an average American consumes makes it clear that the widely reported decline in living standards is pure myth—at least when it comes to the material aspects of life. No one claims, though, that bigger houses, more appliances, better-equipped automobiles, and rooms full of the latest electronic gadgets are all that matters in life. Although most of us work so we can consume more, we also want time off to enjoy ourselves. We want to relax, pursue our hobbies, travel, and visit with families and friends. It would be hollow indeed to assert that Americans are better off if most of us were able to consume more only through longer hours on the job.

Hard work remains one of the country's enduring values, and there's no shame in striving to get ahead. Many of America's greatest success stories involve men and women putting in back-breaking hours to earn the good life for themselves and their families. Most of us, however, aren't so driven. We wouldn't consider ourselves better off if employment stole away too many precious hours of leisure.

Are we becoming a nation of workaholic consumers? Some pessimists see just that. They contend that Americans, faced with declining real wages, are grinding out longer hours and working second or even third jobs in an attempt to maintain the family's living standards. They argue that one paycheck is no longer enough to sustain a middle-class lifestyle, and point out that two-income families, where both husband and wife hold jobs, rose from 33.8 percent of all households in 1970 to 47.3 percent in 1997. They bewail downsizing because leaner and meaner, so celebrated on Wall Street, often translates into harsher working conditions, with companies driving employees harder to make up for reductions in personnel.

If there's anything we can all agree on, it is that life was once lived at a much slower pace. Many Americans go like mad from sunup till bedtime. Nearly everyone complains of a haggard, sleep-deprived, on-the-go lifestyle. A 1996 NBC–*Wall Street Journal* poll found that almost four of five Americans described themselves as very busy. As with the hard-luck stories of the laid off, downsized, and marginalized, anyone who cares to ask enough people can come up with endless anecdotes, all of them no doubt true, that depict time-pressed lives.

As with patterns of consumption, surveys and anecdotes don't tell the whole story. Once again, we need to test them against statistics—cold, hard facts that dispassionately measure how we allocate our time between work and leisure. The numbers show that the average American has never put fewer hours into earning a living than now. Household chores take less time, too. What's more, spending patterns, attendance figures, and participation rates in leisure activities suggest we're squeezing more recreation into our lives than we once did. In short, Americans are getting more free time than ever before, and they're probably enjoying it more. Although today's hectic lifestyles may leave many of us breathless, it's not because we're overwhelmed by work. The brisk pace of modern life shouldn't obscure one fact: Today's Americans aren't working themselves to death.

Accounting for the Hours

Time is the ultimate scarce resource. Each day contains 24 hours. Each week consists of seven days. There's no reprieve from the tyranny of the clock and calendar. Most of us need to budget what time we have, parceling out precious hours to work, sleep, family obligations, and play. Our use of time hasn't escaped scholarly analysis. Government agencies and private researchers collect statistics on how an average American allocates his 24 hours and seven days. Our jobs consume big chunks of our time, but there's been a long-term decline in time spent on the job. An average employee's annual work hours in the United States fell by nearly one-half during the past 125 years—from about 3,070 hours to 1,570 hours. Most important, the trend toward fewer hours on the job hasn't reversed itself in recent decades, when concerns about American living standards have come to the fore.

The accepted norm in U.S. business is a 40-hour week, but it's been almost a half century since the average employee actually worked that long. The statistics put the typical workweek at 34.4 hours in 1996, down from 36.9 hours in 1973. Employees work fewer hours in a number of ways—fewer days, later arrival, earlier departure, longer breaks. In addition to the shorter weeks, the average worker has gained more than two days in paid vacations and more than four days in paid holidays. Putting it all together, average annual work hours are down 10 percent since 1973—the equivalent of 23 work-days a year (see Table 3.1).

How could this happen? It's Economics 101. Decade by decade, American workers have become more efficient, applying technology, better tools, and improved skills to produce more goods and services on the job. We could have taken every bit of our productivity gains in additional consumption—more televisions, more cars, more clothes, or more toys for the kids—and worked just as hard. Doing that, however, wouldn't be true to human nature. Most of us value time off highly. A 1997 *U.S. News & World Report* poll found that 57 percent of Americans consider leisure important, up from 33 percent in 1986. Nearly half of us say society ought to stop emphasizing work and put more value on free time. With that in mind, it's not surprising that we parlayed part of our productivity gains into additional time off. As we get wealthier, we're likely to forego the opportunity to own more material goods, trading higher consumption for additional leisure. Put another way, we're spending less time on the job because we're able to afford it. Increasing leisure is a sure sign of a wealthy society.

Today's Americans even have it easier once they get home from work. The average daily time devoted to household chores has fallen

TABLE 3.1   Work Time

Year	Work-week (hours)	Work-day (hours)	Work-week (days)	Annual Hours (paid)	Vaca-tion (days)	Holi-days (days)	Other Time Off (days)	Annual Hours Worked
1870	61.0	10.2	6.0	3,181	0.0	3.0	8.0	3,069
1890	58.4	9.7	6.0	3,045	0.0	3.0	8.0	2,938
1913	53.3	8.9	6.0	2,779	5.0	3.5	8.0	2,632
1929	48.1	8.0	6.0	2,508	5.5	4.0	8.0	2,368
1938	44.0	8.0	5.5	2,294	6.0	4.5	8.0	2,146
1950	39.8	8.0	5.0	2,075	6.5	6.0	9.0	1,903
1960	38.6	7.7	5.0	2,013	7.0	7.0	9.0	1,836
1973	36.9	7.4	5.0	1,924	8.0	7.5	9.0	1,743
1990	34.5	7.3	4.7	1,799	10.0	11.0	9.5	1,584
1996	34.4	7.3	4.7	1,794	10.5	12.0	10.0	1,570

consistently—from 4 hours, 12 minutes in 1950, to 3 hours, 48 minutes in 1973, to an estimated 3 hours, 30 minutes in the mid-1990s. Eighteen minutes among 24 hours may seem trifling, but over an entire year it adds up to more than four extra days of free time. Fewer hours spent doing housework doesn't necessarily mean our homes and lives are less tidy. Technology has come to the aid of the modern family. Microwave ovens, no-iron fabrics, self-cleaning ovens, frost-free refrigerators, prepared foods, and dozens of other conveniences make housework lighter and faster. In more and more homes, chores are being turned over to hired help—maids, lawn services, dry cleaners, restaurants, financial experts.

Fewer hours spent working and doing chores during a year aren't the end of the good news about Americans' free time. To fully appreciate how much less the average person works, it's important to examine an entire lifetime, not just one week or even one year. Only from their twenties through their fifties do most Americans spend five days a week earning a living. It's in these years, when we're establishing households and raising families, that household chores are the most demanding, too. At both ends of the typical life—in childhood and retirement—most of us work part time or not at all. In 1996 an average lifetime's waking hours devoted to work, both on the job and at home, stood at an all-time low of 21.8 percent, compared with 24.8 percent in 1973 (see Table 3.2).

Most of the gains in additional leisure come in youth and old age. To start with, Americans are taking their first job later in life. In the two decades after 1973, the age at which the average worker entered the labor force increased by nearly a year. With most households better off, there's less pressure on young people to go to work to help the family finances. Some young Americans are no doubt taking the extra time for frivolous pursuits. Most, though, are apparently delaying work to prepare themselves for future jobs. In 1996, 60 percent of high school graduates continued their education, up from 25.4 percent in 1970. The educational experience itself is taking longer, perhaps because there's more to learn, perhaps because, with parents footing the bill, there's less of a hurry to leave campus to earn a paycheck. By 1996, the median number of years students took to graduate from four-year programs had stretched to more than six years.

Even more significant, we're enjoying longer periods of retirement. Americans are leaving the labor force earlier, at an average age of 62.2 years, down from 64 in 1973. Based on life expectancy at the age of starting full-time work, they are also living three years longer than

TABLE 3.2   Less Work, More Leisure

	1870	1950	1973	1990	1996
Activity					
Age starting work (avg.)	13	17.6	18.5	19.1	19.4
Life expectancy at age 20 (age)	62.5	72.0	74.1	76.5	77.1
Retirement age (avg.)	death	68.5	64.0	63.6	62.2
Years on job	49.5	50.9	45.5	44.5	42.8
Retirement (years)	0	3.5	10.1	12.9	14.9
Annual hours worked	3,069	1,903	1,743	1,584	1,570
Annual hours home work	1,825	1,544	1,391	1,290	1,278
Lifetime hours					
Working on job	151,916	96,863	79,307	70,488	67,263
Working at home	96,269	88,885	81,703	79,916	79,747
Leisure	299,315	444,972	488,106	519,736	528,386

they did in the early 1970s. As a result, a typical retirement grew from 10.1 years in 1973 to 14.9 years in 1995. Earlier retirements wouldn't be possible if senior citizens didn't have the financial resources to maintain their living standards. The government reports that older Americans are far wealthier than they used to be. After adjusting for inflation, average net worth of retirement-age Americans rose from $170,839 in 1983 to $324,490 in 1995. What's more, the majority of our senior citizens aren't just sitting on the porch, rocking away their last years. Of the nation's 33.2 million residents over age 65 in 1994, 15.4 million exercised, 4.6 million swam, 4.3 million went fishing, 2.7 million golfed, 2.3 million biked, and 2 million bowled. Older Americans spend more than those under 25 on entertainment and reading.

Although most of the added leisure comes early and late in life, many of us in the prime working years have it easier than our parents did a quarter century ago. When jobs and work at home are combined, the gain in leisure since the early 1970s was a minuscule few minutes a week for employed men. Thanks largely to labor-saving appliances and other helping hands, women who didn't work outside the home reaped 10 extra hours a week of leisure. Women who held jobs outside the home over this entire era benefited from an average six-hour-a-week decline in total work. Unfortunately, not everyone has it easier today. The exception is women who once stayed at home but now work at paying jobs. These women are putting in, on average, about 13 additional hours a week. The logical explanation: A job typically consumes most of the day, and many household chores still await them at the end of it.

The fact that some of us are working harder doesn't nullify society's overall gain in leisure over the past quarter century. As some women have left the home for work, others have given up jobs to raise families, decreasing their total weekly hours of work. The comings and goings of individuals are difficult to keep tabs on, but the net effect has been just a small increase in the overall workforce—an estimated 2.6 percent, not enough to offset the gains elsewhere. We shouldn't forget, too, that all isn't dreary for the women who sacrificed leisure going from homemaking to the job market. They spend less time on housework than a working woman did 25 years ago, and they're compensated with higher incomes.

What about those second and third jobs? Moonlighting increases hours of work and decreases leisure. Holding more than one job, however, still isn't a common practice, despite all the attention paid to it. In 1996, only 6.2 percent of U.S. workers had more than one job, compared with 5.2 percent in 1970. The increase amounts to just 1.3 million workers. The number of men holding more than one job actually fell from 7 percent in 1970 to 6.3 percent in 1995, so the increase in multiple job-holding came among women. In 1996, 6.6 percent of women held second jobs, compared with 2.2 percent in 1970. When asked why they're holding two jobs, fewer than half of these workers cited the need to pay bills or the pressures of debt. Many women take a second job to gain experience, build up a business, or save for the future. Even here, the effects of shorter workweeks and lighter chores cannot be ignored. Only a day-job requiring fewer hours enables many Americans to devote time to a second occupation.

The traditional image of a moonlighter who rushes from one job to another, gobbling down dinner in between, doesn't apply to many workers with more than one job. Surveys show that many second jobs are done at home, especially with the advent of computers, facsimile machines, and electronic mail. What's more, holding multiple jobs usually isn't a permanent lifestyle. Only one in four Americans who work two jobs keep both for five years or more.

When declining working hours, less time spent toiling at home, extended youth, and longer retirement are all added up, the results are mind-boggling: American workers, on average, have added the equivalent of more than five years of waking leisure to their lives since 1973. The University of Maryland's Americans' Use of Time Project confirms the trend toward more leisure. After asking 10,000 people to record hour-by-hour entries in time diaries, researchers found that a typical American has 40 hours of leisure a week, up five hours since 1975.

That translates into almost 11 days a year. John Robinson, the project's director, said: "Like making money, progress in gaining leisure is often hidden, particularly because people have so many choices in how they will spend it that they feel out of control and don't enjoy what leisure time they have." The average American may feel more rushed, but the hard numbers on work and leisure do not support the image of an overworked nation. Despite the complaints about long days of work, we are the most leisure-rich generation in U.S. history.

Working Harder at Leisure

Many Americans, rushing to and fro and swapping stories of cramped schedules with other busy people, may not be impressed by data showing that they spend less time at work. They'll want more proof. Indirect evidence of Americans' gains in free time lies in the country's recreational and cultural pursuits. If so many of us are strapped for spare time, leisure industries ought to be starved for customers. It's just the opposite. We're allocating more time and money than ever to the pursuit of happiness.

We've already seen that the nation owns more boats, more snowmobiles, more recreational vehicles, and more sports gear than a generation ago. We travel more often, and there has been a sharp increase in the number of cruises we take. If we didn't have more free time, Americans probably wouldn't load up on televisions, videocassette recorders, audio equipment, computer games, compact discs, and other paraphernalia for relaxing. Sporting-goods companies wouldn't spend millions of dollars to improve the quality of sneakers, golf clubs, tennis rackets, and bikes unless research indicated that markets for these products are expanding rapidly. Once again, figures don't lie. Per capita recreational spending, adjusted for inflation, jumped from $501 in 1970 to $1,650 in 1995, an average annual gain of 4.8 percent. In the same period, amusement spending, including money spent at theme parks, arcades, and pool halls, jumped more than 5 percent a year. Money spent on clubs and fraternal organizations increased 3 percent a year, as did gardeners' outlays for flowers, seeds, and potted plants. Over the past 25 years, money allocated to fun and games has increased from 5 percent of consumer spending to more than 8 percent.

Increased leisure fueled a boom in participatory sports. From 1970 to 1997, the number of Americans who play golf more than doubled, increasing to 11 percent of the population. The number of golf courses rose by 54 percent, to 15,703 in 1997. In 1970, a quarter of Americans bowled; now, a third of them do. Even after adjusting for population growth, the number of adult softball teams jumped five-fold in 25 years. By one count, the number of sports Americans play now exceeds 100, from arm wrestling to weightlifting. Growing up in the 1960s and 1970s, few of us ever imagined we'd find time for all of the traditional athletic pursuits, let alone such new pastimes as rock climbing, bungee jumping, in-line skating, hang gliding, competitive skateboarding, acrobatic skiing, or snow boarding. Our appetite for outdoor activities includes some that aren't so strenuous: Birdwatchers now outnumber golfers and swimmers.

Spectator sports are expanding, too. Attendance at big-league professional baseball, football, basketball, and hockey games rose from 24,820 per 100,000 people in 1970 to 47,432 in 1993. The increased attendance, by the way, occurred in the face of rising ticket prices, which economists might expect would dampen demand. The average ticket now costs $42.51 for football, $36.32 for basketball, and $40.64 for hockey. The Atlanta Olympics in 1996 set records for ticket sales and television viewing. Auto racing has emerged as a fast-growing sport. NASCAR's Winston Cup series drew 1.5 million paying customers in 1981 and 6.1 million in 1997. Minor-league baseball and hockey are played in more small towns. New leagues and circuits are forming for such sports as women's basketball, softball, indoor soccer, outdoor soccer, arena football, beach volleyball, and seniors' golf. The total hours of sports broadcasts on television increase year by year, the traditional networks being joined by all-sports cable channels. Television-rights fees are an enormous investment in America's leisure time. The National Football League's television contracts, signed in early 1998, total $17.6 billion over eight years. In late 1997, the National Basketball Association's signed a four-year deal worth $2.64 billion. Major-league baseball gets $1.6 billion for five years. College basketball's postseason tournament goes for $1.7 billion for eight years. Would the networks and cable companies keep paying huge rights fees if they weren't confident that millions of Americans had time to tune in?

Meanwhile, cultural activities haven't been neglected. Per capita attendance at symphonies and operas doubled from 1970 to 1994. The number of books sold hit an all-time record of 2.3 billion in 1997. New titles rose from 36,071 in 1970 to 179,282 for the year ending July 1998. Parents and pundits bemoan the hours spent in front of the tube; even so, we now spend more time watching television, including such new offerings as MTV and CNN. The average American now watches more than 3,300 hours of television a year, compared with 2,153 in 1970. In 1994, Americans attended an average of five movies a year, one more than they did in 1970. Despite VCRs and television, new movie theaters are going up at an almost frantic rate, some with dozens of screens.

Pop music concerts, art galleries, aquariums, and theme parks are proliferating, too. The leisure market is so ripe that new entertainments arrive on the scene regularly—ever more sophisticated arcade games, panoramic theaters, and the made-for-television *X-Games*. Gambling is proliferating, with riverboat casinos and lotteries now competing with Las Vegas and Atlantic City. Off shore betting parlors even make betting on-line a reality. Shopping remains one of America's favorite pastimes, and the number of stores and malls is at an all-time high. An average American took three pleasure trips in 1995, up from just one in 1970. The overcrowding of national parks bespeaks of the arrival of a great democracy in free time, with the masses enjoying what was once possible for only a privileged few. The number of visits to national parks, monuments, seashores, and recreational areas jumped 22 percent between 1970 and 1995.

When Americans aren't at work, it's not all fun and games. In addition to giving more money to charity, we're also giving more of ourselves. Almost half of the population finds time for some volunteer work, up from less than a quarter in 1974. The leading beneficiaries of our donations of time are religious organizations—with almost a quarter of the volunteers. Youth development, education, and health-care organizations each get more than 10 percent. Americans devote countless hours to social causes, from planting trees to saving whales. How could a bone-weary and overworked nation find time for all these good works?

Almost every activity entails two costs—time and money. Americans couldn't be spending more money on leisure activities if they didn't have more time. By the same token, they couldn't spend more time attending sports, cultural events, and other diversions without an increase in disposable income. Americans swear they're busier than ever. They may well be right. What's crowding our lives, though, isn't necessarily work or chores. It is the relentless chasing after leisure opportunities in a society that has more free time and more money to spend.

From Home to Market

Two-income households raise questions about whether Americans of the 1990s are sacrificing their lives to their jobs. In the early 1950s, a quarter of U.S. wives worked outside the home, a figure that climbed to 41 percent in 1970 and 61 percent in 1995. Children don't seem to alter the equation much. Among women who have children under six years old and live with their husbands, 62.7 percent held jobs in 1996, up from 18.6 percent in 1960 and 36.7 percent in 1975. More important than the statistics are our memories. We recall an era when one 40-hour-a-week job was enough to support a middle-class family. It now takes 69 hours—the average workweek is down to 34.4 hours—just to get by. Or so the argument goes. The pessimists see working mothers as a sign of the economy's failure, contending that women are being forced to seek employment because many men's jobs don't pay enough to support a family.

This is backward.

Both adults in a two-parent family have always worked. Running a household entails a daunting list of chores: cooking, cleaning, gardening, child care, shopping, washing and ironing, financial management, ferrying family members to ballet lessons and soccer practice. The average workweek of yesterday's housewife, the 1950s stay-at-home mom of the June Cleaver mold, was 52 hours, a more exhausting schedule than the 39-hour workweek her husband typically put in. According to the statisticians' arbitrary view, however, only women who are taking home a paycheck "work." Those who stay at home do something else.

Belittling housework is insulting to women, who still do most of America's cooking, cleaning, and child rearing. More important, it misses how specialization contributes to higher living standards. Before the dawn of the Industrial Age, both adults worked exclusively at home. In the usual scenario of the nearly self-sufficient household, the man constructed buildings, tilled the land, raised livestock. The woman prepared meals, preserved food, looked after the children. Both worked long hours, but living standards rarely rose above subsistence, a reflection of what economists would call low productivity.

Over time, Americans began going to work for money, turning over household tasks, such as growing and canning food, to the market. The farmer became a worker, earning wages to buy food for his family. These days, we hardly bat an eye at paying others to do chores for us. To the extent that they can afford it, modern households hire professionals to clean, paint, tend the yard, figure taxes, care for clothing, take on family responsibilities, and much more. In getting our daily bread, Americans are finding ways to ease the burden of cooking at home. Eating out, once an occasional luxury, has become a way of life, with almost half of adult Americans going to a restaurant on a typical day. In 1996, restaurants received 40 percent of the country's spending on food, double their share in 1972. Even when we eat at home, we often rely on market goods, such as heat-and-serve products, microwave meals, delivery services, and carry-out items. In just the past decade, demand for takeout food has jumped 60 percent. The modern home is a place to live, not a small enterprise. Over all, home production fell steadily from 45 percent of the economy's output at the end of World War II to 33 percent in 1981. Since then, it has dropped by a few more percentage points, a trend that probably won't reverse itself.

Shifting production from home to market makes us better off because the jack of all trades isn't a very efficient fellow. By doing one job well, with the aid of more machinery, equipment, and technology than any home could muster, workers can become more productive, making money to buy what their families don't have the time or resources to provide at home. At first, men usually took jobs outside the home, gaining skills and earning higher incomes. When men went to work outside the home, the family's living standards rose because of the tremendous gains from specialization and exchange. Why do we insist that the same transition for women can only mean a pinch on households' possibilities? It makes no sense to suggest that the economic rules flip-flop when a second adult takes a job. Working women are a sign that families are making themselves better off, not slipping toward poverty.

Both husband and wife holding jobs doesn't mean Americans are working harder. It just means we're working differently—producing more in the market and less in the household. The impetus for this change, by and large, has been opportunities for women outside the home. A rigid division of labor based on sex no longer applies in the labor market. In the Information Age, fewer jobs require sheer brawn and physical strength. Instead, today's jobs call for intellectual and interpersonal skills, favoring the sexes more equally. More women are finishing college and graduate school, making them more valuable as economic assets.

Families are more likely to choose to "do it yourself" when opportunities outside the home are few, when pay is low, or when income-tax rates are high. In recent decades, basic economic trends have favored working women. Wages have risen sharply, more so for women than for men. In fact, the financial contribution of working women in married-couple households is much greater than it once was. In 1970, the addition of a working wife increased median family income by less than 60 percent. In 1995, the gain was 80 percent. Women's skills, higher pay, and greater opportunities are the important factors in creating incentives for two-income households.

Two-income households are a response not to declining wages, but to the greater benefits of working outside the home. The economy is providing greater incentive for a woman to earn a paycheck, letting the family turn to the market for more of what used to be household chores. Many families decide to earn two paychecks because they can redirect their work effort to produce higher living standards, not so they can avoid being trampled in a stampede toward poverty.

The Way We Work

Sometimes it's a good idea to recall how far we've come. That's especially true when confronting the myth that a single-minded drive for greater productivity is turning corporate America into a nastier place. What working conditions did Americans decades ago endure for the sake of productivity? Foul air, bad lighting, poor ventilation, exposure to hazardous substances, long hours, inadequate sanitation, rigid schedules, repetitive tasks, the risk of disease or even death. For most of our forebears, work was no picnic. Believe it or not, Americans used to earn meager paychecks spending long hours winding string into balls, breaking bones in slaughterhouses, stirring glue pots, hauling ore out of mines, boiling lime, and mixing acids.

Few of today's workers face the on-the-job travails of their grandparents. In fact, our jobs have never been less burdensome. Workplaces are safer and more secure. Working conditions have become more pleasant. The pessimists tell us there are no good jobs anymore, but that's not the testimony from Americans themselves. A 1996 Gallup Poll, for example, found widespread job satisfaction at a time when corporate belt tightening was making headlines. Among those surveyed, 88 percent said they didn't worry that their jobs would become obsolete, 84 percent said they had chances to learn and grow during the previous year, 82 percent said they had the opportunity to "do what they do best" every day, 75 percent said their previous work year did not have three or more days where job stress affected family life, 70 percent said management did what was necessary to make the company a great place to work, and 69 percent said they had been compensated fairly in the previous year.

Some facts and figures will help explain why the survey didn't find workers disgruntled, disillusioned, and discouraged. On-the-job deaths and accidents are down. In 1995, only 4 of 100,000 workers died of work-related causes, down from 18 in 1970. The rate of accidents fell from 11 per 1,000 workers in 1973 to 8.1 in 1995. The improved safety comes partly from efforts to reduce hazards, some of it accomplished through employer programs, some of it no doubt prompted by regulation and fear of lawsuits. Another factor is the changing structure of the job market. The most dangerous industries are construction, manufacturing, mining, and agriculture. Their share of total employment fell by 13 percentage points in the past quarter century. A larger portion of American jobs are now in trade, services, transportation, communications, and utilities, all sectors with better safety records.

Despite all the talk of an age of insecurity, most workers are actually gaining security at work. We're taking more of our pay in fringe benefits that protect us from the vagaries of life—job loss, illness, and penury in old age. Unemployment insurance, a state-run program to assist those who have lost their jobs, had expanded to cover 92 percent of employees by 1995, up from 74 percent in 1970. Although the anecdotal nightmare involves families losing health care and benefits as a result of companies' downsizing, workers with employer-paid health care rose from 53 percent in 1970 to 75 percent in 1994. Employees' out-of-pocket payments accounted for 49 percent of health-care costs in 1960, 34 percent in 1970, and just 18 percent in 1994. Americans covered by some kind of employer-sponsored retirement plan increased from 48.3 percent in 1970 to 78 percent in 1994. Fixed-benefit pensions are falling out of favor, being replaced by 401(k) plans and others that permit employees to direct the investment of their own money. Over all, fringe benefits as a percentage of total pay rose from 32.7 percent in 1973 to 41.9 percent in 1995.

We hear a great deal about workers' trembling in fear of a pink slip, but U.S. jobs may not be getting more iffy. Statistics on job tenure date back only to 1983, but they show that since then, the time the average worker stays with one company has risen from 3.5 years to 3.8 years. Among those over age 40, more than a third of us have held the same job for 10 years or more. Above age 50, the figure rises to more than half. Layoffs still occur with regularity, of course, but the fraction of the labor force unemployed for 15 weeks or more isn't any higher now than it was in the early 1970s. A 1994 National Bureau of Economic Research (NBER) study found that the probability of holding a job for a full decade rose slightly between 1973 and 1991. In the dynamic economy of the 1990s, the chances of job seekers finding new employment are pretty good on a purely statistical basis: For every two jobs taken away, three are created.

Are layoffs at "lean and mean" companies making us work harder? That's not easy to measure. In most workplaces, however, work is becoming less onerous. Job sites are overwhelmingly well lit and sanitary. Air conditioning is commonplace. Over the past 25 years, more and more workers have taken advantage of a new generation of benefits, such as educational assistance, exercise facilities, personal leave, and advice on how to avoid illness. Employees who relocate sometimes get assistance in selling homes. From 1988 to 1993, the proportion of female workers at medium and large firms who are entitled to maternity leave rose from 33 percent to 60 percent, and the percentage of male workers entitled to paternity leave jumped from 16 percent to 53 percent. Employer-provided child care is still rare, but the percentage of companies offering it nudged upward from 4 percent to 7 percent between 1988 and 1993.

The watchword in today's job market is "flexibility." Work schedules aren't as rigid as they once were, and more workers set their own hours. Two of five Americans employed outside the home travel to work outside the traditional rush hour of 6:30 to 9 A.M. Change is coming rapidly. According to Hewitt Associates, a global consulting firm based in Lincolnshire, Illinois, the percentage of 1,020 large companies offering flexible hours rose from 39 percent in 1990 to 73 percent in 1997. The percentage of companies offering the option of job sharing, which gives employees abbreviated schedules, increased from 18 percent to 37 percent; of those offering four-day scheduling, from 12 percent to 24 percent; and of those offering the option of working at home, from 8 percent to 20 percent. At many companies, employees now wear comfortable clothing if it doesn't interfere with customer service. Advances in technology—cellular phones, computers, fax machines, electronic mail—created a new class of mobile workers freed from the bonds of the office. Many of us prefer working at home because it offers flexible hours, less stress, and a commute of only a few steps. Telecommuting's ranks swelled to 9.1 million in 1995, up from 100,000 in 1980 and a few thousand in 1970.

Statistics on how Americans use their time provide evidence of an important aspect of an easier worklife—a decline in hours on the job. Workdays are shorter. Vacations are longer. Holidays come more often. There's another wrinkle to it: We're also taking more personal time while at work. Time-diary surveys show that Americans today spend as many as six of their weekly on-the-job hours on leisure pursuits, compared with only one hour in 1965. What are some of the ways employees use their recorded work hours other than to work? Chatting with co-workers. Talking on the phone to friends. Arriving late after dropping the kids off at school or camp. Leaving a half hour early to pick up the kids. Going to parent-teacher conferences. Visiting the doctor or dentist. Going outside to smoke. Playing solitaire on the computer. Browsing the Internet. Selling cookies for the kids. Raising funds for charities. Catching up on a few tasks for a second job. Exercising, perhaps even in employers' facilities. Calling talk-radio programs or contests. Reading the paper, a book, or a magazine. Attending parties or showers. Writing personal correspondence. Running errands. Taking long breaks. Paying bills. Even napping—if the boss isn't looking.

There are still workers who face unpleasant and unhealthy working conditions, but for most of us the days of dreadful jobs are past. Workers once complained about health and safety hazards, inadequate fringe benefits, unpleasant working conditions, and inconvenient or excessive hours. What do we hear about in the 1990s? Meaningful work, respect, empowerment, communication, employee activities, wellness programs, flexible schedules, and family benefits. Most firms strive to meet their employees' needs, not out of the goodness of their hearts but because it's necessary to attract the workers they need to make the company grow and prosper.

For most of us, work is a major part of our lives, taking a big chunk of time as well as serving as a touchstone for who we are. It's not, however, all there is. The vast majority of workers take pride in a job well done and put an honest effort into doing a good job. Even so, we continually seek shorter hours, new recreational outlets, and additional perks on the job. The fact that most of us are getting them provides one of the best examples of how America's market economy is providing what we want.

4 BY OUR OWN BOOTSTRAPS

LAND OF OPPORTUNITY." Anywhere in the world, those three words bring to mind just one place: the United States of America.

Opportunity defines our heritage. The American saga entails waves of immigrant farmers, shopkeepers, laborers, and entrepreneurs, all coming to the United States for the promise of a better life. Some amassed enormous fortunes—the Rockefellers, the Carnegies, the DuPonts, the Fords, the Vanderbilts, to name just a few. Even today, America's opportunity is always on display. Bill Gates in computer software, Ross Perot in data processing, Bill Cosby and Oprah Winfrey in entertainment, Warren Buffett in investing, Sam Walton in retailing, Michael Jordan in sports, and Mary Kay Ash in cosmetics could head a list of the many thousands who catapulted from society's lower or middle ranks to the top. Many millions more, descendants of those who arrived with little more than the clothes on their backs and a few bucks in their pockets, took advantage of an open economic system to improve their lot in life through talent and hard work.

Even pessimists acknowledge that the Gateses, Perots, Cosbys, Winfreys, Buffetts, Waltons, Jordans, and Ashes are getting filthy rich, along with Wall Street's wheeler-dealers, Hollywood moguls, and big-league ballplayers. At the nation's 350 largest companies, top executives' median total compensation in 1996 was $3.1 million, or 90 times what a typical factory hand earns. We often hear that ordinary Americans aren't keeping up, that success isn't as easy, or at least not as democratic, as it once was. At the close of the twentieth century, one disturbing vision portrays the United States as a society pulling apart at the seams, divided into separate and unequal camps, an enclave of fat cats gorging themselves on the fruits of others' labor surrounded by a working class left with ever more meager opportunities.

The most-cited evidence of ebbing opportunity is the *distribution of income*—the slicing up of the American pie. Examining the data, analysts seize on two points. First, there's a marked inequality in earnings between society's haves and have-nots. Second, and perhaps more ominous, the gap between the richest and poorest households has widened over the past two decades. The Census Bureau provides the statistical ballast for these claims. In 1997, the top 20 percent of American households received almost half of the nation's income. Average earnings among this group are $122,764 a year. The distribution of income to the four other groups of 20 percent was as follows: The second fifth had 23.2 percent, with average earnings of $57,582; the third fifth had 15.0 percent, with average earnings of $37,177; the fourth fifth had 8.9 percent, with average earnings of $22,098. The bottom 20 percent earned 3.6 percent of the economic pie, or an average of $8,872 a year (see Figure 4.1).

The case for the existence of a growing rift between rich and poor rests on longer-term trends in the same Census Bureau data. Since 1975, only the top 20 percent of Americans managed to expand their allotment of the nation's income—from 43.2 percent to 49.4 percent.

FIGURE 4.1   Slicing Up the American Pie

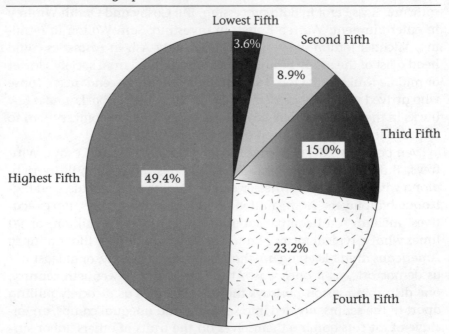

Shares of National Income Earned by Each Fifth of Households in 1997.

FIGURE 4.2   A Caste Society?

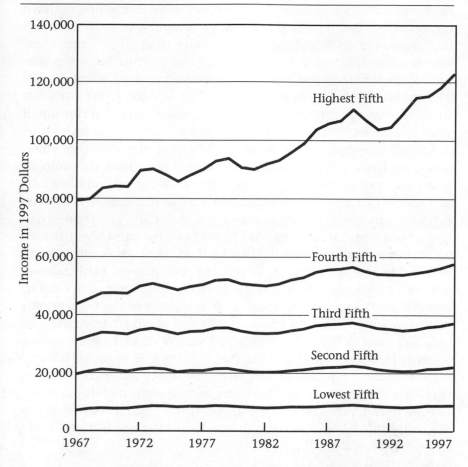

Over the same period, the distribution to the middle three groups slipped slightly. The share going to the lowest 20 percent of income earners fell from 4.4 percent to 3.6 percent. The shift of income toward the upper end of the distribution becomes even more striking when it's put in dollars. After adjusting for inflation, the income of households in the bottom 20 percent increased by only $207 from 1975 to 1997. The top tier, meanwhile, jumped by $37,633 (see Figure 4.2).

Once again, the pessimists have it wrong. The income distribution only reveals how one group is doing relative to others at a particular moment. That kind of you-vs.-me score keeping has little to do with whether any American can get ahead. By its very nature, opportunity is individual rather than collective. Even for an individual, the concept can't be divorced from its time element, an assessment of how well someone is doing today relative to yesterday, or how he can expect to do tomorrow compared to today. How many of us worked our way up? How quickly did we move from one rung to the next? How many of us fell? Studies of income inequality cannot say whether individuals are doing better or worse. They lump together Americans who differ in age, educational level, work effort, family and marital status, gender and race. The sample never stays the same from one year to another, and researchers haven't a clue about what happened to any individual in the income distribution.

Annual snapshots of the income distribution might deserve attention if we lived in a caste society, with rigid class lines determining who gets what share of the national income—but we don't live in a caste society. It takes a heroic leap to look at the disparity between rich and poor and conclude that any one individual's chances of getting ahead aren't what they used to be. Even the most sophisticated income-distribution statistics fail to tell us what we really want to know: Are the majority of Americans losing their birthright—a chance at upward mobility? Static portraits, moreover, don't tell us whether low-income households tend to remain at the bottom year after year. By definition, a fifth of society will always inhabit the lowest 20 percent of the income distribution. We don't know, however, whether individuals and families stay there over long periods. It's no great tragedy if the bottom rung is where many Americans start to climb the ladder of success. To argue that upward mobility is being lost, we would have to show that the poorest remain stuck where they are, with little hope of making themselves better off. Nothing could be further from the truth.

Making It from Bottom to Top

How can we gauge *opportunity*—the prospects for getting ahead? The best way involves identifying individuals and tracking them year by year, capturing the highs and lows of income over a lifetime. When combined with such personal data as age, education, and marital status, individual earnings profiles pinpoint income changes that occur along life's journey. It's no easy task to keep tabs on specific income earners in a mobile, fast-changing society. The statistical mills of government and private industry produce few numbers on long-term earnings—year-by-year data on the income of particular persons. One source of such information does exist: the University of Michigan's

Panel Survey on Income Dynamics, the longest tracking study ever done on Americans' earnings. Since 1968, the university has collected detailed information on more than 50,000 Americans. This mass of data, carefully designed to provide a statistically valid picture of the nation as a whole, has over the years served as the basis for hundreds of studies. A sample from this database allows us to follow the ebbs and flows in income for 17 years. It's a period long enough to capture the real stories of our economic lives—the hirings, firings, raises, promotions, retirements, windfalls, and financial setbacks.

Tracking individuals' income over time gives a startlingly different view of income distribution than the Census Bureau's static analysis. Let's begin where others find the most disappointing trends: with the Americans in the bottom 20 percent of income earners in 1975. The inference typically drawn from the Census Bureau data is that these Americans should be worse off in the 1990s. The University of Michigan sample says it just isn't so. Only 5 percent of those in the bottom fifth in 1975 were still there in 1991. Where did they end up? A majority made it to the top three fifths of the income distribution—middle class or better. Most amazing of all, almost 3 out of 10 of the low-income earners from 1975 had risen to the uppermost 20 percent by 1991. More than three-quarters found their way into the two highest tiers of income earners for at least one year by 1991 (see Table 4.1).

In fact, the poor make the most dramatic gains when one looks at income distribution. Those who started in the bottom 20 percent in 1975 had an inflation-adjusted gain of $27,745 in average income by 1991. Among workers who began in the top fifth, the increase was just $4,354. The rich may have gotten a little richer, but the poor have gotten much richer (see Table 4.2).

The University of Michigan data suggest that low income is largely a transitory experience for those willing to work, a place Americans may visit but rarely stay. Nearly a quarter of those in the bottom tier

TABLE 4.1   Moving On Up

Income Quintile, 1975	Percent in Each Quintile, 1991				
	1st	2nd	3rd	4th	5th
1st (Lowest)	5.1	14.6	21.0	30.3	29.0
2nd	4.2	23.5	20.3	25.2	26.8
3rd (Middle)	3.3	19.3	28.3	30.1	19.0
4th	1.9	9.3	18.8	32.6	37.4
5th (Highest)	0.9	2.8	10.2	23.6	62.5

TABLE 4.2   The Poor Are Getting Richer Faster

Income Quintile, 1975	Average Income, 1975	Average Income, 1991	Absolute Gain
1st (Lowest)	$1,263	$29,008	$27,745
2nd	$6,893	$31,088	$24,195
3rd (Middle)	$14,277	$24,438	$10,161
4th	$24,568	$34,286	$9,718
5th (Highest)	$50,077	$54,431	$4,354

Figures are in 1997 dollars.

in 1975 moved up the next year and never again returned. By contrast, long-term hardship turned out to be rare: Less than 1 percent of the sample remained in the bottom fifth every year from 1975 to 1991. Labor Department data confirm that long-term poverty afflicts only a relatively small number of Americans. In the early 1990s, the median duration of a poverty spell was 4.2 months. Only a third of the nation's 36 million classified as poor by the Census Bureau had been below the poverty line for 24 or more months. With those figures in mind, the long-term poverty rate shrinks to 4 percent, compared to the overall official rate of 13.3 percent in 1997.

Other tiers of income earners in the University of Michigan sample show the same pattern of upward mobility seen in the bottom fifth. Among the second-poorest 20 percent in 1975, more than 70 percent had moved to a higher bracket by 1991, a quarter reaching the top echelon. From the middle group, almost half of the income earners managed to make themselves better off. Even a third of the people from the next-to-highest 20 percent could be found among the top fifth of income earners after 17 years. All through the University of Michigan data, there's a consistent, powerful upward thrust toward the top of the income distribution.

The sample shows, too, that the rise in income can be swift, especially for those with education and skills. More than half of those in the lowest 20 percent in 1975 had reached one of the top three tiers within four years. Two-thirds of these people made that leap within six years, and three-fourths did it in nine years. Not surprisingly, it's the young who move up most quickly. Among respondents 20 to 24 years old in 1975, workers who finished college saw their inflation-adjusted income increase fivefold, to $44,159, in 1991. A typical college graduate with work experience rose from the next-to-lowest bracket to the top one in about a decade. High-school graduates who were in their early twenties in 1975 doubled their average incomes to $30,271 in 17 years. They moved quickly up to the next-to-highest echelon of income earners with a few years of experience, but tended to stay there through 1991. Even high-school dropouts weren't completely shut off from opportunity. Their earnings also rose, although much more slowly than those of any other group, going from $12,741 in 1975 to $20,918 in 1991. They were without question better off, even if they lost ground to their better-educated contemporaries (see Figure 4.3).

The University of Michigan sample also tells us what happened to those who were in the top tier in 1975. Nearly 66 percent of them could still be found in the top tier in 1991, and 23 percent slipped just one bracket, leaving them in the second fifth of income earners. Less than 1 percent of the richest fifth in 1975 plummeted all the way to the bottom of the income distribution in 17 years. The fate of the well-to-do offers a comforting conclusion: Once households move up the income ladder, they rarely get pushed back down again. Those in the middle groups showed a similar tendency to avoid downward mobility.

Tracking individuals gives a truer verdict on upward mobility, but it still doesn't provide a perfect measure of changes in living stan-

FIGURE 4.3   Income Mobility by Education: Even Dropouts Earn More

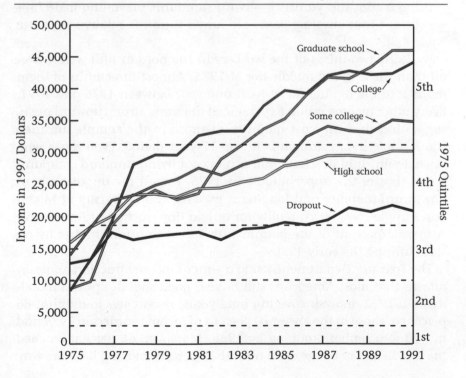

TABLE 4.3   Living Standards on the Rise

| Income Quintile, 1975 | Percent in Each 1975 Quintile, 1991 | | | | | In 5th 1975 Quintile Sometime in 1976–91 |
	1st	2nd	3rd	4th	5th	
1st (Lowest)	2.3	14.0	17.6	26.9	39.2	57.0
2nd	2.1	19.9	19.9	25.2	32.9	52.6
3rd (Middle)	2.2	15.6	24.1	32.0	26.1	48.2
4th	1.0	6.6	16.0	30.0	46.4	78.6
5th (Highest)	0.3	2.5	7.7	20.1	69.4	98.4

dards. Some progress is still overlooked. In cataloguing how much Americans consume, the argument was that income doesn't march in lock-step with living standards. It's just as true here. From 1975 to 1991, overall income in the United States rose, shifting each fifth of the University of Michigan sample upward in absolute terms. As a result, individuals will be better off even if they fail to make any relative gains. A worker at the midpoint of the bottom 20 percent of income earners today, for example, lives better than someone in a similar spot did almost two decades later.

Using a constant yardstick—living standards prevailing in 1975—we can see that absolute gains are larger than the relative ones (see Table 4.3).

By 1991, two-thirds of the workers in the bottom fifth were better off than those in the middle tier of 1975. Almost three-fifths of them made it to the top tier for at least one year between 1976 and 1991. Every other income group experienced the same strong upward push, suggesting that the vast majority of those in the sample attained comfortable living standards in the 17-year period. Even those who failed to finish high school had achieved a living standard comparable to that of the upper middle in 1975. For all the anguish about downward mobility and long-term poverty, the University of Michigan sample shows it's a reality for only a tiny fraction of Americans. A mere 2 percent of the bottom fifth failed to attain higher living standards by the early 1990s.

The Treasury Department, using a similar income-tracking analysis, affirms that most Americans still have a good shot at upward mobility. In a 1992 analysis covering nine years, researchers found that 86 percent of those in the lowest 20 percent of income earners in 1979 had moved to a higher grouping by 1988. Moreover, 66 percent reached the middle tier or above, with almost 15 percent making it all the way to the top fifth of income earners. Among Americans who started out above the bottom fifth in 1979, the Treasury found the same movement up the income ladder. Nearly 50 percent of those in the middle tier, for example, rose into the top two groupings, overwhelming whatever downward mobility that took place (see Figure 4.4).

The Treasury study used a database of income-tax returns from 14,351 households. The sample is entirely different from the University of Michigan's, so there's no chance the Treasury is merely rehashing the same statistics. The study using the University of Michigan data shows more upward mobility, probably because it examines a period twice as long.

In addition to confirming that most Americans are still getting ahead in life, the Treasury study verifies that the quickest rise occurs among the young, an antidote to the prevailing ennui among the so-

FIGURE 4.4   A Second Opinion from the Treasury

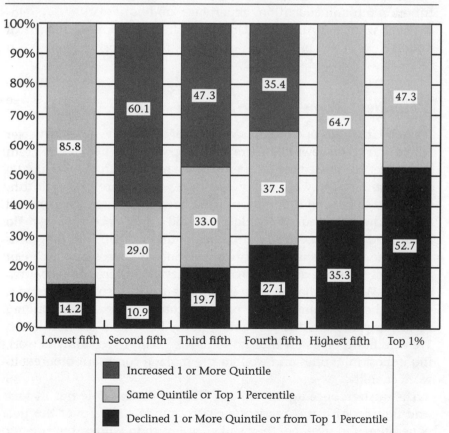

called Generation X. It also found that wage and salary income was primarily responsible for pushing people upward in the distribution, indicating that work, not luck, is the widest path to opportunity. Ours is not a *Wheel of Fortune* economy, where a few lucky individuals win big, leaving paltry gains to the great mass of people. Most of us get ahead because we strive to make ourselves and our families better off.

By carefully tracking individuals' incomes over many years, both the University of Michigan data and the Treasury study show that our economic system is biased toward success. These results should go a long way toward quelling fears of an America polarized between privileged rich and permanently poor. The rich may indeed be getting richer. We ought to have little problem with that. The poor are also getting richer. We ought to celebrate that. Indeed, what's so encouraging is the ability of those who start out in the lowest income brackets to jump into the middle and upper echelons. There's evidence that most Americans are making their way up the income distribution through education, experience, and hard work.

That's what the American Dream, a dream of opportunity, is all about.

Minorities, Women Doing Better

It's a dream that's open to all segments of society. Even if society as a whole isn't going downhill, there's still worry about whether one group or another has missed the prosperity of the mainstream. We've already seen that the poor, while still very much with us, are better off than they used to be, and that bottom-rung households typically consume more in the 1990s than the middle class did a quarter century ago. The remaining concerns center on minorities and women: Are they sharing in the country's upward thrust of living standards and incomes? That's not the same as asking whether they've attained full economic equality. Without a doubt, most minorities and women aren't doing as well as the white-male norm, partly because of such socioeconomic factors as education and job tenure, partly because of discrimination. We can, however, assert that an otherwise healthy economy is working if most minorities and women are making consistent progress toward equality.

The answer, once again, isn't in rhetoric or anecdote but in facts and figures. African-Americans clearly made strides over the past generation. On average, they still earn less than whites, but the gap is shrinking. Among black male, full-time workers with year-round jobs, the average income rose to 72 percent of whites' average income in 1996, compared with 65 percent in 1973. Black women's average income moved from 46 percent of white men's in 1973 to 59 percent in 1996. The disparity in average income between black and white women went from 15.4 percent to 13 percent. After adjusting for inflation, the proportion of African-American families earning more than $75,000 has tripled since 1970, to 9 percent. In 1998 the poverty rate for African-Americans fell to 26.5 percent, the lowest since the government began collecting data on blacks' poverty in 1959.

Minority businesses often face greater hurdles in raising capital, finding skilled labor, and developing markets, but African-American entrepreneurial activity is still flourishing. The census of U.S. businesses, taken every five years, found that the number of black-owned businesses stood at 620,912 in 1992, up 46.4 percent from the previous reading and a whopping 281 percent since 1967. From 1987 to 1992, total sales increased 63 percent to an inflation-adjusted $36 billion. In 1976, they were just $4.5 billion. Most minority enterprises are small, but at least 17 African-American–owned companies have revenues of $100 million or more, topped by TLC Beatrice International Holding's $2.2 billion.

Blacks' college enrollment rose from 1.1 million in 1975 to 1.8 million in 1995. As a result, African-Americans raised their representation between 1983 to 1996 in many high-paying professions, such as financial managers, personnel executives, accountants and auditors, psychologists, and editors and reporters. What's more, minorities are no longer bearing the brunt of hard times. In 1982, the layoff rate was 45 percent greater for blacks than for whites. By 1993, the rate for blacks was the same as that for whites. Minorities actually gained jobs during the 1990–91 recession, whereas in the recessions between 1950 and 1975, minorities suffered job loss at a rate nearly double that of whites.

For Hispanics, economic fortunes have been somewhat mixed. On the positive side, the number of Hispanic-owned businesses rose from 100,000 in 1967 to 422,373 in 1987 and 862,605 in 1992. Sales soared 150 percent, to $86 billion, eclipsing the gains made by African-Americans. The gain since 1967 was a staggering 506 percent. College enrollment among Hispanics jumped from 411,000 in 1975 to 1.2 million in 1995, allowing Hispanics to take a larger share of the good jobs in white-collar occupations. Hispanics' incomes show signs of slipping back, however. Although many families are making their way up the income ladder, the group's overall income hasn't kept pace with that of whites and African-Americans. Hispanics' median weekly earnings fell from 75 percent of whites' in 1986 to 67 percent in 1996. One possible reason: Continuing immigration brings in new waves of low-skilled, low-paid workers, overwhelming the statistical gains of longer-term resident Hispanics who are improving their education and skills.

For women, the past quarter century has brought progress by almost any measure. For starters, women are a growing presence in the business world. They are starting their own companies at twice the rate of men. In the 1990s, women owned 7.7 million businesses in the United States, up from fewer than 402,000 in the early 1970s. The portion of all U.S. companies owned by women rose from 4.6 percent in 1972 to 33.2 percent in 1992. At major corporations, women now hold 10 percent of the top management positions—a figure that represents steady gains but still disappoints women's groups. In the future, more women will no doubt get prestigious titles because the pipeline is filling with candidates: The number of female vice presidents doubled in the past decade and the number of senior vice presidents rose 75 percent. About 40 percent of business travelers are women, up from 1 percent in 1970, another indication that women are taking on more responsibilities in the workplace. Women aren't just taking on the burdens of executive life. They're also reaping the material rewards of success: One-third of today's Porsche buyers are women, up from just 3 percent just a few years ago.

Women are moving into higher-paying, traditionally male jobs. They've had their strongest employment gains among the ranks of managers and professionals. Overall, women make up about 46 percent of the labor force, but hold half of the jobs as managers and professionals. Among financial managers, 50 percent are women, up from 24 percent in 1975. Women fill 45 percent of the ranks of professors, an increase from 31 percent in 1975. Women computer analysts rose from 15 percent to 30 percent of the profession in two decades. A quarter of America's lawyers are women, compared with just 7 percent in 1975. The percentage of police officers and detectives who are women increased from 3 percent in 1975 to 14 percent today.

Education has played a key role in women's economic gains. In 1970, 55 percent of college freshmen were men and 45 percent were women. Today, the ratio is just the opposite. In 1970, only 13 percent of Ph.D.s went to women. Now, the figure is up to 40 percent. In the past quarter century, women's representation among law school graduates jumped from 5 percent to 45 percent. Degrees in dentistry climbed from 2 percent to 40 percent. Medical degrees increased from

8 percent to 38 percent. What's more, women are quickly adopting cutting-edge technologies that enhance employment prospects. They accounted for only 20 percent of Americans on-line in as recently as 1994. By 1998, two out of five Web surfers were women.

With their success in business, the workplace, and academia, women are shrinking the earnings gap between themselves and men. Among full-time wage and salary workers, women on average now earn 75 percent of what men do, up from 62 percent in 1970. The pay gap gets smaller for more recent entrants into the labor force, suggesting it will continue to narrow. Among women aged 20 to 24, pay is almost 92 percent of men's. It's 86 percent for women aged 25 to 29. By contrast, working women over age 50 earn less than 70 percent of what men do. Each year, more women move past their mates in earning power. Among married couples, 28 percent of working wives brought home a bigger paycheck than their husbands in 1995, up from 24 percent just eight years ago.

One piece of data suggests how much more even the economy is becoming: Among workers between the ages of 27 and 33 who have never had children, the wage gap between the sexes all but disappears, with women earning 98 percent of men's wages. As women march out of colleges, graduate schools, and professional programs with newly minted diplomas, it only seems right that, other things being equal, they earn just about what men do.

Variations in pay involve a hodgepodge of variables, not just gender but occupation, age, work experience, education, lifestyle choices, union membership, and motivation. Even expectations vary: A mid-1990s survey by the consulting firm Korn/Ferry found that 14 percent of women aspired to be their company's chief executive officer, compared with 46 percent of men. The differences help explain why minorities and women still earn less. Black and Hispanic workers, for example, have fewer years of schooling, a crucial factor in pay. Many women take time away from work for childbearing and family responsibilities, so they average fewer years in the labor force. For women who leave the workforce, the median amount of time before returning is 4.5 years. As a result, a typical 40-year-old woman may find herself five years behind her male contemporaries in seniority. Motherhood even influences what jobs women take. Some women, knowing that they might interrupt their careers, choose occupations where hours are flexible and skills deteriorate at a slower rate. These jobs are often lower-paying. Women are more likely to work at home, an option that usually doesn't enhance career advancement. Four-fifths of work-at-home women are married and three-fourths have children. According to the Department of Labor, these women put in fewer hours and earn approximately 25 percent less than their on-site counterparts. The choice of working at home apparently involves a significant financial sacrifice, but the flexibility it affords makes it worthwhile for many families.

Differences in social and family situations can lead to economic disparities. Over the years, dozens of statistical studies have attempted to account for inequality in wages and income, looking at such factors as education, experience, and occupation. Wage gaps for minorities and women shrink, but they don't completely disappear. Adjusting for differences in education, for example, brings African-Americans to within 80 percent or 90 percent of whites' incomes. The unexplained 10 percent to 20 percent isn't necessarily a result of discrimination. There might be additional factors that researchers haven't taken into account. By the same token, equal wages wouldn't rule out the presence of discrimination: A group might be considered underpaid if its members get a substandard return on years of schooling or work experience. Wage differences don't equate with racial or sexual discrimination.

Will minorities and women ever catch up to white men? Not as long as work experience, occupational choice, and other factors contributing to earnings gaps remain. The elusiveness of full equality shouldn't blind us to the fact that the U.S. economic system has opened itself to minorities and women in the past quarter century, allowing them to make significant improvements in their status. Overall, minorities and women may continue to lag behind white men because of education, experience, and other socioeconomic reasons. Even so, it doesn't mean minorities and women don't have opportunity for upward mobility. In the age of equal-employment laws, affirmative action, and general disapproval of racist and sexist attitudes, job discrimination based on sex or ethnicity isn't the barrier it once was. For minorities and women, the path to success will lie in the virtues a thriving economy rewards on a consistent basis—education, experience, work effort.

The Common Thread: Lifetime Earnings

If so many Americans are rising through the income ranks, and if only a few of us stay stuck at the bottom, who makes up the lowest fifth of today's income earners? One group is the downwardly mobile, those who once took in enough money to be in a higher echelon. Descent can be voluntary, usually a result of retirement, or it can be involuntary, resulting from layoffs or other hard luck. Just changing jobs sometimes results in a dip in earnings. We've already seen, though, that downward mobility happens to only a small segment of the population. By far the largest number of low-income earners are new entrants into the world of work, mostly young people. Many of us begin our working lives as part of the bottom 20 percent, either as students with part-time jobs or as relatively unskilled entrants to the labor force. Many immigrants, whatever their age, start off with low incomes.

Although they usually start at the bottom, the young tend to rise through the income distribution as they become better educated, develop skills, and gain experience. In fact, income tends to follow a familiar pattern over a person's lifetime: It rises rapidly in the early years of working, peaks during middle age, then falls toward retirement. When the average earnings at each age are placed side by side, it creates a lifetime earnings profile, shaped like a pyramid.

The changes in lifetime earnings over the past four decades tell us quite a bit about the evolution of our economy. In 1951, workers reached their peak earning years in ages 35 to 44, when their average annual earnings were 1.6 times the income of those in the 20-to-24 age group. By 1973, the ratio had risen to 2.4 to 1. By 1993, the peak earning years had shifted to ages 45 to 54, and workers in this highly paid group earned almost 3.2 times more than the 20-to-24-year-olds (see Figure 4.5).

A steeper lifetime earnings profile reflects greater opportunity. One way to see that is to imagine a perfectly flat pattern of lifetime income, with workers earning the same income every year. Paychecks for the middle years of life would match those for the early twenties. This would be a world devoid of upward mobility, offering workers no prospect of getting ahead during their lifetimes, no matter what their effort, no matter how much they improve their worth on the job.

What is behind the faster rise in Americans' lifetime earnings? Most likely, it's the by-product of broad changes in the way we work. When the economy was largely industrial, Americans worked with their hands and their backs. Today, more Americans than ever owe their paychecks to brainpower. The skills of the mind, unlike those of the body, are cumulative. Mental talents continue to sharpen long after muscles and dexterity begin to falter. These facts of physiology and economic development probably explain why the peak earning

FIGURE 4.5   The Steepening of Lifetime Earnings

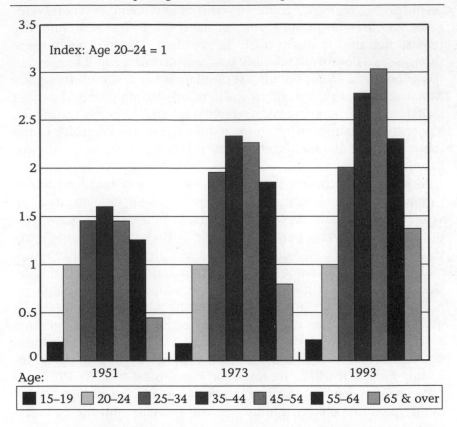

years have shifted to older age groups in the past two decades. As the United States retools itself for a more knowledge-intensive era, as the country moves from a blue-collar economy to a white-collar one, the rewards for education and experience are increasing.

The lifetime earnings profile is the thread that sews together recent trends in upward mobility and income inequality. As today's workers reap greater rewards for what they've learned on the job, earnings become sharply higher with experience. It's not that today's young workers are falling behind their counterparts of earlier generations. On the contrary, older workers are doing so much better than they used to. The result is an increase in the gap between youth and middle age. In the end, the steepening of lifetime earnings leads us to a surprising conclusion: Upward mobility may well be an important factor in the widening gap in income distribution.

All told, this isn't the harsh world seen by those who say the rich are getting richer and the poor are getting poorer. Both rich and poor are becoming better off. Are most of us going nowhere? Quite the contrary; the majority of Americans are busy climbing the income ladder. Greater returns to education and experience can skew income toward the upper end, but we would be foolhardy indeed to become so obsessed with the pecking order that we lose sight of what's really important—opportunity.

A steeper lifetime earnings profile also puts a different slant on the notion of a vanishing middle class. The center of the income distribution isn't a destination. It's just one step on the ladder of upward mobility. Forty years ago, with a flatter earnings profile, families spent most of their working lives in the middle income brackets. Today's more rapid rise in incomes means they move to the top faster, spending less time defined as "middle class." Worries about Generation X's future can be put to rest, too. Those entering the labor force in the 1990s may look at their parents' income and wonder how they will ever attain such heights. They should, however, find a steeper earnings profile encouraging. During their first two or three decades in the labor market, young workers are likely to see their incomes rise more quickly than their parents' did.

In the United States, getting ahead isn't a great mystery. The economy provides opportunity—more, in fact, than ever before—but it's up to each of us to grab it. Success isn't random. Luck and Daddy's money aren't the way most Americans get to the top. More often than not, the rewards go to education, experience, talent, ambition, vision, risk taking, readiness to change, and just plain hard work. Young people aren't guaranteed success any more than their parents were. Their chances will improve, though, if they make the right choices in life. Opportunity lies in the advice given by generations of parents and teachers: Study, work hard, and save. In short, the best advice for economic success is this: Listen to your elders.

Data confirm their wisdom:

Get an education.   Nearly 60 percent of all Americans in the top fifth of income earners graduated from college; in the bottom fifth, just 6 percent did. Only 4 percent of those in the highest tier dropped out of high school; in the lowest income group, the figure is 20 percent. Adjusting for inflation, the median income of households headed by workers with advanced or professional degrees was $92,417 in 1996.

Earnings decline to $56,402 for baccalaureate degrees, $33,036 for high-school diplomas, and $18,203 for dropouts.

Work full time, all year round.   Four fifths of the Americans in the top earnings bracket work 50 or more weeks a year. In the lowest tier, 84 percent work part time, work less than half the year, or do not work at all. Most who work part time, however, do it as a conscious choice. In 1997, only 8 percent of part-time workers said they were looking for full-time work and were unable to find it.

Full-time work is the standard remedy for poverty. Even at the minimum wage of $5.15 an hour, a worker putting in 40 hours a week would earn $10,700, more than $2,500 above the poverty level for a one-person household. Two minimum-wage workers earn nearly $5,000 more than the poverty level for a family of four. Although they are routinely dismissed as menial, minimum-wage jobs aren't necessarily a dead end: Moving up the economic ladder requires stepping onto the first rung.

Save money.   Taking inflation into account, median assets of households, excluding home equity, were $82,254 in 1993's top income-earning echelon; the bottom 20 percent had just $30,541. Not surprisingly, earnings from interest and dividends for the first group were 30 times what they were for the second. Savings can make a big difference, especially for retirement. For individuals age 65 or older in the bottom fifth, 83 percent of income comes from Social Security, a program aimed at subsistence, and only 9 percent from savings. In the top bracket, earnings on savings make up 54 percent of income and Social Security accounts for only 20 percent.

Form a family.   Only 13 percent of the top fifth of income earners live in "nonfamily" households. In the bottom tier, 64 percent do. It's not that poorer Americans lack the instinct for forming families. If that were true, we wouldn't see larger families among low-income workers. More than likely, the encouragement of and responsibility for others pushes most of us to take making a living more seriously.

Be willing to move.   If work paves the way to success, it makes sense to go where the jobs are. The unemployment rate in McAllen, Texas, is 17.2 percent. A few hundred miles away, in Austin, a city on the leading edge of new technology, it's 2.5 percent. Employment opportunities aren't the only variation from region to region. Wages can differ, too, even within the same job category. The nation has been on the move for decades—farm to city, the South to the North, the East to the West: Geographical mobility is one way Americans can find opportunity and close the income gap.

Be willing to retrain. The average hourly wage for a computer programmer is $23.01. A typical textile worker makes only $8.25. What's more, the number of computer jobs is rising, while the opportunities in textiles are diminishing. Jobs come and go as the economy evolves, often benefiting those workers who learn new skills and keep up with the economic changes.

Become computer-savvy. Workers who know how to operate a computer earn an average of 15 percent more than those who don't—and that's doing the same job. We shouldn't be at all surprised: The machine makes those who use it more productive and more employable.

Stick to it. Average income tends to rise quickly in life as workers gain experience and knowledge. Income in households headed by someone under age 25 averaged $27,404 a year. Average earnings nearly doubled, to $43,881, for 25- to 34-year-olds. For those aged 45 to 54, the figure jumped to $65,039. It takes time for learning, hard work, and saving to bear fruit.

Inequality Is Not Inequity

Judging from the public debate, at least some Americans would prefer a more equal distribution of income to a less equal one, perhaps on moral grounds, perhaps as a part of an ideal of civic virtue. There's no *economic* reason, however, to prefer one pattern of income distribution over another. In fact, the income statistics do little but confirm what's obvious: America isn't an egalitarian society. It wasn't designed to be. Socialism, a failed and receding system, sought to impose an artificial equality. Capitalism, a successful and expanding system, doesn't fight a fundamental fact of human nature—we vary greatly in capabilities, motivation, interests, and preferences. Some of us are driven to get ahead. Some of us are just plain lazy. Some of us are willing to work hard so we can afford a lifestyle rich in material goods. Some of us work just hard enough to provide a roof overhead, food, clothes, and a few amenities. It shouldn't come as a surprise that our incomes vary greatly.

Income inequality isn't an aberration. Quite the opposite, it's perfectly consistent with the laws that govern a free-enterprise system. In the early 1970s, three groups of unemployed Canadians, all in their twenties, all with at least 12 years of schooling, volunteered to participate in a stylized economy where the only employment was making woolen belts on small hand looms. They could work as much or as little as they liked, earning $2.50 for each belt. After 98 days, the results were anything but equal: 37.2 percent of the economy's income went to the 20 percent with the highest earnings. The bottom 20 percent received only 6.6 percent. This economic microcosm tells us one thing: Even among similar people with identical work options, some workers will earn more than others.

In a modern economy, incomes vary for plenty of reasons having little to do with fairness or equity. Education and experience, for example, usually yield higher pay. As industry becomes more sophisticated, the rewards to skilled labor tend to rise, adding to the number of high-income earners. Location matters. New Yorkers earn more than Mississippians. Lifestyle choices play a part, too. Simply by having an additional paycheck, two-income families make more money than those with a single breadwinner. Longer retirements, however, will add to the number of households with low income, even if many senior citizens live well from their savings. Demographic changes can twist the distribution of income. As the Baby Boom enters its peak earning years, the number of high-income households ought to rise. Economic forces create ripples in what we earn. The ebb and flow of industries can shift workers to both ends of the income distribution. Layoffs put some Americans into low-income groups, at least temporarily. Companies with new products and new technologies create jobs and, in most cases, share the bounty by offering workers higher pay. In technology industries, bonuses and stock options are becoming more common. Higher rates of return on investments—with, for example, a stock-market boom—will create a windfall for households with money riding on financial markets.

In and of itself, moreover, income distribution doesn't say much about the performance of an economy or the opportunities it offers. A widening gap isn't necessarily a sign of failure, nor does a narrowing one guarantee that an economy is functioning well. As a matter of fact, it's quite common to find a widening of income distribution in boom times, when almost everyone's earnings are rising rapidly.

All it takes is for one segment of the workforce to become better off faster than others. However, the distribution can narrow in hard times, as companies facing declining demand cut back on jobs, hours, raises, and bonuses. In fact, we often see a compression of incomes in areas where people are sinking into poverty.

There's no denying that our system allows some Americans to become much richer than others. We must accept that, even celebrate it. Opportunity, not equality of income, is what made the U.S. economy grow and prosper. It's most important to provide equality of opportunity, not equality of results. There's ample evidence to refute any suggestion that the economy is no longer capable of providing opportunity for the vast majority of Americans. At the end of the twentieth century, upward mobility is alive and well. Even the lower-income households are sharing in the country's progress. What's more, data suggest that the populist view of America as a society torn between haves and have-nots, with rigid class lines, is just plain wrong. We are by no means a caste society.

5 STILL ON TOP OF THE WORLD

Rising from defeat in World War II, Japan's economy came on like a juggernaut. The country rebuilt its industrial base, looked around for markets, and saw across the Pacific Ocean the world's largest, wealthiest nation—the United States. At first, Japan sold Americans cheap knockoffs, but it soon moved up to transistor radios, televisions, motorcycles, and inexpensive cars. As their economy came of age, Japan's companies created markets for such innovative products as Sony's Walkman and Nintendo's video games. Eventually, Japan Inc. achieved perhaps the ultimate in exporting by selling luxury cars into Cadillac country.

Competing on price and quality, the Japanese relentlessly won market share in the United States. In doing so, they provided great benefits to American consumers, not only directly but also indirectly. Competition drove down the prices of televisions, computers, and other electronic gadgets. To regain sales lost to the Japanese, U.S. automobile companies renewed their focus on quality, eventually regaining parity with imported models in most consumer surveys. Just as important, new products arrived on the market sooner. American engineers demonstrated the first prototype videotape recorder in 1951 at Bing Crosby's recording studio in Los Angeles. California's Ampex Corp. devised a commercial model in 1956, but the company doubted Americans wanted to watch movies at home. Sony set out to make the VCR a household product in the 1970s—and, along with other Japanese companies, it succeeded. If not for the Japanese, it might have taken much longer for the VCR to become a fixture in America's living rooms.

By the 1980s, the Japanese had become so successful that U.S. business and political leaders sounded an alarm. Japan became an

American obsession. We were told the United States would benefit by emulating the strategic genius of Japan Inc. and the diligence of Japanese workers. We were told that in just a few years Japan would eclipse the United States as the world's foremost economic power. We were told that Japan was unfair and predatory, that our nation was at risk if we didn't impose trade restrictions that would stop Japan's relentless advance.

Asia's menace didn't stop with Japan. South Korea, Taiwan, and even tiny Singapore and Hong Kong emerged as threats to American business. When China began to modernize, it arose as the next candidate, after Japan, poised to supplant the United States in the world economy. In the dog-eat-dog world of international competition, our country, critics lamented, was toothless, our workers coddled, unwilling to work, poorly educated for the new technologies. Our companies were too focused on the short-term bottom line to match the strategic vision of our overseas rivals. Decline was regarded as inevitable. The era of American economic supremacy would crumble.

This view of America's ability to compete in the world economy became pervasive in the 1980s. Commissions and think tanks issued somber reports calling for increased savings and investment, better education, greater spending on research and development. Nothing is wrong with these prescriptions—by and large they would do any economy good. The assessment of the patient's health, however, was way off base. The only scenario seldom taken seriously was the one that jibes with the facts: Our economy, the most dynamic and powerful in history, was still outperforming all others, and it was well positioned to continue leading the pack into the twenty-first century.

How America Stacks Up

By the mid-1990s, Japanophobia had cooled. Japan's economy had slipped into a prolonged funk, and Japan Inc. no longer looked to be an unstoppable force, even though its exports and investment money still poured forth. In 1997, other Asian countries stumbled, their currencies plummeting and stock markets in full retreat. In fact, it was the United States, not Japan or Asia's Tigers, that began to look like a world beater. American companies became more productive, more innovative, more profitable, and more capable of reasserting themselves in world markets. Overall, America's economy grew twice as fast as Japan's from 1991 to 1997. In industry after industry, U.S. producers gained ground or held their own—not only against the Japanese but also against the rest of the world. For all the anguish about the loss of America's dominance in the world economy, the United States still ranks as the top producer of jet aircraft, computers, telecommunications, medical technology, high-tech petrochemicals, food and beverages, movies, software, pop music, financial and legal services, tourism, and thousands of everyday consumer products. In 1993, Americans once again became kings of semiconductor production, their market share surpassing Japan's for the first time since 1986. By 1996, the United States was making 46 percent of the world's semiconductors, compared with 36 percent for Japan and 18 percent for other countries. One reason for the American resurgence is a trend toward customization of computer chips, a more profitable segment of the industry that U.S. companies do better. Despite Japan's prowess as an automaker, the top producer is the United States, even if we exclude the output of Japanese-owned American factories. Detroit's Big Three automobile producers had 37 percent of the world's output in the mid-1990s, compared with 30 percent for Japan. General Motors remains the top automobile producer worldwide, with 8.4 million vehicles in 1996. And Ford comes in second, with production of 4.8 million vehicles in 1996, nearly a million more than Toyota, Japan's top company.

America is still the largest economy on Earth, at $8.5 trillion. The United States still leads the major industrialized countries in per capita income and job creation (see Table 5.1).

Even the manufacturing sector, so often portrayed as a basket case in international competition, staged a comeback in the 1990s, increasing both output and employment after the end of the early-1990s recession. The United States now boasts 11 of the world's top 15 most profitable publicly traded companies. The total value of America's publicly traded companies eclipses that of every other nation by a factor of five. In most industries, our companies are healthy and profitable. Of the 162 U.S. companies that rank among the world's 500 largest, profits in 1996 were $214 billion, compared with $41 billion for runner-up Japan's 126 companies. At a time of solid growth with low inflation, our stock market led all others in the 1990s by a wide margin, a signal that investors had confidence in the future of the American economy. American workers lead all major industrial nations in productivity. The country is on the cutting edge of technology. For example, after pioneering a technique called "parallel processing," the United States once again claimed the world's fastest

TABLE 5.1   Per Capita Income, Job Creation Among Nations

Country	Per Capita Income 1996	New Jobs 1980–96	Percent Gain
United States	$28,338	27,405,000	27.6
Japan	$23,667	9,600,000	17.6
Germany	$21,594	980,000	3.7
France	$20,915	480,000	2.2
Italy	$20,346	−150,000	−0.7
United Kingdom	$18,983	1,610,000	6.5
Canada	$21,929	1,395,000	23.4

Monetary figures are in 1997 dollars.

computer, a machine with 9,152 U.S.-made Pentium microprocessors. The United States possesses an incredible 40 percent of the world's computing power.

Our country even holds the lead in international trade. By reputation, Japan is the world's great exporting nation. Statistics tell a different story. United States, not Japan, is the top exporter—and American companies, unlike their Japanese rivals, don't have the huge U.S. market to export into. The scorecard for 1996: America's overseas sales of goods and services were $871 billion, compared to Japan's $456 billion. The U.S. share of world exports has remained constant, about 13 percent, over the past quarter century, further evidence that America isn't less competitive than it used to be. The final word comes from the prestigious World Economic Forum, a Swiss research consortium that each year analyzes dozens of indicators for the major economies. In its *World Competitiveness Report*, the Forum has declared the United States the best overall performer every year since 1992. In recent years, the report has praised America's overall economic vitality, openness to trade and investment, infrastructure for business needs, sophisticated financial markets, and prowess in science and technology. The *World Competitiveness Report*'s only reservations about the U.S. economy centered on the quality of the labor force and government policies, including a budget deficit that has since disappeared. Otherwise, the country ranks in the top three on every other important economic asset.

The broad statistics used to compare one nation to another sound precise. We can, for example, find a table that shows a U.S. manufacturing worker earning $18.24 an hour, or $1.13 less than his counterpart in Japan. Should a blue-collar American envy his Japanese counterpart? To answer the question of who's better off, we need data on the cost of living in each country. In reality, nearly all international yardsticks fall prey to a mass of distortions, not the least of which is fluctuating exchange rates. From 1985 to 1995, the dollar's value fell from nearly 260 yen to less than 100. In some of the statistical tables, Japan's per capita income soared from $11,124 to $40,726, making Japan, in dollar terms, a fabulously wealthy society. The average Japanese, however, wasn't really that much richer, and his family still lived in cramped quarters likened to "rabbit hutches." The average American wasn't relatively poorer, especially because few Japanese companies raised the dollar prices of their goods to make up for the rise in the value of their nation's currency. Foreign-exchange markets operate on supply and demand, so they usually provide objective values for currencies. Even so, simple exchange-rate conversions don't necessarily yield meaningful international comparisons of income and earnings, at least not for purposes of measuring what's most important—living standards. Economists attempt to get around the vagaries of exchange rates by putting international comparisons on a "purchasing-power parity" basis. This methodology attempts to equate currency values with domestic price levels. Table 5.1, showing the United States leading other industrial nations with a per capita income of $28,338 in 1996, comes from purchasing-power parity data.

One way to circumvent the fuzziness in international income statistics is the consumption test, the yardstick used earlier that showed that Americans have more of just about everything in the past quarter century. International comparisons are across space instead of time: How does a typical American household fare when measured against other countries' families? No item-by-item inventory of consumption by country exists. What is available from a dozen advanced industrial nations, however, strongly suggests that Americans are far better off than consumers in other parts of the world.

In the United States, more than 90 percent of households own radios, televisions, vacuum cleaners, clothes washers, and microwave ovens. Other nations have achieved that rate of ownership of some appliances, but none has yet reached that level for all items. Nearly every household in the 11 countries has at least one television, for example, but U.S. families are more apt to own two or three, the better, presumably, to avoid conflicts over what to watch. As a result, Americans have 901 televisions for every 1,000 people, compared to 650 for runner-up Japan. American families lead the world in ownership of dishwashers and clothes dryers. We're at or near the top in telephones and cellular devices. We're more likely than the Japanese to own videocassette recorders, even though Japan Inc. produces most of them. In the number of personal computers owned per capita, the United States rate is more than double that of its nearest competitor. Putting it all together in an index of 13 common appliances gives the typical American household a wide lead over families in any other nation. Macroeconomic data confirm that the United States ranks as the superpower of consumption. Private spending on goods and services accounts for two-thirds of the economy, a higher fraction than any other major industrial nation. Yet Americans also lead the world in holding financial assets, so we're not necessarily consuming while others save (see Table 5.2).

Mere counting doesn't capture all of the American advantage in living standards. Because Americans have larger houses, we can accommodate more stuff. Our televisions, refrigerators, washers, stoves, and microwaves are larger, too. Homes are better insulated and better equipped—for example, much more likely to have air conditioning, central heat, garages, and second and even third bathrooms. Americans' incomes go further because they pay less for many basic products. Nearly all consumers in foreign countries pay more for food, gasoline, airline tickets, telephone calls, utilities, clothing, household supplies, and movies. Perhaps the advantage for the American consumer can be summed up by McDonald's Big Mac, rapidly becoming a fast-food staple all over the world. In minutes of work, the double-decker burger is slightly more expensive in Germany and costs at least 40 percent more in every other industrialized nation than it does here.

The myth of America's decline as an economic power may rest to some extent on unrealistic perceptions of the nation's place in the world economy. The United States came out of World War II a victor unscathed. In fact, the war shook the country out of the decade-long Great Depression, the economy's low point in the twentieth century. We sailed into the postwar period with an unnatural dominance, which couldn't be sustained once the rest of the world, including Japan and Germany, returned to normal. In 1950, the United States produced nearly half of the world's total output. By the mid-1990s, that proportion was down to less than a quarter. Were we worse off? No way. The size of the U.S. economy more than quadrupled over those 45 years. Per capita income tripled. Indeed, the revival of the world economy after the devastation of World War II ought to count as one of this country's greatest contributions, not just lessening the likelihood of another world war but contributing to our own prosperity as well.

TABLE 5.2 Americans' Living Standards Still Stand Out

Product Ownership	U.S.	Belgium	Denmark	France	Germany	Italy	Nether-lands	Spain	Sweden	Switzer-land	U.K.	Japan
Percent of Households:												
Clothes Washer	90	88	74	88	88	96	89	87	72	78	88	99
Dishwasher	53	26	36	32	34	18	11	11	31	32	11	*
Microwave	86	21	31	19	36	6	22	9	37	15	48	73
Radio	99	90	98	98	84	92	99	95	93	99	90	75
Television	98	97	98	95	97	98	95	98	97	93	98	99
Clothes Dryer	82	39	30	12	17	10	27	5	18	27	32	15
Vacuum Cleaner	99	92	96	89	96	56	98	29	97	93	98	99
VCR	83	42	63	35	42	25	50	40	48	41	69	69
Personal Computer	40	22	30	20	20	14	25	11	29	23	25	18
Other:												
Phones per 100 people	63	46	61	56	49	43	53	39	68	61	50	49
Cell phones per 1000 people	128.4	23.2	157.3	23.8	42.8	67.4	33.2	24.1	229.4	63.5	98.0	81.5
TVs per 1000 people	776	464	536	579	550	436	495	490	476	461	612	619
Autos per 100 people	57	41	31	42	49	51	38	na	41	44	35	33

Statistic	U.S.	Belgium	Denmark	France	Germany	Italy	Nether-lands	Spain	Sweden	Switzer-land	U.K.	Japan
Competitiveness ranking	1	23	8	21	14	30	4	27	17	7	12	18
Unemployment rate: 1996	5.4	9.8	6.0	12.4	9.0	12.0	6.3	22.2	10.0	3.7	8.2	3.4
Long-term unemp. rate	0.8	5.4	2.8	4.2	1.9	5.9	3.7	10.6	0.6	0.8	3.6	0.4
% Job growth: 1970–96	61.0	-0.1	10.4	8.1	3.7	5.1	35.4	1.8	4.4	na	8.0	28.0
% Job growth: 1980–96	27.6	-2.7	3.9	2.2	5.2	-0.7	24.1	12.2	-4.9	na	6.5	17.6
GDP per capita: 1996	$28338	$22261	$22833	$20915	$21594	$20346	$21292	$15231	$19615	$25873	$18983	$23667
Life exp. at birth: 1997	76.0	77.2	77.3	78.6	76.1	78.2	77.9	78.5	78.2	77.8	76.6	79.7

(continues)

TABLE 5.2 (continued)

Statistic	U.S.	Belgium	Denmark	France	Germany	Italy	Netherlands	Spain	Sweden	Switzerland	U.K.	Japan
Crude death rate[a]	8.8	10.3	10.4	9.0	11.1	9.9	8.7	8.9	11.3	9.6	11.2	7.9
Suicide rate[b]	11.8	17.9	20.4	19.8	13.8	7.1	9.6	6.6	14.7	19.6	9.3	15.1
Portion of the population aged 25–64 that's college educated	24.4	10.1	13.7	9.2	12.6	7.5	21.4	11.0	12.2	8.4	11.7	13.3
Percent of manufacturing employment in high-tech industries	21.0	*	12.3	18.4	20.1	10.9	15.7	*	13.8	*	19.4	21.8
R&D scientists and engineers per 1,000 labor force	7.6	4.4	4.1	5.2	5.9	3.1	4.0	2.6	2.6	4.0	4.5	9.2
Old-age dependency ratio (%)	18.5	24.3	23.0	23.3	24.4	24.7	19.7	22.4	27.4	23.0	24.8	23.2
Earnings of women relative to men (1980 = 100)	113.0	*	*	*	*	*	*	*	100.0	*	108.0	99.0
Tax rate for all social security programs	21.0	37.9	*	50.3	40.6	54.3	56.6	38.3	36.1	12.9	22.2	26.6
Financial wealth per capita	$64402	$23957	*	$28388	$27338	$33060	*	$11853	$9258	*	*	$38818
Work injury rate[a]	26.9	41.1	16.4	34.5	69.8	43.1	11.1	58.3	17.5	37.5	7.9	*
Work injury death rate[b]	2.4	3.6	2.2	5.1	7.6	6.6	*	15.2	2.2	4.4	1.5	5.1
Big Mac, minutes work	8.1	11.4	11.6	14.0	8.2	14.3	10.8	17.4	13.3	12.2	13.6	8.9
Student:teacher ratio	16	7	11	14	19	10	15	17	11	*	18	18
Student:computer ratio	7	13	*	11	19	32	16	*	*	8	*	25
Pace of life (rank:1 is fastest)	16	*	*	11	3	5	9	*	7	1	6	4
Nobel Prize recipients	178	2	3	10	26	4	4	0	10	8	46	4

[a] per 1,000
[b] per 100,000

Straight Talk on Trade

In the 1990s, the United States retains its position as the most potent economic force on this planet, which brings us to something of a conundrum: How did so many of our countrymen come to believe that America was losing competitiveness? As with living standards, fault-finding works by distilling reality down to one or two indicators—then fashioning them into the worse possible scenario. The case for a competitiveness crisis usually rests on the merchandise trade deficit. In the early 1970s, imports and exports were roughly in balance, as three years of small surpluses offset three years of small deficits. Since 1976, the country has sunk deeper into deficit, culminating in a world-record $198 billion in 1997. With the economic crisis in Asia likely to curtail exports, 1998 saw even heavier red ink. Meanwhile, other countries posted huge surpluses. Japan's bilateral surplus in merchandise trade with the United States rose from $1.9 billion in 1980 to $56 billion in 1997. In the 1990s, China has emerged as a major surplus country, its merchandise exports to the United States topping imports by nearly $50 billion in 1997. The fact that Americans, year in and year out, bought more than they sold in competition with other countries indicated to many observers that the country could no longer cut it. Even more ominous, the persistent deficits seemed to suggest that other nations were taking advantage of the United States by refusing to buy the goods and services we produced.

The deficit that causes so much hand-wringing reflects only merchandise trade, a category that includes oil, automobiles, clothing, electronic gadgets, and other tangible goods. It misses a lot of commerce between nations. For the United States, the red ink in merchandise trade has been partly offset by a surplus in such services as movies, insurance, medical care, banking, consulting, tourism, and much more. In 1997, the nation's positive balance in services totaled $87.8 billion, a figure rarely reported on the evening news. Even more significant is a third category of international transactions, the flow of capital. The gloomy view of international finance focuses on money leaving the country, as investors diversify their portfolios with foreign stocks and U.S. companies build plants and open offices overseas. We forget that foreigners put their money into the United States. Not surprisingly, the powerful American economy, with its wealthy consumers and booming stock market, has become a magnet for foreign investment. Since the early 1980s, annual capital flows into the United States for real estate, stocks, bonds, and government securities have skyrocketed from $58 billion to $733.4 billion. Annual capital outflows—essentially, U.S. purchases of foreign assets—rose from $87 billion to $478.5 billion. As a result, the United States showed a capital inflow of $254.9 billion in 1997. Behind these numbers are millions of decisions about saving and investment. A country that saves more than it invests—Japan, for example—will send its excess money abroad in the form of investment. The United States invests more than it saves, so it imports capital.

The merchandise, services, and capital accounts don't have to balance independently. Nor, for that matter, do the bilateral dealings of any two nations. Over all, though, a nation's international transactions must, by the logic of double-entry accounting, always come out equal. The term "balance of payments." It means that, minor statistical discrepancies aside, what America pays to the rest of the world always matches what it gets back. The same holds for every other nation. What ensures this result in the marketplace is the relative value of currencies. If services didn't sell across borders and if financial flows were slight, exchange rates would adjust international prices to bring merchandise trade into balance. That's the world of 25 years ago, when imports and exports showed a rough equivalence. What has changed? Countries have opened their markets to services and freed up their capital markets, and we've seen a rush of money across borders. For the United States, rising surpluses in services and investment are the flip side of growing deficits in merchandise trade (see Table 5.3).

The trade deficit is a red herring. Few critics take time to explain that we aren't losers in our economic dealings with other countries. Some Americans might want to welcome foreign investment, especially since it enriches us by pumping up stock prices and financing the building of factories that employ U.S. workers. They would prefer to have surpluses in merchandise trade, too. The combination simply cannot work. The trade deficit and capital surplus are two sides of the same coin. Other countries' surpluses in goods earn them dollars to purchase more of our services and invest in America. If we don't buy from foreigners, they can't buy from us and invest with us. This is the only outcome that makes sense. If we really were importing without regard to economic laws, the United States would be consuming at the expense of other nations—in effect taking advantage of other countries, many of them less fortunate. It's a fairer world than most of us suspect: Every country gives as much as it gets.

The long-running furor of the merchandise-trade deficit can be turned on its head: What it really signifies is that the United States re-

TABLE 5.3   Balance of Payments, by the Numbers: Billions of Dollars in
1997

Merchandise exports	679.3	
Merchandise imports	−877.3	
Merchandise balance	−198.0	
Service exports	258.3	
Services imports	−170.5	
Services balance	87.8	
Overall goods and services		−110.2
Income from U.S. assets abroad	241.8	
Income paid out on foreign assets	−247.1	
Net Investment income		−5.3
Foreign investment in the U.S.	733.4	
Americans' foreign investment	−478.5	
Net inflow of capital		254.9
Unilateral transfers		−39.7
Statistical discrepancy		−99.7
Net balance on account		0.0

mains the best place to invest—by a large margin. In the mid-1990s,
direct investment from overseas in the United States was more than
double that in any other country. Japan's trade surpluses, by the way,
reflect the opposite. The Japanese economy, where profits and interest rates are low and prices are high, hasn't been a good place to invest. Not surprisingly, reasonable Japanese, looking at the prospects
at home, have decided instead to put their capital into the United
States, where returns are better than in Japan. The United States
could rack up merchandise-trade surpluses if it chose to. One way
would be to decide to save more, a solution that comes at the price of
consuming less of both domestic and foreign goods. Another way is
to make the U.S. economy less attractive, perhaps with a severe recession. No one would want to invest here, capital would flow out instead of in, and, through the hydraulics of exchange rates and the
balance of payments, Americans would end up shipping out more
goods than they import.

Would anyone celebrate? Probably not.

Understanding the balance of payments clears up the biggest mis-
conception about trade, but many Americans still fear open markets.
Advocates of trade protection condemn imports and foreign ownership as harmful to the country's well-being, although they seem quite
willing to encourage exports. They blame foreign competition for
ravaging whole industries—textiles, shoes, steel, televisions, a hand-

ful of agricultural products. Critics bemoan our open trading system, contending that it failed to protect the nation's good factory jobs, that other nations somehow bested us by taking away our manufacturing industries. The remedy, at least among those of this mind-set, involves fencing out imports, an action that supposedly would save the jobs for American workers.

Protectionism possesses political, perhaps even patriotic, appeal, but it would ruin the U.S. economy. It's important to realize that doing business abroad enriches the United States, just as it does every other country. Imports are vital, especially to a modern economy. Other nations provide hard-to-find natural resources, such as platinum and tungsten. Bananas and coffee would be expensive to produce at home. We'd pay a lot more at the gasoline pump if we couldn't buy foreign crude oil. Even where Americans could meet their own needs, open trade delivers pluses for the economy as a whole. At a bare minimum, imports increase the variety of products available in the United States. Think of all the products introduced from abroad—from transistor radios in the 1960s to compact disc players in the 1980s. Perhaps most important of all, pressure from imports, just like competition from domestic producers, forces U.S. companies to keep prices low and product designs up-to-date. All of these forces help spread the gains from trade to the masses. In the past, when imports were expensive, only the wealthy could afford them. Open trade and cheaper transportation have turned America's shopping malls into international bazaars. The great accomplishment of American capitalism has been to democratize consumption of the world's goods and services, giving the average family the foreign wines, foods, clothing, and household furnishings that only Rockefellers and Kennedys once enjoyed.

The traditional defense of free trade remains as true today as it was when promulgated by David Ricardo, the nineteenth-century British economist. Countries will attain higher living standards if they produce the goods and services in which they possess a *comparative advantage*. Simply put, nations will be better off if they use their time, energy, and resources doing what they do best, then sell the products abroad in exchange for what other countries do best. Specialization will make all nations better off. The classic example, formulated by Ricardo himself, involves Portuguese wine and English textiles. Wine required 80 units of labor in Portugal and 120 in England. Textiles needed 90 units in Portugal and 100 units in England. Without trade, a Portuguese vintner's labor bought less than one unit of domestic textiles. If a Portuguese merchant bought textiles in England, however, the return on one unit of wine would be 1.2 units of textiles, or 35 percent more. Similarly, each unit of British textiles could be exchanged for 35 percent more wine in Portugal than at home. Portugal would be richer—that is, consume more of both wine and cloth—if it concentrated on wine-making and bought textiles from Britain. The result holds, by the way, even though Portugal, with its relatively cheap labor, could make both products at a lower cost.

Comparative advantage typically results from a society's stock of resources, natural and acquired. A nation's endowment includes workers, land, minerals, machinery, technology, and natural beauty. In the modern world, countries can enhance their comparative advantages by investing in technology and workers' skills. As economies have become increasingly open over the past three decades, there has been a revision in the international division of labor. U.S. industrial structure isn't suited to making products requiring large inputs from unskilled, low-paid workers. As a result, the United States has been relinquishing to other countries labor-intensive manufacturing, such as textiles and shoes. Comparative advantage for the United States, as revealed by recent trade patterns, lies in large-scale agriculture, high-technology products, services, medicine, and finance, to suggest just a few areas. From 1989 to 1997, for example, machinery and other capital goods as a proportion of total U.S. exports rose from 40.5 to 42.4 percent. Auto parts and engines rose from 9.8 to 10.7 percent of the total, and manufactured consumer goods increased from 10.0 to 11.3 percent. During this period, the share of exports made up of raw materials, including food and industrial supplies, declined. We are also expanding overseas sales of banking, consulting, entertainment, and other services. In 1980, overseas sales of merchandise exceeded services by 5 to 1; by 1997, the ratio had declined to 2.7 to 1. The international division of labor isn't entirely black and white. In textiles, for example, American companies, using computerized looms, automated stitching machines, and sophisticated marketing, can stay competitive in linens, T-shirts, and high-fashion garments. Low-priced garments that need hand stitching, such as shirts and blue jeans, can usually be made more cheaply abroad.

And what about the import-battered industries where jobs are lost? It can't be denied that these industries exist, but recent experience shows that rising imports haven't done any harm to the overall economy. Between 1980 and 1987, when the U.S. deficit rose to its peak of

3.6 percent of total output, industrial production gained 17 percent. Manufacturing did even better, increasing 23 percent. The 1990s provided a replay. As the deficit tripled between 1992 and 1997, the economy surged ahead by 24 percent in industrial production and 27 percent in manufacturing. What's more, there's no compelling evidence that employment is suffering. America had its most vigorous job growth when trade deficits were swelling in the 1980s and 1990s. The unemployment rate fell in all but two of the 14 years of rising red ink in trade. In the recession of 1990–91, the deficit shrank but unemployment rose. Big-picture macroeconomic forces, not imports, determine the number of jobs. Trade plays a role in determining the types of jobs available. Imports diminish prospects in low-wage professions, surely bad news for workers in low-skilled manufacturing. Many of the industries where the United States boasts a comparative advantage, however, rely on advanced machinery, sophisticated management, and educated workers. They are above average in terms of pay and working conditions. In the 1990s, the Commerce Department reports, wages are 15 percent higher in export industries. Over two centuries, the United States has become a rich nation by moving up to high-productivity jobs, almost always at the expense of low-paying ones. The eve of the twenty-first century is no time to stop doing this.

The American economy is wide open to trade and investment—just as it should be. The average U.S. tariff is just 2.8 percent, lower than that of any other economy except Hong Kong's and Singapore's. With the exceptions of sugar, textiles, and a handful of other products, there are few nontariff barriers to trade and investment. Trade is an integral part of the process through which an economy improves its productivity, income, and living standards by concentrating its efforts in the goods and services with higher value in the marketplace. The United States cannot move on to tomorrow's industries if it uses trade restraints to cling to yesterday's. Higher living standards don't come from hoarding what we've got and protecting the status quo from change.

A familiar bumper sticker reads: BUY AMERICAN, THE JOB YOU SAVE MAY BE YOUR OWN. On the face of it, the idea makes sense. If Americans spend their money in America, it will keep their countrymen employed. The fallacy of the exhortation shows up as borders shrink. Why not buy Texan? After all, the state doesn't gain much when its residents buy from New Yorkers, who may or may not buy from Texas. Better yet, wouldn't Dallas consumers help their local economy by refusing to purchase goods and services made in Houston—

and vice versa? The argument reaches its ultimate absurdity when we consider buying only from our own neighborhood or our own family. Obviously, we'd give up a lot of what we consume. Buying close to home won't make us better off, especially if we pay higher prices, accept lower quality, or do without because what we want isn't made in this country. Trade makes us better off only because of *imports*. They are the gains from trade. Exports, the side of the trade equation many regard as beneficial, actually are a *cost* of trade. When we sell overseas, we are giving up goods and services that could be consumed at home. The broader the market, the more opportunity it provides for companies and workers to do what they do best. A national market is better than a local one, a global one better than a national one. "Buy American" isn't the pathway to prosperity. It's a prescription for poverty.

In the real world, most international transactions aren't dictated by the preferences of some agency or institute. They are for the most part the outcome of market forces—that is, voluntary transactions. No one is forcing Americans to buy Japanese cars and camcorders, Italian clothing, Mexican beer, or French wines and cheeses. No one is forcing British or Arab investors to seek the safety and profitability of the American economy. Consumers and companies involve themselves in international trade and investment because it suits them. They believe it makes them better off. Some Americans campaign to block foreign investment, even though it amounts to a tiny fraction of the U.S. economy. America's physical wealth, its land, labor, and infrastructure, can't be readily bought and shipped overseas, so it's hard to understand what all the fuss is about. Foreign-owned assets and companies in the United States are still governed by U.S. law, thus safely under our control.

Once the fallacies about foreign trade and investment are laid to rest, it's hard to understand why anyone could object to America's *fully voluntary* dealings with the rest of the world. We should appreciate how open markets benefit us—as consumers, first and foremost—by increasing competition, variety, and value in the marketplace. We need to acknowledge that foreign investment helps provide jobs for Americans and boosts the value of Wall Street investments. Our $877 billion in merchandise imports in 1997 may anger U.S. industrialists and union workers. Manufacturing jobs have been lost to import competition, no doubt about it. The protectionist alternative, however, is far worse. Self-sufficiency is an expensive illusion—and chasing it cannot fail to make Americans worse off. Turning the nation's back on trade proved disastrous in the late 1920s, when the Smoot-Hawley tariff, the most protectionist law passed in the United States, triggered the economic crisis we now refer to as the Great Depression.

Leading the Followers

Up until the current boom, many Americans worried that our country's economic growth hadn't been keeping pace with that of other nations. Once again, they found numbers to make their case: Some of our competitors are moving forward at two, three, or even four times the speed of the United States in terms of their per capita output. From 1973 to 1990, the years of the Asian economies' heady growth, per capita output in the United States increased by an average of 1.5 percent a year. By contrast, average annual gains were 3.1 percent for Japan. While the United States seemed to crawl along, such developing countries as Korea, Taiwan, Thailand, and, most recently, China posted double-digit growth rates.

No economy the size of the United States' can match developing nations' growth—at least not in percentage terms. Expanding at the rates achieved in the 1980s by even the slowest of the Asian nations would require a nearly $500 billion burst of economic activity, equivalent to re-creating on our shores an economy the size of Australia's every year. A spurt of that magnitude would no doubt overheat the American economy. We would face severe shortages of labor and other inputs. Inflation almost surely would spiral into double digits, forcing policy makers to cool everything with higher interest rates. Trying to grow too fast will lead only to recession and ruin. A mature economy ought to strive for a sustainable rate of growth that produces lasting jobs and keeps inflation under control. We've done that for almost two decades.

If other nations continue to grow faster, are we doomed to be overtaken? Not likely. An up-and-coming economy, one that's posting eye-popping growth rates, can't quickly zoom to the top of the heap. When the United States grows by 3 percent in a year, it adds $950 to per capita income. For China, one of the fastest-growing developing nations, tripling the U.S. growth rate would increase the economy by just $300 per capita in a year. As a result, the average Chinese finds himself slipping more than $600 further *behind* an average American. Even with rapid growth, it would take China generations to reach the living standards of today's Americans—if its economic thrust doesn't slow. And that's a big if. High-flying countries can't vault forward at the same pace forever—a fact underscored by the troubles afflicting Asia's economies in the late 1990s.

The reason: It's much easier to play catch up. Envision an explorer wielding a machete to cut a path through a dense jungle. He goes forward slowly, hacking his way, destination not clearly seen. Those who come behind him have a much easier time of it. They see the path. They know where they're going. They can move faster, gaining ground on the trailblazer, at least until they near the front and begin to encounter the thick undergrowth. That's just what happens with economies. The most advanced nations open the way for others by pioneering industries, markets, technologies, business systems, and infrastructure—in effect, creating a successful model. Less developed countries, coming along later, quickly adopt what works and exploit existing markets, and they expand rapidly.

As other countries have surged ahead in the past 45 years, the U.S. lead in per capita income has dwindled. Even so, the United States still hasn't lost the top spot—and it's not likely to do so (see Figure 5.1).

When they get closer to America's level of development, other countries will tend to slow down, their growth rates converging with ours as per capita incomes come into balance. That has surely been true of Asia's "miracle economies," all of which grew more slowly in the 1990s than they did in the three previous decades. For example, Japan outdid the average annual growth rate of the United States by 6.8 percentage points in the 1960s, by 1.7 percentage points in the 1970s, and by 1.5 percentage points in the 1980s. In this decade, the United States is growing faster than Japan. If the economic crises in South Korea, Thailand, Indonesia, and other Asian nations linger, their economic progress will no doubt slow as well.

Over time, other countries may well continue to gain ground on the United States by posting higher rates of growth. Keeping score among nations, however, doesn't get us very far. There would be no jockeying for position if the United States and all other countries grew in lock-step at 1 percent a year. Our material lives would be better if the U.S. economy expanded at 3 percent, even if a handful of other nations managed growth rates of 10 percent or more. Whether it's Afghanistan or America, what ought to matter most is absolute standards of living, not relative well-being. We ought to ask whether we're better off than *we* used to be, the question broached by comparing today with the early 1970s. On this basis, America's economy continues to perform well. By the same token, the United States doesn't benefit when other countries' economies stumble. On the contrary, you're better off if your neighbor's

FIGURE 5.1 As Nations Grow Richer, Economic Performance Converges

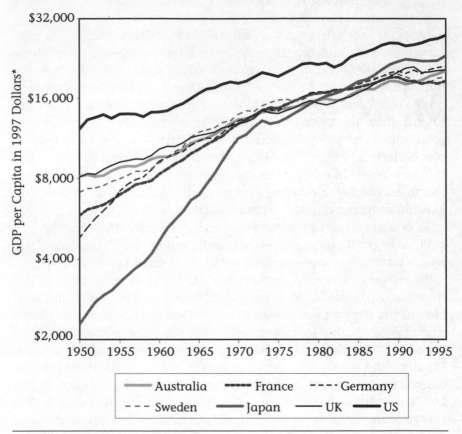

*Adjusted for purchasing power parity.

For decades, the United States was the unchallenged leader in per capita GDP growth. Since the 1950s, GDP in other countries has risen faster than, but failed to match, the U.S. level.

rich than if he's poor. Prosperity abroad provides opportunities for U.S. exports and business deals.

The economic pessimists are wrong in their critique of America's place in the world economy, just as they were wrong about declining living standards and incomes. An overwhelming array of facts and figures proves that every bit of it amounts to pure myth. America is not poorer. Incomes are not falling. America is not slipping behind the rest of the world. In terms of living standards, the United States is doing quite well. We can now turn to the task of debunking myths about America's jobs.

PART TWO

Myths About Jobs

6 THE UPSIDE OF DOWNSIZING

*T*HEY WERE THE COOPERS, makers of wooden barrels and tubs; the Chandlers, producers of candles; the Sawyers, the cutters of lumber. They were the Carters, conveyors of goods on wagons. The Colliers, who mined coal. The Turners, operators of lathes, wheels, or other rotating devices. They were the Farmers, the Hunters, the Fishers, the Fowlers, the Archers, and the Wheelers. The Dyers, the Gardeners, the Glovers, the Hoopers, the Shoemakers, the Tanners, the Taylors, the Walkers, and the Weavers. The Bakers, the Butchers, the Barbers, the Brewers. The Crockers, the Cooks, the Carpenters, the Clarks, the Colemans. The Miners, the Masons, and the Millers. The Porters, the Potters, and the Planters. The Shepherds, the Shearers, the Spinners, the Salters, the Singers, and the Spicers. Sometimes their jobs were specialized—for instance, the Tuckers day after day made small tucks in cloth. The Fullers were workers who fulled cloth, increasing its weight by shrinking, beating, or pressing. Other occupations were broad—the Wrights, who fabricated wheels and wagons, or the multitude of Smiths, all molders of metals.

Their trades and talents were diverse, but they had this much in common: Their work was important to them—so much so, in fact, that it became their identities, their very names, passed down along with skills and tools from one generation to the next. In the America of the 1990s, many of us carry reminders of the long-ago practice of adopting surnames based on occupations. Dallas's telephone book lists 1,191 Carters, 2,796 Millers, 7,347 Smiths, 1,362 Turners, and 1,455 Wrights, none of them likely engaged in their ancestors' occupations.

Even today, our work remains an essential part of who we are. One of the first questions we usually ask upon meeting new people is what they do for a living. In the modern era, of course, job titles don't become names. At your next office party, you won't run across a Jack Stockbroker or a Jill Programmer. And for good reason. None of us knew at birth what job we would have as adults. What's more, occupations come and go with jarring regularity, so we're almost certain our identities will last longer than our jobs. According to one study, an American entering the labor force today will hold five jobs before retirement, four of which haven't been created yet.

It's one thing to leave a job, quite another when the job leaves us. Even in a decade marked by a robust seven-year expansion, Americans can't escape the harsh reality that many workers will lose their jobs. Some companies lay off workers because products don't meet the test of the marketplace and business is on the skids. Even where demand remains healthy, enterprises run into trouble if they fail to stay competitive on cost or quality. Other companies issue pink slips as new technologies and new production methods make it possible to serve customers, old as well as new, with fewer employees.

During the first few years of the 1990s, millions of Americans found themselves out of work as firms closed down, cut costs, relocated operations, and introduced labor-saving technology. The panic-button rhetoric of the times saw it all as ominous and unprecedented: Americans heard time and again that the country's good jobs were being wiped out, never to return again. The old standby term "layoffs" hardly conveyed enough drama to capture the misfortune visiting our factories and offices. So the media borrowed a euphemism first used by corporations cutting jobs: *downsizing*. It became the watchword for the employment crunch that dominated discussion of the economy in the first half of this decade. The numbers glaring from the headlines were certainly big enough to provoke anxiety: 74,000 jobs cut at General Motors, 60,000 at IBM, 50,000 at Sears, 40,000 at AT&T. Those were only the largest, the most prominent. Hundreds of other companies announced layoffs involving enough workers to command at least a few inches in the *New York Times*, and many more jobs vanished without fanfare. A U.S. Department of Labor survey found that companies dismissed 17.4 million workers between 1990 and 1995.

Hand-wringing over downsizing more or less ended—for this business cycle, at least—as the economy created new jobs; by April 1998 the unemployment rate had fallen to 4.3 percent, a rate not seen since 1969. Good times have not, however, meant an end to layoffs. Companies continue to adjust their labor forces to stay competitive. In 1997 and early 1998, labor-force reductions included 19,900 at Eastman Kodak, 19,000 at AT&T, 9,200 at Woolworth's, 9,000 at Citicorp, 9,000 at International Paper, 8,700 at the defense contractor Raytheon, and 6,400 at Levi Strauss. During this period, job reductions involving 50 or more workers were running at a rate of 1.2 million a year.

Our initial instinct is to interpret job losses as signs of failure—something wrong with us or with the system. To many Americans, a pink slip signifies personal defeat, and downsizing can seem to be a verdict that cast-off workers are no longer valuable human resources. To others, it reflects a breakdown of the loyalty that once held company and worker together in a common purpose. Viewing layoffs as a sign that the system is out of whack, some critics even proposed that government reward the "good" companies that don't cut jobs and punish the "bad" ones with taxes, sanctions, and regulations.

Such proposals arise out of a misunderstanding of what's going on. Layoffs aren't a sign of failure, not for the economy, not even for most workers. Job losses hurt Americans and their families, no doubt about it, but downsizing can't be properly understood apart from the economy's overall health. In a free-enterprise system, layoffs are only one aspect of a dynamic process that reallocates resources to boost efficiency and satisfy changing consumer tastes and preferences.

The turbulence isn't just about lost jobs. It's also about new opportunities. In fact, one place to find job creation is in the very industries of the high-profile downsizers of the early 1990s. As Sears struggled, Wal-Mart Stores added 624,000 jobs between 1985 and 1996. Overall, publicly held retailing companies, including such specialty stores as Home Depot, Circuit City, and Office Depot, showed a net gain of 1.9 million workers. While IBM trimmed its workforce, other computer-related companies expanded theirs. EDS, a leading data-processing company, increased employment by 60,000, and Microsoft, the dominant force in software, added 19,500 workers. The top names in computer hardware—Hewlett Packard, Sun Microsystems, Compaq, Silicon Graphics, Dell, and Gateway 2000—pumped up employment by a combined 93,000 jobs. AT&T trimmed its payrolls; MCI, Sprint, and other long-distance providers grew by at least 80,000 workers. At the same time, a boom in cellular telephones meant thousands of jobs at such newcomers as Airtouch Communications, 360 Communications, and Nextel Communications. Employment in the cellular business increased from 15,927 at the beginning of 1990 to 109,387 at the end of 1997, a net gain of 93,460 jobs in just eight years. General Motors downsized, but U.S. autoworkers found more than 130,000 new jobs as Honda, Toyota, Nissan, and other Japanese companies opened U.S. plants. Another 304,198 Americans worked at dealerships selling Japanese cars in 1996.

TABLE 6.1 Job Creation and Destruction, 1985–96

Industry	Downsizers	Jobs Lost	Upsizers	Jobs Gained
General Merchandisers	Sears	–131,000	Wal-Mart	+624,000
	K-Mart	–65,000	Dayton Hudson	+90,000
			J. C. Penney	+59,000
Specialist Retailers	Woolworth	–37,000	Limited	+97,800
			Gap	+55,000
Mail, Package, and Freight Delivery	Federal Express	–33,988	UPS	183,600
Food and Drug-stores	Safeway	–45,385	Publix	+62,902
			Food Lion	+56,081
			Albertson's	+51,000
			Walgreen	+39,800
			Kroger	+33,849
Telecommunications	AT&T	–207,200	Lucent Tech.	+124,000
	GTE	–81,033	MCI	+42,840
			Sprint	+20,609
			Bell South	+14,259
Computers, Software, Data processing	IBM	–164,920	Seagate Technology	+82,300
			Intel	+27,200
			Microsoft	+19,563
			Sun Microsystems	+16,300
Aerospace/Defense			Lockheed Martin	+102,200
			General Dynamics	+80,200
Electronics and Electrical Equipment	General Electric	–65,000	Motorola	+48,800
Entertainment			Viacom	+79,100
			Disney	+75,000

Job cutting takes place alongside job creation. In the past decade, America's publicly traded companies reported a hodgepodge of experiences, some showing healthy workforce growth, others forced to downsize (see Table 6.1).

The mix of the past decade's gainers and losers isn't at all random. For the most part, the economy is shifting labor resources toward industries that produce what customers want to buy. Workers move out of sectors where they're no longer needed. Growing demand in financial services, entertainment, travel, and leisure products reflect our rising living standards. In retailing and restaurants, businesses are catering to our preferences for convenience and lower prices. Some employment gains stem from demographic changes. Health

TABLE 6.2   Job Creation by Firm Size

Firm Size (Number of Employees)	By Firms in Business Throughout 1991–95	By Firms Started or Closed 1991–95	Net Change
1–4	1,003,000	2,840,000	3,843,000
5–19	503,000	2,943,000	3,446,000
20–99	155,000	2,391,000	2,546,000
100–499	26,000	985,000	1,011,000
500–4,999	17,000	176,000	193,000
5,000 or more	–469,000	–2,906,000	–3,375,000
Total	1,235,000	6,429,000	7,664,000

care, without doubt, is gaining importance as a source of jobs as the leading edge of the Baby Boom begins its march through middle age. The areas of the economy that have lost jobs over the past decade are traditional industries—mining, metals, chemicals, utilities, and automobiles. For the most part these are older sectors, most in mature markets, whose roots date back a century or so. The longer industries are around, it seems, the less likely they are to encounter a spike in demand and the better they become at raising productivity.

Big companies provide a handy database for illustrating the ebb and flow of employment at individual firms, but they only scratch the surface of job creation and destruction in the United States. In fact, smaller businesses are the economy's primary engine of employment growth. Companies with fewer than 500 workers accounted for virtually all the job growth from 1991 to 1995 (see Table 6.2). Grass-roots job creation takes place every day in just about every community, as new restaurants, dry cleaners, specialty shops, small manufacturers, and other businesses sprout up wherever entrepreneurs see opportunities. Small operations often cut jobs, too. These businesses are in many cases undercapitalized, their owners inexperienced or just unlucky, so the mortality rate is high.

Because they go on everywhere all the time, the ebbs and flows of employment are hard to track. Over all, though, the economy adds more than it subtracts: The United States created jobs for 32 million workers from 1982 to 1997, an increase of 33 percent. In no other 15-year period did the U.S. economy create that many jobs. Despite all the angst about lost jobs and diminishing opportunities, downsizing wasn't the dominant theme of the 1990s.

"The Churn": Engine of Job Growth

Day in, day out, companies and individuals in a capitalist economy act on the most powerful of motives—the drive to make oneself better off. Call it self-interest, the profit motive, or simply greed, it's what makes the economy tick. Entrepreneurs, sensing an opportunity to make money, start businesses or introduce new products, and hire workers as consumers demand more of their goods and services. Sooner or later, the smell of profit lures competing enterprises, which offer newer and better products or lower prices. Marketplace rivalry pressures existing companies to become more innovative or efficient. Those that fail don't keep their customers or their workers. As this process grinds onward, jobs come and jobs go.

Through relentless turmoil, the economy re-creates itself, shifting labor resources to where they're needed, replacing old jobs with new ones. A descriptive, shorthand term for the perpetual turbulence in the labor market is "the churn," a metaphor taken from the way water swirls and eddies, every movement the result of the same inexorable forces. Whereas the expression "downsizing" focuses solely on the discomfiting side of economic change, the image of the churn captures the whole process, the good along with the bad, the jobs that companies create as well as the ones they let go. The Austrian economist Joseph Schumpeter's seemingly contradictory description of capitalism's constant renewal is "creative destruction." In *Capitalism, Socialism, and Democracy*, Schumpeter writes: "The fundamental impulse that sets and keeps the capitalist engine in motion comes from the new consumers' goods, the new methods of production or transportation, the new markets, the new forms of industrial organization that capitalist enterprise creates."

The churn isn't new. Throughout history, each generation of jobs has given way to the next. At the very beginning, in fact, there was but one job, held by just about everybody—survival. Prehistoric humans spent their days hunting and foraging for food. Over the millennia, with the introduction of agriculture and other technologies, the work required to obtain food, clothing, and shelter diminished, even as the number of mouths to feed increased. With life becoming less of a daily struggle, early societies eventually had enough surplus labor to move beyond the production of basic necessities. In time, consumption expanded to include ever faster transportation, ever more elaborate furnishings and accessories, ever more intricate gadgets, ever more varied entertainments. Jobs multiplied and evolved, becoming more specialized with each passing era. While farmers continued to till the soil, societies began to provide work for priests, soldiers, artisans, merchants, and entertainers, to name just a few broad classes of occupations. We've come so far now that Americans find work as pet orthodontists, personal trainers, information managers, tour guides, marketing directors, and telephone psychics. The connection of *what we want* with *what we do* is hardly happenstance: Both result from the workings of the churn, the economic process that delivers new products, new jobs, and progress.

The mix of American jobs changed dramatically between 1900 and 1960, then changed just as much between 1960 and 1997. Such traditional occupations as retail clerk, teacher, and secretary are still prominent in the mid-1990s, but some interesting new entries pop up among the top 30 jobs. They deal with financial services, mathematics, computers, technology, and higher education (see Table 6.3).

A host of new jobs, including many that didn't even exist a few decades ago, now provide work for an expanding labor force. The computer performs so many routine tasks that it's not at all surprising that the ranks of programmers and operators has swelled beyond 2 million. Work associated with the facsimile machine, a staple in most offices and many homes, has added jobs for nearly 700,000 Americans since 1980. The United States is already seeing the arrival of new jobs associated with the Internet, including hundreds of thousands of "Webmasters," the hip term for designers of Web sites. Some old jobs, many of them once vital to the economy, have been made obsolete. Employment has dwindled to statistical insignificance for carriage and harness makers, boilermakers, milliners, blacksmiths, and watchmakers. Dozens of other occupations employ just a fraction of what they did in their heyday (see Table 6.4).

The churn isn't tidy. New jobs are often far from exact replacements for old ones. Ascendant companies and industries—and the workers they require—differ in unpredictable ways from what came before them. Although retraining helps employees fit themselves into new jobs, some find the transition difficult, and they end up worse off. Overall, though, the gains outweigh the hardships. History tells us that the churn spurs economic progress. It reallocates labor to produce the goods and services that meet consumers' needs and wants. It allows us to produce more with the resources we have. Despite its unsettling aspects, the churn pushed the economy toward higher productivity, bigger corporate profits, lower inflation, and greater competitiveness. America could never have achieved its material abundance without the downsizing, restructuring, and re-creation of the economy that comes with the churn. As harness makers faded away and computer programmers arrived, America's total employment increased steadily—from 29 million in 1900 to 68 million in 1960 to almost 130

TABLE 6.3   America's Top 30 Jobs Since 1900

1900		1960		1997	
Job	Workers	Job	Workers	Job	Workers
Farmers	5,674,875	Retail salespersons and managers	4,351,867	Retail salespersons	6,887,000
Agricultural laborers	4,410,877	Farmers and farm managers	2,525,907	Teachers	4,798,000
General laborers	2,577,951	Teachers	1,683,667	Secretaries	3,692,000
Servants	1,453,677	Truck and tractor drivers	1,662,723	Truck drivers	3,075,000
Merchants	790,886	Secretaries	1,492,964	Financial salespersons	2,613,000
Clerks	630,127	Private household workers	1,281,740	Janitors and cleaners	2,226,000
Salespeople	611,139	Farm laborers	1,244,276	Farmers and farm managers	2,177,000
Carpenters	600,252	Manufacturing laborers	960,998	Cooks	2,126,000
Railroad workers	582,150	Bookkeepers	936,270	Nurses	2,065,000
Miners	563,406	Carpenters	923,837	Engineers	2,036,000
Teamsters/coachmen	538,933	Waiters and waitresses	896,273	Freight and stock handlers	1,930,000
Teachers	438,861	Engineers	871,582	Vehicle mechanics and repairers	1,898,000
Launderers	385,965	Vehicle mechanics and repairers	862,363	Police officers and guards	1,886,000
Dressmakers	346,884	Apparel and textile workers	808,378	Nursing aides, orderlies, attendants	1,875,000
Iron and steel workers	290,538	Construction workers	751,085	Bookkeepers	1,735,000
Machinists	283,145	Assemblers	686,754	Health technologists and technicians	1,693,000
Painters	277,541	Janitors and sextons	621,027	Accountants and auditors	1,625,000
Bookkeepers	254,880	Sewers and stitchers	617,029	Wholesale commodities brokers	1,507,000
Cotton mill workers	246,391	Cooks	597,056	Waiters and waitresses	1,375,000
Tailors	229,649	Typists	543,801	Mathematical and computer scientists	1,494,000
Blacksmiths	226,477	Machinists	515,532		
Firefighters	223,495	Mfg. checkers, examiners, inspectors	514,135		
Shoemakers	208,903				
Sawyers	161,624				
Masons	160,805				

Housekeepers	155,153
Printers	155,147
Seamstresses	150,942
Physicians	132,002
Tobacco factory workers	131,452
Police officers and guards	513,200
Cashiers	491,906
Packers and wrappers	491,695
Accountants and auditors	476,826
Deliverymen and routemen	438,002
Painters	416,040
Launderers and dry cleaners	412,042
Attendants (hospital, nursing home)	408,587
Total of top 30 jobs (42.6 percent of employment)	28,997,562
Total employment	67,990,073
Total of top 30 jobs (78.7 percent of employment)	22,894,127
Total employment	29,073,233

Investigators and adjusters	1,417,000
Assemblers	1,338,000
Carpenters	1,335,000
Precision production supervisors	1,262,000
Heavy-equipment operators	1,125,000
Computer programmers/operators	1,011,000
Receptionists	1,005,000
Postal clerks, mail carriers, messengers	977,000
Engineering technologists/technicians	960,000
Professors	869,000
Total of top 30 jobs (46.3 percent of employment)	60,012,000
Total employment	129,558,000

TABLE 6.4   The Churn: Jobs Then, Jobs Now

Destruction	Now (1997)	Then	Year
Railroad employees	205,000	2,076,000	1920
Carriage and harness makers	*	109,000	1900
Telegraph operators	*	75,000	1920
Boilermakers	*	74,000	1920
Milliners	*	100,000	1910
Cobblers	*	102,000	1900
Blacksmiths	*	238,000	1910
Watchmakers	*	101,000	1920
Switchboard operators	173,000	421,000	1970
Farm workers	796,000	11,533,000	1910
Bank tellers	446,000	495,000	1980

Creation	Now (1997)	Then	Year
Airplane pilots and mechanics	255,000	0	1900
Auto mechanics	905,000	0	1900
Engineers	2,036,000	38,000	1900
Medical technicians	1,693,000	0	1910
Truck, bus, and taxi drivers	3,547,000	0	1900
Electricians/electronic repairers	774,000	*	1900
Optometrists	62,000	*	1910
Professional athletes	92,000	*	1920
Fax machine workers	699,000	0	1980
Computer programmers/operators/ scientists	2,247,000	160,613	1970
Actors and directors	136,000	34,643	1970
Editors and reporters	257,000	150,715	1970
Medical scientists	77,000	3,589	1970
Dieticians	101,000	42,349	1970
Special-education teachers	384,000	1,563	1970
Physicians	724,000	295,803	1970
Pharmacists	200,000	114,590	1970
Authors	137,000	26,677	1970
TV, stereo, and appliance salespersons	254,000	111,842	1970
Webmasters	500,000	0	1990

*Less than 5,000.

million in 1997. The churn, however, isn't just a matter of more jobs. It also creates better jobs. As the U.S. economy has evolved, the recycling in the labor market has tended to benefit workers, despite the occasional sting of the pink slip. On balance, paychecks have grown fatter. Workweeks have gotten shorter. The backbreaking toil of farms and sweatshops has given way to the comfort of air-conditioned offices.

The workings of the churn aren't predictable. Nevertheless, the Department of Labor gives it a try every five years or so. The "official" outlook gets a lot of attention, but it doesn't fully anticipate the churn's impact on the job market. Let's look at the soothsaying from 1981, far enough back in time to see whether projections have panned out. The Labor Department overpredicted job growth for bank tellers, telephone operators, typists, janitors, assemblers, and tailors. It underpredicted the need for computer personnel, engineers, economists, accountants, auditors, and lawyers. The Labor Department counted too much on a continuation of the old economy of then-routine jobs. It failed to appreciate how quickly the Information Age would transform the way Americans work. For example, the Internet came out of nowhere and took off, creating demand for workers with computer skills. By one estimate, 500,000 Americans worked in jobs tied to the Internet in 1997, making an average annual salary of $62,800. The Labor Department's current projections, taking the economy through the year 2005, anticipate great demand for computer-related skills. That's a safe bet. Opportunities are also expected in a host of service-sector industries—health care, physical therapy, legal and medical assistants, finance, hospitality, teaching, and security. What jobs will decline? The Labor Department singles out pressroom personnel, telephone operators, and clerks that handle routine office paperwork. These tasks are being replaced by computer technology. No doubt by the time 2005 rolls around, there will be unanticipated changes in what Americans do to earn a living.

Economic forces don't roil only labor markets. Employers are also buffeted by the churn (see Table 6.5). In the early years of this century, firms engaged in metals, oil refining, meatpacking, and basic machinery dominated the U.S. economy. They were, in their own ways, the technology leaders of their day. They had introduced new products and new production methods, emerging as national suppliers to an early industrial economy. Although General Electric, AT&T, and the big oil companies stay among the largest U.S. industrial concerns decade after decade, newcomers are always driving toward the top of the corporate elite. In the past decade, such companies as Microsoft, Intel, and Hewlett Packard jumped into the top echelon, testimony to the growing importance of the microchip. Merck, Eli Lilly, Pfizer, and other drug companies reflect the advances in pharmaceuticals. Near the end of the twentieth century, a list of the top 100 companies in terms of market value also shows the economy's shift toward consumer goods, technology, retailing, finance, and services. Companies in these industries are moving up the ladder. So are Disney and Time Warner, a reflection of the rise of the information and

TABLE 6.5 New Companies Rising to the Top: Rankings by Market Value

Rank	1917	1945	1967	1987	1997
1	U.S. Steel	AT&T	IBM	IBM	General Electric
2	AT&T	General Motors	AT&T	Exxon	Coca-Cola
3	Standard Oil (N.J.)	DuPont	Kodak	General Electric	Microsoft
4	Bethlehem Steel	Standard Oil (N.J.)	General Motors	AT&T	Exxon
5	Armour & Co.	General Electric	Standard Oil (N.J.)	General Motors	Intel
6	Swift & Co.	Union Carbide	Texaco	DuPont	Merck & Co.
7	International Harvester	Humble Oil & Refining	Sears, Roebuck	Ford	Philip Morris
8	DuPont	Sears, Roebuck	General Electric	Merck & Co.	IBM
9	Midvale Steel & Ordinance	U.S. Steel	Polaroid	Amoco	Procter & Gamble
10	U.S. Rubber	Texas Co.	Gulf & Western	Digital Equipment	Wal-Mart Stores
11	General Electric	Coca-Cola	DuPont	Philip Morris	Johnson & Johnson
12	International Mercantile Marine	Standard Oil (Ind.)	Xerox	Chevron	Bristol Meyers Squibb
13	American Smelting & Refining	Standard Oil (Calif.)	Minnesota Mining & Manufacturing	Sears, Roebuck	DuPont
14	Anaconda Copper Mining	Chrysler	Standard Oil (Calif.)	Mobil	American International Group
15	Standard Oil (N.Y.)	Kodak	Mobil	Bell South	Pfizer
16	Phelps Dodge	Gulf Oil	GTE	Kodak	Hewlett-Packard
17	Singer	International Nickel	Avon	Standard Oil	Eli Lilly & Co.
18	Jones & Laughlin Steel	Socony-Vacuum Oil	Hewlett-Packard	Hewlett-Packard	Citicorp
19	Westinghouse Electric	Kennecott Copper	Procter & Gamble	Coca-Cola	Mobil
20	American Tobacco	Pennsylvania Railroad	Standard Oil (Ind.)	Wal-Mart Stores	AT&T

entertainment sectors. And there's McDonald's, the quintessential expression of America's taste for fast food.

The churn is just as relentless in the corporate sector as in the labor market. Of today's 100 largest public companies, only five ranked among the top 100 of 1917. Half of the firms in the top 100 are newcomers over just the past two decades. Although flux is a constant for the economy, the process seems to be taking place faster. In the 60 years after 1917, it took an average of 30 years to replace half of the companies in the top 100. Between 1977 and 1998, it took an average of 12 years to replace half of the companies, a near tripling in the rate of replacement, or "firm churn." With technology and markets changing so quickly, firm churn probably will continue to accelerate. As with the churn of jobs, there's no mistaking where the jumbling of America's corporate pecking order is taking us—to a post-industrial economy, one that provides what Americans want.

What propels the churn is better ways of providing what consumers want. Nearly all of us have a need to get from one place to another. For millennia, the human race moved about on muscle or wind power. The steam engine was a world-shaking invention, leading in 1807 to Robert Fulton's famed "folly," the *Clermont*. The 133-foot paddlewheeler ran up the Hudson River from New York City to Albany in a record 32 hours, achieving the great average speed of 5 miles per hour. In England, George Stephenson built the first viable steam locomotive in 1825. One of his engines pulled 38 cars at speeds of 12 to 16 miles per hour. For the first time in history, it became possible to travel on land at speeds faster than the pace of a galloping horse.

Compared with animal or wind power, steam greatly reduced the time and expense of travel and shipping—and in so doing changed the economic realities of everyday life. At sea, fleets of steamships, bigger and faster with each passing year, made the goods of other countries cheaper and more readily available to American consumers. On land, railroad tracks spread across the United States, allowing increasingly powerful locomotives to find their way to nearly every corner of the county. Even more than the steamships, the railways cut shipping costs and forged a national market, bringing the benefits of competition to isolated American consumers. As advances in transportation technology expanded markets, Americans' living standards rose.

Railroads and steamships didn't end the evolution of transportation. In the early twentieth century, automobiles arrived, offering the convenience of powered, personal vehicles that took drivers wherever they wanted, whenever they wanted. As cars rolled off assembly lines and roads and highways fanned out, America was well on its way to becoming an automobile-obsessed nation. By the 1930s, trucks were heading for every part of the country, packed with the products of factory and farm. Within a few decades, the airplane became a competitor to cars, trains, and ships. Propeller-driven aircraft and, later, jets lopped hours and even days off travel time. Mail moved faster. Goods could be delivered anywhere in the world in hours. Year by year, aircraft companies added refinements, such as bigger, quieter engines and better navigation systems. Only the themes of almost two centuries of advances in America's transportation technology remained constant: faster, cheaper, farther, safer, more convenient, and more comfortable.

Railroads, automobiles, and airplanes meant great strides in transportation, but they weren't unalloyed benefits. New industries rose to compete with the horse-and-buggy trade, sailing vessels, and canal-based transport. As new forms of transportation captured the market, existing jobs disappeared by the millions, often quite quickly. In the middle of the nineteenth century, 2 percent of Americans worked in water transport. Today, it's down to less than a tenth of 1 percent. In 1900, the peak year for the occupation, the country employed 109,000 carriage and harness makers. In 1910, there were 238,000 blacksmiths. Today, these jobs occupy at most only a few thousand Americans. Railroads eclipsed earlier modes of transport, but they themselves lost ground in competition from automobiles, long-haul trucks, and airplanes. The number of Americans working on the railroads peaked at 2.1 million in 1920. Only 202,000 of us make a living from trains today (see Figure 6.1).

The lost jobs have been offset by new ones. As the automobile went from backfiring public menace to everyday necessity, it created a multitude of new occupations: car designers; assembly-line workers; mechanics; parts manufacturers; truck, bus, and taxi drivers; used-car salesmen; traffic cops; and parking-lot attendants. Americans earn their paychecks racing cars, making safety seats for children, servicing catalytic converters, and staffing counters at the local auto-parts stores. The automobile's impact spilled over into dozens of other sectors of the economy. The oil industry owes much of its prosperity to the automobile. Among the jobs there: roughnecks, geologists, refinery hands, pipeline workers, and gas-station attendants. Nonexistent in 1870, the automobile and related industries now employ 7.5 million Americans, more than 5 percent of the labor force. Airplanes

FIGURE 6.1   Railway Employment

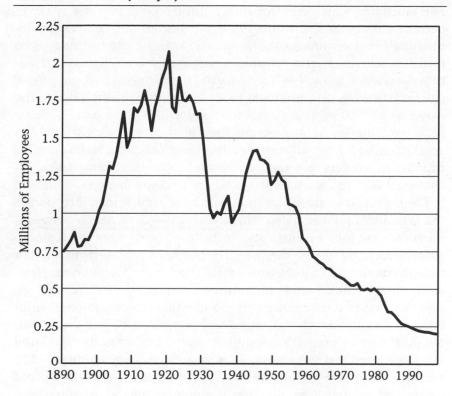

triggered a similar job reshuffling. Opportunities opened for pilots, flight attendants, aircraft mechanics, assemblers, baggage handlers, ticket agents, and dozens of other occupations. The aviation industry, employing a few hundred people in the early 1920s, boomed to more than 1 million jobs in the mid-1990s.

Advances in transportation spilled over into communications. Suppose companies in New York and San Francisco want to conclude a business deal. On the eve of the Civil War, the quickest way to exchange information was the federal government's Pony Express, which could haul documents across the country in 8 to 10 days. The telegraph connected the country in 1861, but complex legal documents could be sent only at a prohibitive cost. With the coming of transcontinental railroad after 1869, mail service became cheaper and faster: Documents could be sent coast to coast in a few days. Telephones linked the coasts in 1913. Starting in the early 1920s and continuing over the next 50 years, airplanes sped up mail delivery. Overnight delivery services entered the market in the 1970s, but, in work time, it cost roughly twice what Federal Express charges today. Fax machines, which can transmit a printed page in a few seconds, became commonplace in the 1980s. In this decade, computers created the latest communications wrinkle with nearly instantaneous transmission via electronic mail. In time and money, the cost of getting documents from New York to San Francisco has become practically nil. How we communicate today bears little resemblance to the way we did it 40 years ago, not to mention 140 years ago. The evolution of communications technology shows up in our jobs: Pony Express riders no longer gallop across the American West, but a growing number of workers owe their livelihood to Internet companies, including 9,000 who work for the industry leader, America Online.

The evolution of transportation and communications incorporate the grand themes associated with the churn—job losses in dying industries, new jobs in emerging industries, great benefits for consumers. Over the years, the scenario has been replayed millions of times in thousands of industries—farm machinery, telephones, television, plastics, hand-held calculators, computers, medical devices. They've spawned all manner of job creation—programmers, engineers, actors and directors, technicians, petrochemists and many others. At the same time, it's nearly impossible to find millwrights and telegraph operators these days. They've gone the way of buggy-whip makers (see Table 6.6). An inventory of job gains and job losses could go on and on, but it would show a common theme: Technological change doesn't allow the economy to stand still. Innovation and competition fuel the churn. New ideas, new products, new technologies, new markets, and new forms of industrial organization upset the status quo, rerouting demand from existing companies and industries. In doing so, it destroys existing industries and jobs, those eclipsed by the arrival of new products that make consumers better off.

When we fret over the tragedies of the churn's downside, we tend to lose sight of its very powerful and important upside. What's really going on is a healthy recycling of labor resources. It's conservation, not carnage.

Downsized but More Productive

The popular lament depicts downsizing as an idling of resources. That's true only in the short run. Cast-off workers aren't wasted in a free-enterprise system. In time, the vast majority move on to newly

TABLE 6.6   Technological Unemployment

New Product	Labor Needed	Old Product	Labor Released
Automobile	Assemblers Designers Road builders Petrochemists Mechanics Truck drivers	Horse/carriage Train Boat	Blacksmiths Wainwrights Drovers Teamsters RR workers Canalmen
Airplane	Pilots Mechanics Flight attendants Travel agents	Train Ocean liner	RR workers Sawyers Mechanics Ship hands Boilermakers
Plastics	Petrochemists	Steel Aluminum Barrels/tubs Pottery/glass	Miners Founders Metalworkers Coopers Potters Colliers
Television	Electronic engineers Actors Reporters Electricians	Newspaper Theater Movie Radio	Reporters Actors
Computer	Programmers Computer engineers Electrical engineers Software designers	Adding machine Slide rule Filing cabinet Paper	Assemblers Millwrights Clerks Tinsmiths Lumberjacks
Fax machine	Programmers Electricians Software designers	Express mail Teletype	Mail sorters Truck drivers Typists
Telephone	Electronic engineers Operators Optical engineers Cellular technicians	Mail Telegraph Overnight coach	Postal workers Telegraph operators Coach drivers
Polio vaccine	Chemists Lab technicians Pharmacists	Iron lung	Manufacturers Attendants

created jobs in expanding industries. It's understandable for workers to view their own jobs as important. For the economy as a whole, though, the resources are the skills and talents of the workers, not the particular jobs that they hold at any one time. One of the churn's great ironies is that the bad news of job losses is part and parcel of the good news of economic progress.

The most important feature of the churn is that it raises living standards. In 1800, it took nearly 95 of every 100 Americans to feed the country. In 1900, it required 40. Today, it takes just 3. The downsizing of agriculture, however, hasn't left the nation hungry. Quite the contrary, the United States enjoys history's greatest agricultural abundance—and much more. The workers no longer needed on farms have been put to use providing new homes, furniture, clothing, computers, pharmaceuticals, appliances, medical assistance, movies, financial advice, video games, gourmet meals, and an almost dizzying array of other goods and services. Today's Americans would have much less of just about everything if farming hadn't endured one of history's most wrenching downsizings. It was an unsettling experience for families caught in the poverty, foreclosures, droughts, and financial panics that led to the exodus from farming. Most of the mass migration from rural to urban life occurred generations ago, so today's Americans retain only fuzzy memories of the dislocations. What we have in place of long hours in the fields is the wealth of goods and services that comes from allowing the churn to work, wherever and whenever it might occur.

Telephone service provides a more up-to-date example of how the economy as a whole benefits as some workers lose their jobs (see Table 6.7). In 1970, the telephone industry employed 421,000 switchboard operators, and Americans made 9.8 billion long-distance calls. By 1996, telephone companies had reduced the number of operators to 164,000. Yet consumers didn't see a corresponding reduction in their long-distance connections. In 1996, they rang up 94.9 billion calls. The telecommunications industry could handle more calls with fewer workers because of a surge in productivity, largely due to innovations in switching technology. An average operator handled only 64 calls a day in 1970. By 1996, the figure had jumped to 1,585—a staggering gain in efficiency. The old technology simply couldn't keep up. At the productivity level of 1970, today's volume of long-distance traffic would require 4.1 million operators, or 3.2 percent of our labor force, instead of the 0.14 percent it actually takes. Americans would be worse off in two ways: We would lose whatever goods

TABLE 6.7   Dialing for Pennies

	1970	1996	No Progress[a]
Long-distance calls	9.8 billion	94.9 billion	94.9 billion
Switchboard operators	421,000	164,000	4.1 million
Calls per day per operator	64	1,585	64
Operators as share of labor force	0.51%	0.14%	3.21%
Work time to buy a 5-minute coast-to-coast call	40.3 minutes	7 minutes	40.3 minutes

[a] The no-progress scenario assumes zero productivity gains over the past quarter century. It answers the question: At 1970 productivity levels, how many operators would we need to handle the 1996 volume of calls? We couldn't employ that many, of course. We would make do with fewer telephone calls at higher prices.

and services displaced telephone workers produce elsewhere in the economy, and we would pay six times as much for our long-distance telephone calls.

The miracle of increasing productivity isn't limited to small segments of the economy. Americans worry a great deal about dwindling employment in such industries as textiles, apparel, basic metals, manufacturing, agriculture, and automobiles. We call these "declining industries." Are they? The number of jobs says so. In most cases, however, dwindling employment hasn't been accompanied by a decline in output. In textiles and apparel, industries that saw a decline of almost 700,000 workers from 1970 to 1995, the actual production from U.S. factories rose. Adjusted for inflation, the gain was 62 percent for textiles and 55 percent for apparel. At least half a dozen other so-called declining industries are actually expanding, including steel, coal mining, railroad transport, and farming (see Table 6.8). If we look only at jobs, manufacturing appears to be suffering a long-term decline. America's factory employment has fallen to 18.5 million, down from a peak of 21 million in 1979. As a portion of employment, manufacturing has slipped from 35 percent in 1953 to barely 14 percent today. Thousands of high-paying jobs in the manufacture of construction machinery, household appliances, and other products have disappeared in the past decade or so, most likely forever. Manufacturing hasn't gone away—or even declined. In 1995, the nation's factories churned out $1.3 trillion in goods, up an inflation-adjusted 109 percent from 1970. We're manufacturing more than ever but doing it with fewer people. To arbitrarily restore to the U.S. economy the 3 million manufacturing jobs lost since 1979 would require rolling back the productivity gains made during the past 15 years. The country would be much poorer for it. In reality, the number of shrinking sectors in the

TABLE 6.8   More Output, Fewer Workers

Industry	Employment, 1970	Employment, 1995	Increase in Output	Productivity Gain
Apparel	1,363,800	935,800	55%	126%
Textiles	974,800	663,200	62%	138%
Steel	627,000	241,600	15%	197%
Coal mining	145,100	104,400	59%	121%
Railroad transport	633,800	238,400	29%	244%
Agriculture	3,463,000	3,440,000	132%	134%
Manufacturing	19,367,000	18,524,000	100%	110%

Note: Productivity is measured per worker, not per hour.

economy turns out to be quite small. One is footwear: Employment declined by 81 percent since 1970—from 212,700 to 40,500. At the same time, domestic output fell 73 percent.

Looking at a microcosm of the decade's high-profile downsizing can show how job losses fit into the process that drives the economy forward. The sample consists of 10 large companies that shed labor in the 1990s, each mentioned time and again in accounts of America's layoffs. All told, they jettisoned almost 850,000 workers between 1990 and 1995. These companies—and dozens like them—are the very ones the critics of downsizing portray as hardhearted, uncaring, and unpatriotic (see Table 6.9). The 10 firms' data reveal another set of facts that are typically overlooked but deserve just as much attention as job losses. For starters, there are productivity gains. Because of production cutbacks, the collective output of the 10 firms fell by an inflation-adjusted 8.2 percent from 1990 to 1995. The companies required 34.4 percent fewer employees. The silver lining: Output per worker surged more than 26 percent, or an average of 5 percent a year. As a group, these downsizing companies' average annual productivity gains were over three times the economywide rate of roughly 1.5 percent. Rising productivity plays a vital role in rising living standards, so it's incongruous to celebrate productivity gains yet denigrate the downsizing that's essential to the process.

More often than not, the wisdom in the hard-nosed decision to downsize wins Wall Street's approval. As companies become more productive and thus more profitable, share prices rise. Stock-market gains from 1990 to 1995 among the 10 companies in the sample averaged more than 130 percent, compared with 86 percent for the S&P 500 companies overall. This vote of confidence ought not to be dismissed as some capitalist perversion that places profits above people.

TABLE 6.9 Less Equals More

Company	1990 Sales[a]	1990 Employment	1990 Stock Price	1995 Sales[a]	1995 Employment	1995 Stock Price	Jobs Cut	Productivity Change
Sears	$66,689	460,000	$25³/₈	$36,510	275,000	$39	185,000	-8.8%
IBM	$82,233	373,816	$113	$74,657	252,215	$91³/₈	121,601	29.7%
K-Mart	$38,223	370,000	$14¹/₄	$35,963	250,000	$7⁷/₈	120,000	33.1%
General Electric	$69,599	298,000	$28³/₄	$72,673	222,000	$72	76,000	33.8%
General Dynamics	$12,132	98,100	$12⁵/₈	$3,678	27,700	$59¹/₈	70,400	7.1%
Digital Equipment	$15,590	124,000	$54⁷/₈	$14,335	61,700	$64¹/₈	62,300	61.4%
McDonnell Douglas	$19,482	121,190	$6¹/₂	$14,873	63,612	$46	57,578	37.5%
Boeing	$32,879	161,700	$45³/₈	$20,252	105,000	$78³/₈	56,700	-5.3%
General Motors	$150,146	761,400	$34³/₈	$175,205	709,000	$52⁷/₈	52,400	22.6%
GTE	$21,892	154,000	$29¹/₄	$20,711	106,000	$43⁷/₈	48,000	31.8%
Total	$508,865	2,922,206	$100[b]	$468,854	2,072,227	$230³/₄	849,979	26.2%

[a] Sales in millions of 1997 dollars.
[b] Equally weighted index, 1990 = 100.

A rising stock market reflects investors' assessment that these companies have taken difficult steps that will make them more competitive and more productive in the future.

So far, these 10 companies are more productive, and stockholders are richer. As good as that may be, the most important gain to *society* is yet to come. To see that, we need to revisit the 850,000 employees cut loose. Remember this above all else: The real wealth lies in the worker, not the job. As displaced employees find new work, they add to U.S. economic output from other firms, new ones as well as existing ones. A precise calculation of the contribution of 850,000 trained and employable Americans isn't possible, but a reasonable estimate might come from the output of an average worker—roughly $58,000 a year. The labor recycled from downsizing just 10 big firms could increase the country's total output by $49 billion a year—not a bad bonus hidden in the usually glum assessments of layoffs.

Did all 850,000 laid-off workers find new jobs and add to America's abundance? No one can say for sure. In a complex economy, there's no way of tracking each and every worker from layoff to new job, but the vast majority of displaced employees probably found work without much trouble. This isn't a heroic assumption: As these men and women began to look for work, unemployment was declining and the number of new job openings averaged 525,000 a month in the mid- to late 1990s, more than double the growth of the labor force. In fact, many companies found it difficult to find enough qualified workers in 1997 and 1998. Being out of work is, for most Americans, a relatively brief experience. Half of those who lose their jobs find another within six to eight weeks; two-thirds find one within 14 weeks; and seven-eighths within six months. The workers let go by these 10 companies had job skills and work history, making them employable. Most no doubt did move on to new jobs in sectors that needed additional labor to expand. What's more, recent studies show that many newly created jobs pay as well or better than those that are falling by the wayside. The 1997 *Economic Report of the President* reveals that 7 of 10 jobs created from 1993 to 1996 were in occupations paying better-than-average wages. The Council of Economic Advisers says the biggest employment gains are coming in managerial and professional positions, a reflection of the shift to services and knowledge-based industries.

In a nutshell, that's the upside of downsizing, a process continually reshaping the U.S. economy. When headlines report the latest layoffs and workers worry about their jobs, it can be hard to step back and appreciate the workings of the capitalist system. Yet that's what we must do, if not individually at least as a society. We have a tremendous stake in allowing the churn to grind forward, putting our labor resources to work raising living standards, to give us more for less. We can't get around it: The churn's promise of higher living standards can't be reaped without job losses. No amount of wishful thinking or dazzling new policy can make it otherwise. The benefits of the churn spread across the whole population—new products, lower prices. The losses usually hit a relatively few individuals. We'd all cheer for a system that worked its magic on *other* industries, protecting our own. Unfortunately, that's not possible. The capitalist system cannot—indeed, should not—offer guarantees to anybody. Downsizing companies will be vilified for making what appear to be hardhearted decisions. When passions cool, however, there ought to be time to recognize that, in most cases, the dirty work had to be done. It's the churn that allows companies to carve away inefficiency, keeps firms competitive, spawns new technologies, and delivers new products into the marketplace. As ruthless as the downsizing may seem, it is a critical part of the free-enterprise system that has made the United States a wealthy nation.

Problem or Progress?

As the churn grinds onward, it allows us to satisfy more of our needs and desires, making most of us better off. Quite rightly, we call this progress. It's not a painless process. The relentless forces of economic change mean lost jobs, missed paychecks, uprooted families, depleted savings, and shattered dreams. The hardships are real. Many Americans, faced with free enterprise's uncertainties and the dislocations from forces beyond their control, might wish to step off the churn's wild ride. Indeed, there is almost always clamor against companies laying off workers, closing plants, and investing in labor-saving technology. The public seldom applauds the churn—at least in the short run, while markets are adjusting to new economic realities. Too often, those who face hard times in declining sectors can't see the new possibilities ripening in emerging industries.

Worry about the downside of economic progress isn't new. Martin Van Buren, when governor of New York, wrote a letter to President Andrew Jackson seeking help for canal workers threatened by a new menace—the locomotive (see Figure 6.2). Van Buren, a future president, was entirely correct in his basic assumption: The arrival of the

FIGURE 6.2   Save Jobs on the Canals

To President Andrew Jackson

   The canal system of this country is being threatened by the spread
of a new form of transportation known as "railroads." The federal
government must preserve the canals for the following reasons:
   One. If canal boats are supplanted by "railroads," serious unemployment will result. Captains, cooks, drivers, hostlers, repairmen and
lock tenders will be left without means of livelihood, not to mention
the numerous farmers now employed in growing hay for horses.
   Two. Boat builders would suffer and tow-line, whip and harness
makers would be left destitute.
   Three. Canal boats are absolutely essential to the defence [sic] of
the United States. In the event of the expected trouble with England,
the Erie Canal would be the only means by which we could ever move
the supplies so vital to waging modern war.
   For the above-mentioned reasons, the government should create an
Interstate Commerce Commission to protect the American people
from the evils of "railroads" and to preserve the canals for prosperity.
   As you may well know, Mr. President, "railroad" carriages are pulled
at the enormous speed of 15 miles per hour by "engines" which, in addition to endangering life and limb of passengers, roar and snort their
way through the countryside, setting fire to crops, scaring the livestock
and frightening women and children. The Almighty certainly never intended that people should travel at such breakneck speed.

Martin Van Buren
Governor of New York
January 31, 1829

railroad did threaten the livelihood of everyone who worked on the
canals. In fixating on existing jobs, however, Van Buren ignored
what was really going on. The new form of transportation would provide one of history's great spurs to economic progress and new jobs.
   Van Buren's concerns may seem comical now, but they provide a
splendid example of arguments used time and again in opposing the
churn. His arguments echo in present-day America, where advocates
of saving jobs call on government to enact measures to protect workers from the vagaries of the free-enterprise system. Indeed, there are
almost always proposals to thwart layoffs, plant closings, more flexible labor practices, and import competition.

These policies are almost always a mistake. If labor isn't allowed to migrate to different sectors of the economy in response to fundamental changes in the economy, new products and efficiency gains will fail to materialize. Existing labor would be stuck in unproductive uses, making horse-drawn wagons instead of cars, vacuum tubes instead of computer chips—a small calamity over a short period but a catastrophic one over the long haul. Imagine the absurdity of a well-intentioned program that 100 years ago might have aimed at keeping blacksmiths and harness makers employed. Had our ancestors somehow been able to freeze the jobs of those bygone days, we would now be spending billions of dollars to keep blacksmiths and harness makers employed in useless jobs. We would be depriving ourselves of what their labor could produce in more productive pursuits.

The jobs of the past imply the products and productivity of the past. Viewed in macrocosm and with the benefit of hindsight, it is easier to see that downsizing is simply conservation—recycling of the economy's valuable labor resources. Few Americans would willingly return to life as it was before the automobile and airplane. The loss would be all that has been gained by generations of new technologies.

Shedding labor is how companies stay fit. Market discipline—in effect, consumers' scrutiny—pushes relentlessly at companies, forcing them to economize on resources, including labor. If companies refused to adjust to market realities, they might encounter worse pitfalls down the road, with buckets of red ink and even bigger layoffs. In all likelihood, companies with surplus labor will produce only at higher cost and risk losing business to "lean and mean" competitors or foreign competition. Over the long haul, downsizing comes down to a matter of sheer survival. Failing to trim a bloated workforce can leave a company uncompetitive and put its very future in jeopardy. If companies don't survive, *none* of their workers will have jobs to go to.

An economy remains vibrant only if it can redistribute its labor resources in response to changes in demand and advances in technology. Failure to adjust will lead to stagnation and then decline. Efforts to protect jobs by short-circuiting the churn will ultimately produce higher unemployment, slower job growth, and lower productivity in the long run. A comparison between the United States and the European Community (EC), two highly developed economies of similar size, bears this out. While American labor markets remain relatively free, many EC nations, hoping to avert job losses, have saddled employers with burdensome rules on when and how they can dismiss workers. They've given greater powers to unions. Europeans have made dismissing workers particularly difficult for the small-business sector, an engine of job growth in the United States. The red tape and reproach involved in cutting a company's workforce makes employers wary of hiring new workers in the first place. In affluent northern Europe, moreover, where the minimum wage exceeds $10 an hour (social insurance included), it's hard for young, unskilled workers to get a start. The high cost of adding low-productivity employees means few new opportunities open up. Workers then cling tenaciously to existing jobs, using their political clout to maintain the status quo. As a result, too many of Europe's labor resources remain frozen, and companies find it difficult to respond quickly and aggressively in the marketplace. The inability to make changes in jobs and staffing, moreover, makes European companies slow to introduce new technology and new products. Japan's vaunted "lifetime" employment system seemed for decades to be an exception to the rule that flexible employment practices are better. The country had both job stability and rapid growth. In the 1990s, however, Japan's economy has been stuck in a prolonged recession, unable to free itself from the strangulation of its rigid practices in industry and the labor market.

The EC may have "saved" existing jobs, but it has done so at a high cost in economic performance. Growth has been slower than that of the United States. Productivity gains have been meager. More telling, the effort to maintain employment has largely hindered job creation. The United States had added 11 million jobs since 1990, a gain of 9 percent, while in the EC the number of jobs rose by 4 million, or just 3 percent. Most of the new jobs in Europe have come in the government sector. Private employment actually fell between 1970 and 1994. For most of this decade, the EC's joblessness has been at 11 percent or more, double the U.S. rate. Worse yet, more than 40 percent of the EC's unemployed have been out of work for a year or more. In the United States, only about 11 percent of the unemployed have been without a job that long. Europeans are quite aware of their lackluster record in job creation. In the late 1990s, promises of new jobs have been the centerpiece of election campaigns in Germany, Sweden, France, Spain, and other countries. It's not easy, however, to get rid of entitlements once they're put in place.

Some may say American downsizing has "gone too far." There's no denying the upheaval caused by letting economic forces work. Yet we cannot ignore the much greater cost of forcing companies to maintain the status quo. To society, the valuable resource is the worker, not the job. Efforts to preserve jobs may well succeed, but these policies will rob the economy of its vitality and deprive this generation and future ones of the progress that lifts living standards. What makes the American economy strong is our willingness to endure the churn and let it enrich our economy over and over again.

If people will pay for more and better products, entrepreneurs will try to find new ways to produce them. Thus, a free-enterprise system provides its own fuel for the churn. In this way, the economy will move forward—as long as labor and other resources are able to move from old industries to new ones. The new always looms as a threat to the old. Resisting the temptation to protect the old requires courage and foresight: The pain of lost jobs is immediate, while the payoff from the churn comes mainly in the long term. Job creation and job destruction are forever intertwined. Both are key elements in the process that raises its living standards. Societies that deny the churn by trying to freeze employment actually retard the formation of new jobs and new sources of income. Societies that allow the churn to work reap the rewards of more employment, better jobs, and higher living standards.

7 SOMEBODY ALWAYS FLIPPED HAMBURGERS

AMERICANS NOW EAT MORE MEALS than ever at restaurants. We take our clothes to dry cleaners, our cars to mechanics, our busted appliances to repair shops, our dogs and cats to veterinarians. We go to barber shops and beauty salons for hair care. Two-career families drop off young children at day-care centers. To care for our homes, we hire maids, gardeners, plumbers, carpenters, electricians, carpet cleaners, chimney sweeps, exterminators, architects, interior decorators, and home-security companies. Keeping our finances and personal affairs in order requires lawyers, accountants, stock brokers, insurance agents, financial planners, and bankers. Whether we're buying a loaf of bread or a new car, we usually go looking for a sales clerk. New clothes fit better after the tailor gets done. Our taxes pay the salaries of schoolteachers, police officers, mail carriers, garbage collectors, and, yes, Internal Revenue Service agents.

Getting from here to there would be a Lewis and Clark adventure without travel agents, ticket takers, baggage handlers, and flight attendants. When taking it easy, we sample the talents of a dazzling variety of entertainers—television stars, athletes, actors, comedians, singers, musicians, magicians, and dancers, to suggest just a few. For personal fulfillment, we employ fitness instructors, tutors, librarians, psychics, tour guides, and music teachers. To maintain our health, we turn to doctors, nurses, dentists, social workers, massage therapists, psychiatrists, and pharmacists. No matter how well we take care of ourselves, we will all eventually need a funeral director.

All this—and much more—is the service sector. Yet despite the benefits it provides, the service sector doesn't get much respect. Americans hear time and again that these industries are weeds in the economy's garden. The rise in services, we're told, is a symptom of an

139

economy losing out to overseas competition, its output increasingly devoid of material substance. As services displace manufacturing, we're supposedly left poorer than our parents, saddened by the loss of national prestige. Service jobs get a bad rap. They're usually characterized as low-paying, low-skilled, low in productivity, low in status. They offer scant prospects for advancement and crowd out the economy's good jobs. One putdown captures the essence of service-sector phobia: "We're becoming a nation of hamburger flippers." This bleak vision has been repeated so often that few question it.

We shouldn't let this putdown pass without showing how inaccurate it is. If Americans are to understand the economic forces shaping their lives, they can't let themselves be hoodwinked by catchy phrases. A more thoughtful analysis reveals that the emergence of services in the modern economy isn't a sign of failure, or the result of policy makers' bungling. It's simply another sign of the economy's moving forward, a reflection of the evolution of what we consume and how we produce.

Sprawling and Diverse

Just what are services? Our national accounting system splits economic activity into goods-producing and service-producing sectors. *Goods* is the province of the tangible, what we can put into a bag, load onto a cart, or haul on a flat-bed truck. A car. A computer. A cotton shirt. They're all goods. With goods, production and consumption usually take place at different times and places. *Services* involves intangibles, often as fleeting as listening and offering advice. For the most part, services are what others do for us, so they're inseparable from the workers who deliver them. Unlike goods, services are usually consumed at the moment they're produced—a haircut, a doctor's care, a baseball game.

In practice, the dichotomy is somewhat arbitrary. Goods and services really aren't all that different. Both have value, both are useful. Both can be bought, sold, and even bestowed. They're just alternative ways of satisfying consumers' needs. A few examples will show the inconsistency. If an American worker earns a paycheck on an assembly line making garbage trucks, it's celebrated as manufacturing, supposedly good for the economy. If another worker hangs on the back of the truck collecting trash, this is denigrated as services, even though the only real value of the vehicle is its use in the removal of waste. If a consumer buys a new car, it counts in the goods category. Renting or repairing one is services. Either way, the customer is paying for transportation. Building a television set is goods; providing it with cable programming is services. Making a key is manufacturing; duplicating it is services. Stone used in buildings shows up as goods, but the same rock sculpted into a statue becomes a service performed by an artist. Printing a book counts as goods, but copying some of its pages is services. If an astigmatic American purchases eyeglasses, that's goods. A visit to an eye surgeon for a laser procedure counts as services. In both cases, what the consumer gets for his money is the same—corrected vision.

The most noteworthy characteristic of the service sector is its relentless expansion. Two centuries ago, the United States had a predominately agricultural economy in which 90 percent of Americans worked on farms. At the start of the 1900s, agriculture was still the leading occupation, employing more than 45 percent of workers in the private sector. Services provided a quarter of U.S. jobs. By 1920, manufacturing, mining, and construction—collectively, the goods-producing industries—had eclipsed agriculture as a source of employment. By 1930, services, largely ignored in the fanfare over the Industrial Age, had already slipped past goods in providing employment for Americans. Jobs in goods-producing industries reached their peak in the early 1950s, then started to ebb. Services, meanwhile, marched steadily forward, employing 50 percent of private-sector workers for the first time in the 1960s and reaching 70 percent at the end of the 1980s (see Figure 7.1).

This brief review tells us that the rise of services isn't a modern aberration. It's familiar to our grandparents and even to their forebears. What's more, the surge in per capita income over these decades shows that the shift to services came in lockstep with a rise in American living standards. Services are the mark of a more affluent society, not a poorer one.

As we approach the twenty-first century, services dominate the economy, providing more than two-thirds of the nation's output and employing 78 million Americans, roughly three-fourths of the private-sector workforce. The biggest providers of service jobs are retail and wholesale trade, health care, and the business professions. In addition, roughly 20 million Americans work for national, state, and local governments, and most of them hold service jobs (see Table 7.1). Even in industries typically cast as goods-producing, a growing number of jobs require service-type skills. In manufacturing, for example,

FIGURE 7.1   America's Jobs (A) and Output (B) Move to Services

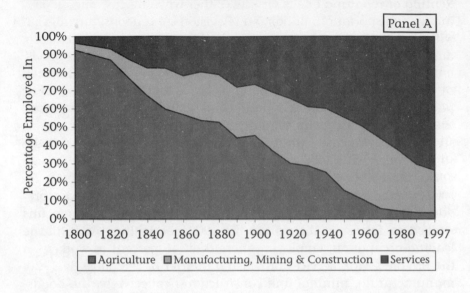

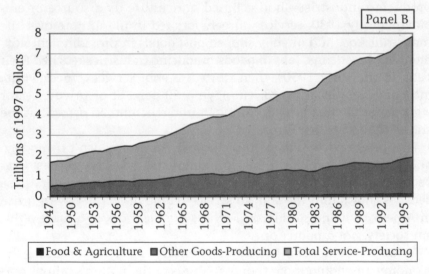

many workers aren't actually involved in producing the company's widgets and whatnots. They may administer, design, advertise, or sell. In 1972, 32 percent of "manufacturing" workers had managerial, professional, sales, technical, or service jobs. By 1997, the white-collar contingent at a typical manufacturing facility had risen to 42 percent.

In addition to providing an overwhelming majority of America's jobs, the service sector is a hotbed of entrepreneurial activity. Every day, Americans open new restaurants, cleaners, consulting businesses, repair shops, marketing firms, and entertainment and recreational facilities. New businesses pop up to take advantage of the latest fads and trends. With the boom in in-line skating, for example, companies lured kids off the streets and parking lots by opening indoor parks with ramps and chutes. There are, believe it or not, bars where patrons pay to breathe pure oxygen. For businesses providing services, barriers to entry are usually low, start-up costs are typically less than they are in manufacturing enterprises, and potential customers are often plentiful. It's not surprising, then, that since 1980, the number of service-producing establishments has grown one-third faster than the number of goods producers (see Figure 7.2). By 1995, the roster of service firms totaled 5.3 million, nearly five times the count for goods producers. The service sector has so many firms because it lends itself to small-scale enterprises. The average service firm employs just 14 workers, less than one-third the number for a typical manufacturing company.

Besides growth, the other grand theme of services is diversity. The "service" label encompasses a broad assortment of jobs, including neurosurgeons, college professors, truckdrivers, and dishwashers. It includes some of the newest professions—for example, Webmasters, the computer wizards who design Internet pages—and the oldest— such as teachers, priests, and cooks. The service sector includes some of the most stable and the least stable jobs. This sector has the most self-employed workers, the most moonlighters, the most people who work at home. Workers in service jobs range from the highest paid and best educated to the lowest paid and least educated. National Basketball Association players, the top earners among athletes in American team sports, make an average of $2.6 million a year. Corporate attorneys with 10 years' experience have a median annual salary of $95,000. A computer whiz can expect to earn about $55,000, a financial manager $45,000. Teachers' pay averages $40,000 a year, and bus drivers earn $22,000. Janitors make $16,000 a year, and cashiers, many of whom put in less-than-full workweeks,

TABLE 7.1 A Snapshot of Where Americans Work: Employment by Occupation (in thousands)

Industry	Total Employed	Executive, Administrative and Managerial	Professional Specialty	Technicians and Related Support	Sales	Administrative Support, Including Clerical	Other Services	Precision Production, Craft, and Repair	Machine Operators, Assemblers and Inspectors	Transportation and Material Moving	Handlers, Equipment Cleaners, Helpers, and Laborers	Farming, Forestry, and Fishing
Total employed	131,287	19,223	19,323	4,323	16,077	18,622	17,236	14,355	7,768	5,184	5,183	3,989
Goods-producing	34,286	4,800	2,381	800	855	2,772	374	9,100	6,320	1,449	2,150	3,281
Agriculture	3,818	113	132	55	38	139	32	44	14	42	27	3,180
Mining	614	86	71	24	19	66	8	193	32	94	19	1
Construction	8,860	1,463	158	62	62	449	40	5,001	79	525	1,003	17
Manufacturing	20,994	3,138	2,020	659	736	2,118	294	3,862	6,195	788	1,101	83
Service-producing	97,001	14,423	16,942	3,523	15,222	15,850	16,862	5,255	1,448	3,735	3,033	708
TCPU	9,101	1,253	543	324	281	2,328	260	1,258	128	2,192	513	22
Trade	27,458	2,645	598	186	11,514	2,250	5,307	1,493	381	1,036	1,940	110
FIRE	8,530	2,425	415	151	2,171	2,798	310	169	5	13	19	52
Other Services	46,049	6,814	14,391	2,633	1,227	7,186	9,238	2,156	916	453	541	494
Government	5,863	1,286	995	229	29	1,288	1,747	179	18	41	20	30

NOTE: Data are for August 1998. TCPU stands for transportation, communication, and public utilities. FIRE stands for finance, insurance, and real estate.

FIGURE 7.2   Growth Lies in Services

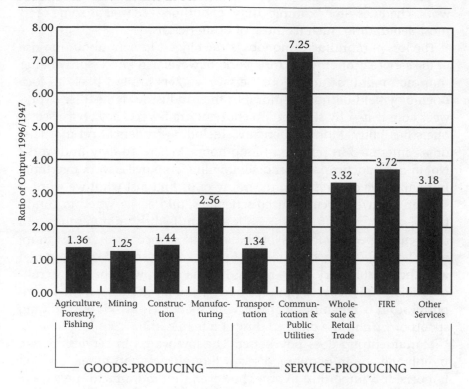

earn $12,300. Average pay in service-producing jobs is $11.80 an hour, which, we hear quite often, trails the average manufacturing wage of $13.20 an hour, including overtime.

The service sector shows the same breadth in other characteristics. Average weekly hours range from 60 or more for top white-collar professionals to as few as 29 in retailing, a sector that depends heavily on part-timers. The unemployment rate can be relatively high—about 9 percent among maids and other household workers, for example. Or it can be relatively low—2.1 percent for managers and 2.6 percent for technicians. Union membership goes from practically nil in finance, insurance, and real estate to 43 percent in government and 28 percent in transportation and public utilities. Working conditions vary from the amenities of the plushest penthouse suite enjoyed by corporate liquidators to the long hours cops on the beat spend in extreme heat and cold, often on tired feet. The level of physical risk ranges from the safe and secure office to the dangers firefighters face in burning buildings and truckdrivers face on the nation's highways.

In the service sector are found some of the economy's most flexible work schedules—for example, those of authors—as well as some of its most demanding, such as those of obstetricians.

The loss of manufacturing jobs is the biggest lament about the rise of the service economy. Factory work, however, isn't necessarily better than non-manufacturing jobs. Service workers are less likely to face unemployment because demand in their industries is steadier. Workweeks are generally shorter; job changes are fewer. The service sector offers flexibility. Many Americans, including students and mothers, aren't interested in putting in long hours. Where do they find work? Not in manufacturing. Most assembly-line employees work overtime. In retail trade and restaurants, many of us find just what we want— shorter workweeks, customized schedules, and easier working conditions. Many manufacturing jobs are dull, dirty, dangerous, and dead-end, especially for the low-skilled. The service sector has its share of undesirable tasks, but the worst service tasks should be compared with the worst factory jobs—not, as is often done, with the best. Scrubbing floors may leave a janitor's back aching, but he'll get little sympathy from a machine operator who spends eight hours changing spools of yarn in the din and dust of a textile mill.

Manufacturing does pay better. The low wages in services reflect mainly the pay in retailing, a sector that attracts part-timers and job hoppers. It is important to note, however, that manufacturing's wage edge is eroding. For many years now, pay in services has been rising relative to pay in goods. In 1980, average hourly wages in manufacturing were 20 percent higher than those in services. By 1997, the gap had narrowed to a nearly insignificant 1 percent. If we exclude retailing, U.S. service-producing jobs now actually pay an average hourly wage 5 percent higher than that in manufacturing (see Figure 7.3). There's no reason to believe that the trend toward higher wages from service jobs will reverse itself. Sometime in the next few years, services may well become better-paying than manufacturing on the whole. The bottom line: The service sector isn't just producing a good many jobs. It's creating many good jobs.

What, then, of the hamburger flippers? This much can't be denied: The fast-food industry's rapid expansion created a lot of new jobs. In 1948, there were a mere 9,723 Americans working in these restaurants. By 1997, there were nearly 3 million, making fast-food service one of the fastest-growing sectors in the post–World War II era. The pay isn't high. A 1994 Bureau of Labor Statistics survey found average wages in fast-food outlets to be only 50 cents above the 1994 fed-

FIGURE 7.3   Hourly Earnings in Manufacturing and Services

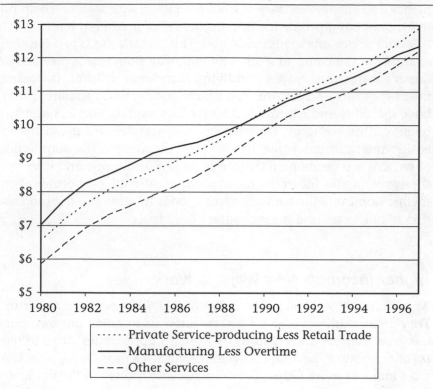

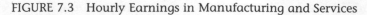

eral minimum wage of $4.25 in 43 states and most metropolitan areas. The top-paying places averaged just $5.50 an hour. Those who portray fast-food workers as the standard for the service sector, however, ignore what's unusual about their jobs. The restaurants rely heavily on teenagers, temporary employees, and workers with little or no job experience. Nearly 70 percent of fast-food workers haven't yet celebrated their twentieth birthday. A high proportion of the counter help and cooks are part-timers, with an average workweek of 29.5 hours. And there's a rapid turnover rate. Nearly half the employees stay on the job one year or less. Few of the fast-food industry's characteristics apply to the service sector as a whole, and it's misleading to portray fast-food workers as the norm.

One benefit of fast-food jobs is that they give American teenagers exposure to the workaday world. Industry analysts estimate that Mc-Donald's alone provided the first job for 1 in 15 U.S. workers. Even if they never again fry another burger for pay, young Americans often learn the importance of arriving on time and doing assigned tasks in fast-food establishments. The fast-food industry has brought convenience and cheaper food—just what the public wants—while helping teach our young people the responsibilities of holding a job.

Service-sector anxiety is misplaced. This sector's rise is just another example of the churn at work. Moving away from goods production doesn't mean that wages and living standards will fall. It doesn't mean that most Americans won't have good jobs, especially if they have the skills and education the new jobs require. Services aren't a blight on the economy. Far from it. More services will mean richer, easier, and more enjoyable lives for most consumers. The dominance of services is a permanent feature of the U.S. economy, and is in fact the wave of the future in all modern industrial economies. Two themes dominate the transition from goods to services—the progression of our tastes and the evolution of our tools.

Higher Incomes, New Ways to Work

As consumers, we Americans value highly what services do for us. They make our lives easier: Caterers allow us to enjoy our own parties, and tax preparers help us as April 15 approaches. Trips to our favorite resort or the Super Bowl make our lives more enjoyable. Services make us more secure, providing us with money in the bank, insurance policies, 24-hour roadside assistance, and alarm monitoring. Most important, perhaps, services save us time—the scarcest of resources. After hiring a lawn service to spruce up the yard, we've got a couple of hours open for golf on Saturday afternoon. Paying an accountant or home remodeler buys us extra hours of leisure that, more often than not, we use to enjoy other services, such as entertainment and travel.

Services reflect consumer choice. We could do many service jobs for ourselves—with the risk, of course, of flooding the basement, short-circuiting the neighborhood's power supply, or wrenching our backs. We often find it better, if not safer, to earn money where we're competent and pay professionals to handle the daily chores and life's little emergencies. By the way they spend their money, Americans are signaling to the market that they want more services, and the economy is providing them.

Why do we prefer more services? Mostly, it's because we're getting richer. Consumers spend more on services as their incomes rise. For a household with a budget of $14,000, less than half of all spending goes to buying services. For consumers with fatter wallets, the proportion expands steadily. When incomes reach $70,000, outlays for services rise to nearly 60 percent of consumption. The relationship between higher income and more services isn't a quirk of the United States in the late twentieth century: It holds over time and across borders. From 1947 to 1997, as average income in the United States nearly tripled, the proportion of spending on services rose from 43 percent to 56 percent. High-income countries such as Canada, France, and Finland spend relatively more on services than poorer countries, such as India and Thailand (see Figures 7.4a, 7.4b, and 7.4c).

What do these patterns say? Consumers first satisfy basic needs, mainly for goods. After that, we begin to buy whatever makes life more pleasant and more fun. It's partly a practical matter. As we fill our stomachs with food, our garages with cars, and our homes with gadgets, we don't want another meal, another station wagon, another home-entertainment system. Additional income goes to hiring helping hands, taking vacations, indulging in entertainment—and that's the service sector. In 1857, the German economist Ernst Engel formulated what has become known as Engel's law, which identifies three categories of consumer spending. Engel observed that as families made more money, they changed their spending patterns, spending relatively less money on necessities: food, clothing, and shelter. Spending for these so-called inferior goods increased more slowly than income. Spending on so-called normal goods, such as home furnishings and transportation, increased at the same rate as income. The third category was luxuries, or so-called superior goods. For these, the rate of spending outpaced the increase in income. Engel's law applies to goods as a whole. Demand for food, clothing, and shelter—indeed, for most manufactured products—doesn't keep pace as incomes increase. From necessities to wants, then to conveniences and on to luxuries and amusements, tastes evolve as people and societies grow wealthier.

Relative prices provide another insight into Americans' demand for services. Services have been becoming more expensive since at least the late 1940s. When we compare the relative cost of goods and services, we now pay twice as much for services as we did in 1947 (see Figure 7.5). Two factors work to raise services' relative value. First, income-driven demand for services is increasing, putting upward pressure on their relative prices. Second, new technology is reducing the cost of producing goods, making them relatively less expensive. The significance of this change shouldn't be overlooked. Usually, peo-

FIGURE 7.4   Higher Spending, More Services

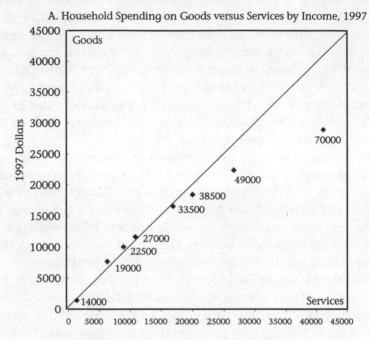

A. Household Spending on Goods versus Services by Income, 1997

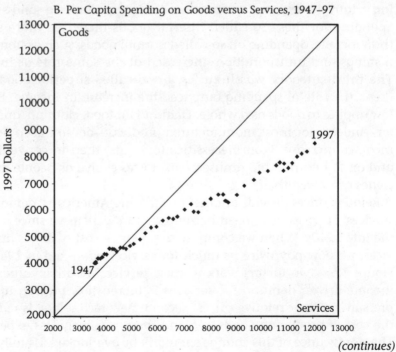

B. Per Capita Spending on Goods versus Services, 1947–97

(continues)

FIGURE 7.4   *(continued)*

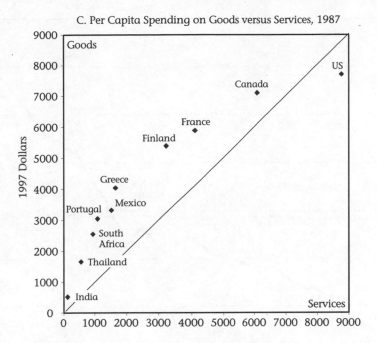

C. Per Capita Spending on Goods versus Services, 1987

ple buy less as prices go up. The fact that demand for services keeps rising in the face of higher relative prices indicates the strength of consumers' preferences for them. As a society, we're putting a higher value on services.

An increasing affinity for services even extends to how we consume goods. A chicken dinner can illustrate how consumers behave as more money flows into their pockets. The very poor might buy chickens to raise in their own yards, and they might eat even the less desirable parts. Those who are a little better off might go to a grocery store to purchase a whole chicken, then cut it up and cook it. A family that's another rung up the ladder can afford to purchase pre-prepared pieces, choosing breasts or legs. Neighbors with even higher incomes might stop by Boston Market for prepared chicken dinners or, if they cook at home, they might choose packaged breasts stripped of skin and bone. Finally, members of an even richer household might go to a fancy restaurant for the chef's specialty—chicken cordon bleu. The chicken remains more or less constant. What's added in the progression from poor to rich are the services of butchers, cooks, and waiters. As we become wealthier, we might pay more to enjoy a chicken dinner, but the chicken, a good, becomes a smaller

FIGURE 7.5   Relative Prices: Services versus Goods

part of the price. We pay extra for services. We do it simply because we feel services make us better off, not because we're settling for some inferior form of consumption.

The same phenomenon occurs throughout the economy, with nearly everything consumers buy. The rich rarely do their own washing and ironing. They take taxis, limousines, and jets, seldom buses. A poor family's source of entertainment might be a television topped by rabbit ears. A higher-income family can afford more varied fare—movies, amusement parks, cable television, and travel, all of which are mainly services. For just about everything on consumers' shopping lists, the difference between low- and high-priced alternatives is generally additional services.

By themselves, the shifting tastes of a richer nation would drive the economy toward producing more and more services. The trend gets an additional push from advances in technology—the tools we use at work. Because of rising productivity, most of us no longer till fields, feed assembly lines, or dig into the earth. Even those Americans who work in jobs that dominated the economy of previous generations don't use plows, sledgehammers, or pickaxes anymore. Technology has liberated us. Machines have taken on much of the routine drudgery that was our grandparents' lot in life. We're now free to do other tasks. The principal tool we use on today's jobs is ourselves. We work with our minds, our personalities, our "people skills." We haven't invented machines to substitute for those human attributes, at least not yet. Compared with the work of the Industrial Age, jobs using workers' innate talents are better—less burdensome, more interesting, and, in many cases, better paying.

Technology doesn't just reduce the need for physical labor. It also increases the need for services. With the Internet, electronic mail, cellular telephones, and satellite transmissions providing so many new ways to communicate, it's not surprising that more Americans are making a living as communicators. As computers give us the power to offer customized services, companies are hiring more workers to do this. Because the advances in sciences vastly improve the ability of doctors and nurses to help us, more Americans are making their living in the health professions. Because today's work requires so many of us to use computers, we've put more Americans to work teaching and tending to employees' needs. The global reach of technology allows organizations to become bigger, more diverse, more expansive. Keeping it all humming requires more employees in administration and management. The tools of modern times are thrusting us headlong into the twenty-first century, when even more of our work will involve producing services rather than goods.

Our demand for more services creates opportunities for all kinds of service workers. It helps to view the service sector as having three branches: household services, personal services, and information services. Over the past four decades, there has been a rapid growth in household services, replacing the cooking, cleaning, child care, and other work once done primarily by family members. These services are moving into the cash economy largely because of the higher wages women, who traditionally performed most of these tasks at home, can earn working in the cash economy. The growth of household services probably reflects the changes in the size and composition of households. Over all, families are smaller than they used to be. In addition, many more households have two wage earners. There just aren't as many hands around to do the chores. In 1950, an average household had roughly 1 person over age 16 available for housework and errands. Now, the ratio has slipped to 0.67 per family, meaning private businesses have had to find ways to do the work that was previously done by as many as 14 million at-home workers. With more women working, there's less time for chores and more money to pay someone else's salary. By hiring household help and eating more meals in restaurants, we're probably just shifting work to the market. For example, today's America isn't preparing more meals per capita than in the past—it's still basically breakfast, lunch, and dinner—but a higher proportion of the meals once cooked and served at home are now prepared in restaurants. To echo the critics of the service sector, *somebody* always flipped hamburgers. Forty years ago it was Mom. Today, it's teenagers working at McDonald's, short-order cooks at diners, or master chefs at fancy establishments.

Americans are also spending more money on a second category, called personal services, which includes health care, transportation, grooming, and entertainment. These often involve giving the customer a personal touch, a bit of pampering. On a flight from Dallas to London, first-class and coach passengers arrive at the same time. The higher fare pays for differences in the pleasures and perks of the experience. The proliferation of extras that cater to consumers' tastes for luxuries shows that Americans are eager to allocate their income gains to services. It's just more evidence of the country's rising standards of living. Only a wealthy society could afford to pay for dating services, pet grooming, and car detailing.

The third broad class of services centers on information—communication, education, retail and wholesale trade, financial services, legal advice, scientific research, engineering services, computing services, and so on. These have grown rapidly over the past two decades in conjunction with an explosion of information technology. The personal computer, the fax machine, the Internet, the cellular phone, cable television, satellite dishes, even improved weather-forecasting radar—they all provide more and faster information. Not long ago, investors needed a ticker-tape machine to find out how their stocks were faring. Now, the information comes in an instant via the computer or a paging device small enough to carry in a pocket or purse. The electronic hardware, the goods component, keeps getting cheaper, while the information, the services component, grows more valuable and more convenient as it becomes more universal.

As societies get richer and more technologically advanced, they demand more of all three types of services (see Figure 7.6). Most of the hand-wringing over service jobs involves those that replace household services. Many of these are the low-paying occupations cap-

FIGURE 7.6   Higher-Paid Service Jobs Lead the Way

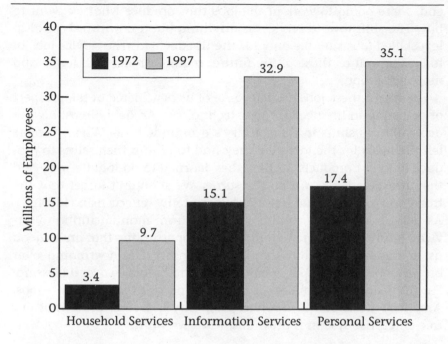

tured in the caricature of hamburger flippers and other menial workers. The household-services classification, however, is the smallest of
the three branches—by far. Personal services provide nearly four
times as many jobs. Information services provide more than three
times as many. What's more, the rate of increase in the number of
jobs in household services has been slowing. The average annual increase in the number of these jobs was 6.3 percent in the 1970s, 4 percent in the 1980s, and just 2.5 percent so far in the 1990s. The
movement into the market of work traditionally done in the home
has largely run its course. The movement of women into the labor
force, a monumental shift in society over the past few decades, has
stabilized. As consumers satisfy their needs for restaurant meals and
maids, growth in demand for household services almost surely will
slow further and level out. Most of the future growth in the services
sector will come from personal and informational services, which
offer the better jobs.

Although it's become fashionable to disparage service industries
and their jobs, the great truth of free-market economies is that we
consumers dictate what we produce and where we work. We are both
producers and customers. It's inconsistent for us as consumers to

want mostly services yet as workers to produce mostly goods. In the end, we're going to work at the jobs that produce what we want to buy. The shift toward services is anything but a downward spiral to low-skilled jobs suitable only for the ill-educated. The service jobs of today, as well as those of the future, require higher skill levels and more education.

The rise of these jobs has left some of us bewildered at the prospect of adjusting to the needs of new technology. Anxiety almost always accompanies shifts in the country's economic base. When farmers left the fields for the factories, they had to retrain themselves to produce different products. In time they learned to do it quite well, and they prospered. We will do the same. We shouldn't forget that the transition to a more service-oriented economy reflects rising incomes. As today's Americans continue to move from manufacturing to services, many will find new employment opportunities that are as good as or better than what they leave behind. Hand-wringing over growth in services employment amounts to brooding over a blessing. Far from signifying failure, or condemning us to less desirable jobs, America's transition to a service economy is further proof that our free-enterprise system is providing what we want.

8 THE ECONOMY AT LIGHT SPEED

BUILD A BETTER MOUSETRAP, and the world will beat a path to your door. The fallacy in Ralph Waldo Emerson's famous maxim lies in mistaking what the customer wants. People don't want better mousetraps. They want dead mice. Similarly, people don't want daily newspapers, magazines, CNN, or the Internet, they want information. People don't want records, tapes, or compact discs; they want music. People don't want cars, trains, planes, boats, or bicycles; they want transportation from one place to another. Our needs are eternal, but the ways of meeting them are limited only by human ingenuity and imagination. In a dynamic economy, there's a relentless quest for new, better, or cheaper ways to give people what they want.

Many of capitalism's champions contend that the system works as companies compete against one another, luring consumers with lower prices, better service, or higher quality. This familiar notion has it only half right. When we find bargain air fares, see long-distance telephone rates plummet, or get a good deal on a new car, we reap the benefit of competition for market share. To another level of competition we owe the very existence of airplanes, telephones, and automobiles. What raises living standards over time isn't companies vying for customers in existing industries. It's competition from new goods and services and new production techniques, bringing about new industries, new jobs, and higher living standards.

"New and improved," a phrase we see on everything from toothpaste to transmissions, translates into "old and obsolete" for existing goods and services. As consumers, we all benefit from innovation. We must. After all, every successful new product passes the test of the marketplace: If people don't want it, they won't buy it. Patented inventions that didn't make it illustrate the point. No market exists for boomerang bullets, eyeglasses for chickens, escape hatches for coffins, and fire-escape parachutes. There's no profit in producing what won't sell, so companies and workers must progress to new goods and services, not just now and then but continuously. The term we've used for this process is "the churn." Technology provides its fuel. In the United States more than anyplace else, we've reaped the rewards of the human impulse to make ourselves better off by improving life for everyone else. Thousands, if not millions, of inventions and innovations—some trivial, some world-shaking—keep the American economy in a constant state of flux.

If nobody came up with new ways to meet human needs, there would be little reason for change in an economy. In fact, progress once occurred at a snail's pace: An Italian farmer of the seventeenth century lived, worked, and died pretty much like the Roman farmer who tilled the same land in the first century B.C. For most of human history, jobs passed like an inheritance from one generation to another. Technology edged forward slowly, new ideas taking decades or centuries to spread. Our ancestors weren't any less clever than we are. Before the advent of steam power in the early 1800s and electricity a few generations later, they produced important innovations: paper, plows, printing presses, sails, sextants, telescopes, windmills, smelting furnaces, and architectural arches, to name a few of the most important.

It just took them some 6,000 years to do it.

Technology's Ebb and Flow

Even in an era of supercomputers and space travel, technology isn't always regarded as a boon. Amid the modern world's hustle and bustle, it's common to find nostalgia for the simpler ways of times gone by. Technophobes cringe at programming the videocassette recorder or installing new peripherals on the computer. Apocalyptical literature, science-fiction movies, and neo-Luddite campaigns portray technology as a dark force that enslaves and dehumanizes people.

That's the technology of myth. The technology of reality is a vital part of what spurs economic progress and raises living standards. In prehistoric times, human knowledge wasn't complex. Stone Age "high tech" may have been as rudimentary as knowing how to strike flint on rock to ignite a fire. Even at that basic level, we can see that technology improved lives. Our ancestors who had fire kept warmer at night, ate hot food, and slept more soundly, worrying less about attacks by saber-toothed tiger or marauding tribes. Fast-forward several millennia, and it's the same story. Modern technology is more elaborate, of course, but it still satisfies the same basic human needs. We're warmed by increasingly efficient gas and electric furnaces. We're nourished by food flown in fresh from all over the world and heated in microwave ovens. We're protected from danger by locks, alarm systems, and 911 operators.

Most treatises on the U.S. economy rely on dry data that look at where we've been and, with a little figuring and fiddling, use it to predict economic growth and buying power. Mere numbers, though, can't tell us what may be just over the horizon, what inventions and innovations will burst onto the market to enrich our lives and accelerate the churn. In anticipating the economy's future, it's far more important to understand how technology soaks into society. Once we do, we will see how well the U.S. economy is positioned for the future.

A first important lesson: Every invention doesn't create the same ripples in the economy. The parachute is very useful, especially when an airplane's engines conk out while flying at 30,000 feet. It's not, however, a world-shaking invention. In changing the way we live, the parachute pales before the internal-combustion engine. Some inventions matter more than others. They carry greater weight largely because they serve a multitude of purposes and spawn further invention. The wheel, the plow, the printing press, and the steam engine are early examples of technologies that generated significant ripples. Without electricity, which was harnessed for household use more than a century ago, the modern family would have few of the conveniences we take for granted. No televisions. No refrigerators. No air conditioning. No popcorn poppers. Pivotal technologies aren't just a study in history. They keep coming along decade by decade. A list of the most important inventions and discoveries since the Civil War probably would include such recent advances as microprocessors, computers, DNA research, and the Internet (see Table 8.1).

The impact of inventions on the economy isn't just a matter of their inherent importance. Another factor is the extent to which new products replace existing ones, and, as a result, existing jobs. Inventions that render the status quo obsolete will cause more disruption in the labor force than those that create entirely new industries. As a way of communicating over long distances, the telephone is quick and personal. Once the country was wired for telephone service, it provided a big improvement over the previous technology, but it wasn't good

TABLE 8.1   Top 10 Inventions and Discoveries Since the Civil War

1.	Electricity	1873
2.	Microprocessor	1971
3.	Computer	1946
4.	DNA	1953
5.	Telephone	1876
6.	Automobile	1886
7.	Internet	1991
8.	Television	1926
9.	Refrigeration	1913
10.	Airplane	1903

news for the 75,000 telegraph operators displaced since 1920. Advances in transportation and telecommunications destroyed thousands of jobs among railway workers and switchboard operators. The blow can be particularly hard when displaced workers can't easily adapt to the new technology. In newsrooms, electronic typesetting and pagination create jobs for programmers, software designers, computer specialists, reporters and editors. The losers have been blue-collar workers in newspapers' backshops—linotype operators and paste-up workers. It's unlikely that many of them easily switched to the white-collar occupations in the newsroom.

Not all inventions cause such tumult. A new product that isn't a close substitute for what's already on the market won't ravage many industries or affect many jobs. The movie camera, the cellular telephone, space technology, and most wonder drugs caused relatively little disruption. They expanded our horizons and didn't compete head to head with existing goods and services. Technological change, moreover, isn't as upsetting if labor from declining industries can easily shift to emerging ones. Many of America's first autoworkers came over from the shops that made horse-drawn carriages. Assembling a car, it turns out, wasn't all that different from making a wagon. Actors and reporters shifted to television after it arose to compete with movies and radio. With a little training, their skills were adaptable.

The most significant aspect of modern technology is how quickly it bursts upon us. Innovation sweeps over modern societies in great waves. A glance backward over the twentieth century shows how quickly the material aspects of life can improve. In 1903, Wilbur and Orville Wright launched mankind into the aviation age with a 12-second, 120-foot flight at Kitty Hawk, North Carolina. A few years later came novocain, chemotherapy, neon lights, vitamins, sonar, and AM radio. Decade by decade, America witnessed a stream of innovations, inventions, and discoveries: television, jet aircraft, space travel, atomic energy, lasers, organ transplants, gene splicing. In the past quarter century, our lives have been enriched by personal computers, compact discs, videocassette recorders, pocket calculators, microwave ovens, cellular telephones, fax machines, satellite dishes, video games, laser printers, color copiers, high-speed modems, instant information via the Internet, and literally thousands of other new products. Particularly astounding are the medical advances, from organ transplants and laser surgery to new diagnostic tools and drugs that treat cancers, viruses, ulcers, depression, allergies, baldness, AIDS, and other maladies.

As rapid-fire communication spreads information faster and consumers become more sophisticated, technologies are entering our lives faster. Within 16 years of the introduction of the personal computer, a quarter of U.S. households owned one. For the cellular telephone, introduced in 1984, the time shrank to 13 years. Judging by what's taken place in the past few years, the Internet is coming into common usage even faster. In bygone days, things didn't move as fast. Decades might have passed before new products became part of everyday life. The first mass-produced automobiles chugged down America's dusty roads in the early 1900s, but the country still had more horses than cars into the 1920s. It took 55 years to get automobiles to a quarter of the population. It took around 35 years before the telephone penetrated one in four homes. Although it existed in the early 1870s, electric power didn't become nearly universally available, even in urban areas, until 50 years later. The technology for television proved itself in the 1920s, but it didn't reach America's living rooms in large numbers until the early 1950s (see Figure 8.1).

If trends toward faster dispersion of new products continue—and there's no reason to believe they won't—marvels yet to come will enter our daily lives even more quickly in the future. They will transform the churn: The time required for labor markets and corporate fortunes to adjust will shrink. New jobs will pop up in just a few years—like Webmasters did in this decade. New companies will emerge out of nowhere, as Netscape and dozens of other Internet-related companies did in the 1990s.

Why is technological progress coming so much faster? The answer starts with the fact that technology is cumulative. Each invention makes the next one easier by providing the stepping stones to future innovation. As society accumulates more know-how, it sets the stage

FIGURE 8.1   Spread of Products into American Households

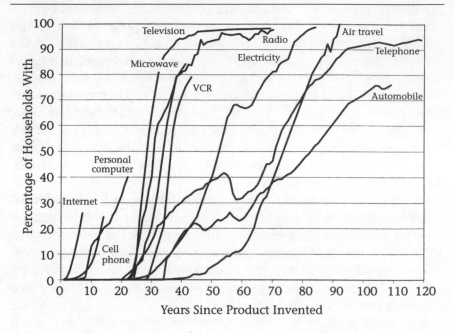

for an ever faster and more varied inventions. The intellectual lineage of the personal computer, for example, stretches back nearly two centuries. In 1801, the French inventor J. M. Jacquard devised a binary-control system with "1" and "0" on punched cards to program a loom to weave cloth in a preset pattern. In 1867, Christopher Latham Sholes invented the typewriter to quickly produce line after line of legible letters. Thomas Edison produced the light bulb around 1880, eliminating the fire hazards of candles and gaslights. Two years later, Edison started the electricity business by opening the world's first power station in New York. John Logee Baird produced the first working television in 1925. Intel's Ted Hoff, Federico Faggin, and Stan Mazor invented the microprocessor in 1971, which became the indispensable component of the hand-held calculator. Each of these inventors gave us useful products. None intended to contribute to the invention of the personal computer. Indeed, they had no idea such a device might someday come into being. Yet binary programming, electricity, the typewriter keyboard, the cathode-ray tube, the microprocessor, and literally hundreds other inventions were commonplace when West Coast hobbyists and entrepreneurs fashioned the first crude personal computers in the mid-1970s.

Personal computers developed out of technology accumulated over generations. They're now part of mankind's tool kit, available to spawn new waves of invention and innovation. If there's any alchemy in free enterprise, it is *technology spillovers,* a term for the phenomenon whereby one innovation hurries along the next ones. We couldn't imagine the Internet without computers. A worldwide network, in turn, is igniting further advances—search engines to explore the World Wide Web, gadgets that access the Internet via television sets, software to design home pages, and intelligent agents that sift through the oceans of information floating in cyberspace. The personal computer's ripples extend beyond electronics. Computational biology, a branch of science that uses computers to locate and code genes, illustrates how computers are putting technology on a faster track. Biologists are now identifying 6 to 10 new proteins a week, and the process will quicken as computers become even more powerful. Over time, the Internet probably will become a powerful piece of our technological heritage: It will reduce the cost of new discoveries by putting whole libraries of the latest research on-line at the touch of a finger.

Market size also influences how quickly technology moves into our lives. Had Alexander Graham Bell lived on a small island with a few hundred residents, there would have been little gain from inventing the telephone. The expense of buying a telephone, compared to walking across the street to talk to neighbors, would outweigh the benefits. Fortunately for Bell—and for Americans who now transmit voice and data communications over telephone lines—the telephone entered a growing economy, with millions of potential customers spread out on a continental scale. It's simply a matter of payoff— more customers, more sales, more profits.

Population isn't the only way markets grow. Cheaper transport can make it profitable for companies to enlarge their distribution area. Information technology pumps up demand as more consumers find out what's on the market. Higher incomes and lower prices allow more of us to afford the latest products, with all their new bells and whistles. In the early 1980s, for example, buying an IBM personal computer required more than 33 percent of an average family's disposable income. In the mid-1990s, a PC enhanced with power and peripherals cost less than 8 percent of the typical household's take-home pay. For today's new products, and for innovations yet to come, markets are increasingly global. In the past two decades, free-trade initiatives have cracked open once-closed markets in Asia, Europe, and Latin America. In the 1990s, new products enter markets with hundreds of millions of potential customers, so the potential gains from innovations are becoming enormous.

In speeding up technology, a growing storehouse of knowledge plays a role, as do larger markets and wider communications, allowing ideas to spread more quickly. Mere knowing how isn't enough, though. Until entrepreneurs and companies devise new goods and services or introduce more efficient production methods, great ideas remain curiosities for scholars and tinkerers, without much significance to daily life. The path from figment to fact involves designing prototypes, obtaining financing, manufacturing, marketing, and managing. The United States is well endowed with companies and workers proficient at these tasks. They don't do it out of generosity or duty. Self-interest provides the motive, free enterprise the indispensable institutional framework. Capitalism gives individuals with an industrious spirit a chance to profit from their ideas. It's no coincidence that England, where capitalism got its head start, became the first hotbed of invention.

Technological change accelerates in societies with free-market incentives and entrepreneurial talent. It speeds up in economies with a rich stock of inventions with significant spillovers. Technology flourishes where new products spread quickly and markets are big and growing. All this describes the United States as it approaches the twenty-first century. Our relatively unfettered free-enterprise system offers abundant incentives to deliver successful products to the market. The rewards can be mind-boggling. Ask Microsoft's Bill Gates. Ask Nike's Phil Knight. Ask the film mogul George Lucas. In recent decades, dozens of bona fide billionaires rocketed out of nowhere to make the *Forbes* 400 list of richest Americans. In 1994, three out of four of them made their fortune in businesses, up from three out of five a decade earlier. The industries are varied: 53 of the richest Americans made their fortunes in media-related businesses, 52 in finance, 30 in manufacturing, 28 in real estate, 27 in oil and gas, 18 in retailing, 18 in technology, and 15 in software. Incentives aren't just for the filthy rich. Rank-and-file workers look for industries that will pay higher wages and offer opportunities for advancement. Through self-interest, our economy shifts money, manpower, and other resources away from yesterday's goods and services to what consumers will buy today and tomorrow.

Stepping up invention and innovation move the economy forward at a faster pace. They also speed up the churn, no doubt bringing new rounds of upheaval in jobs and companies. New technology generates economic change. It's simply a fact of life in a modern economy, not something to be feared or resisted. We ought to welcome it, eyes wide open to the dislocations that will result. Allowing the churn to work is our guarantee of future progress.

Here Today: Tomorrow's Technology

Even in the hurly-burly of a free-enterprise economy, technologies don't advance overnight. They still take decades to mature. The marketplace always lags behind the laboratory. That's reason for optimism about America's future. It implies that we've only begun to reap the rewards of the cutting-edge industries pioneered in the past several decades. America's computer business has grown huge. In all likelihood, though, there's still room for expansion, especially with the export potential of hardware, software, and peripherals. The same applies to cellular communications, the Internet, and medical technology. Opportunities are likely to continue to show up in other rapidly expanding sectors—leisure industries, entertainment, health care, financial and legal professions, information businesses, satellite communications, and high-tech electronics.

Existing technology will carry the economy for a while, but what's beyond it? How can we know the economy will continue to provide rising living standards? The best assurance of tomorrow's progress lies in our inventory of technology. Since the start of recorded history, inventions and innovations have been the wellspring of human progress. They drive the churn, producing new products that raise our living standards and new jobs that pay better. By one estimate, more than half of the store of human knowledge has been produced over the past four decades. It's already spawning new products and building new industries—with more no doubt on the way.

The United States leads the world in creating new technology and introducing new products. The number of scientists and engineers working in the United States has doubled since the early 1970s. Many of them are the best in the world: The United States leads all other nations with 224 Nobel Prize winners, compared with 92 for Great Britain, the runner-up. More than half of all U.S. patents have been issued in the past 40 years. The number of new products put on the market has tripled since 1980, and with so much research and development under way, companies are likely to continue to offer new goods and services at a furious pace. In today's world, with instant communications and global markets, no country's endowment of technology is limited to what it can develop on its own. International technology transfers are commonplace. The United States has seen other countries borrow American companies' know-how in computers, software, and aerospace. In the same way, our country can capitalize on the inventiveness of foreigners. Japan's expertise with robotics and automated production techniques, for example, has already been adapted by U.S. companies. Thanks to untold billions of dollars in research and development, the world already offers a cornucopia of technology, the raw material of new products. This much we can be sure of: This country isn't about to run out of promising ideas. Future growth isn't a matter of wishful thinking. It's guaranteed—if we capitalize on what has already been invented or discovered.

Emerging technologies are already incorporated in many new products, and they're available for additional applications. We're harnessing simple beams of light—part of our universe since God said, "Let there be light"—into an array of useful products. *Lasers* play music in compact-disc systems. Focused beams of light can also read bar codes, drill, weld, cut, carve, and measure. Medical uses include destroying tumors and smoothing the wrinkles in skin. Radiance Services Co. in Bethesda, Maryland, markets laser devices that clean everything from the enamel on our teeth to the metal surfaces of our car's engine. *Optics,* a branch of physics that focuses on light's ability to transmit information, makes possible fiber-optic cables that can send the contents of the entire Library of Congress coast-to-coast in less than 20 seconds. *Holography*, a process that creates three-dimensional images, is available for devices to thwart counterfeiters and make fool-proof identification devices. *Photonics,* which makes use of light's energy, allows us to tap sunlight to generate electricity. Each advance in liquid-crystal displays (LCDs) brings brighter, clearer, and larger screens for computers and televisions. IBM, Hewlett Packard, and Xerox are trying to beat Japan's electronic giants in producing flat screen panels just three inches deep to replace television screens and computer monitors.

Computer technology provides the foundation for thousands of innovations. *Artificial intelligence* involves programming computers to "think" more as humans do. Eventual applications include self-navigating cars, diagnostic tools, information sorting, and household appliances that will be able to make up the family's grocery list. In 1997, an IBM computer finally achieved the mental agility to outmaneuver a world champion chess player. Shortly afterward, General Electric introduced a program that mimics legal reasoning. Scanners can measure the human body inch by inch, creating the possibility of custom-fitted clothing and shoes at the touch of a button. RoboShopper, an add-on to Internet browsers, sifts through the vastness of cyberspace to find the exact jacket, tennis shoes, or car the user wants to buy. *Recognition technology*, a close relative of artificial intelligence, allows machines to detect shapes, sounds, and smells. They can verify signatures; confirm identities by scanning faces, fingertips and eyes; translate words from English into Russian; sniff out gas leaks; and certify the aroma of every bottle of perfume. In 1996, a Kentucky company introduced Dragon Dictate, software that dispenses with the keyboard by putting users on speaking terms with their computers. Dragon Dictate can recognize 120,000 spoken words.

Virtual reality offers more than just fun and games at the arcade. Its emerging uses include remote surgery, guiding micromachines, and training pilots, soldiers, and firefighters. Researchers at Georgia Tech and Emory University developed virtual-reality systems to treat such disorders as acrophobia, the fear of heights. One company quickly adopted the technique to treat fear of flying. Computers make possible *noise-reduction technology*. By taking advantage of the properties of sound waves, devices can drown out the racket of airplanes, motor vehicles, industrial machinery, and household appliances. This technology also makes wireless transmissions clearer.

Robotics is taking the monotony out of assembly jobs and the danger out of such tasks as fighting fires, defusing explosives, or cleaning up toxic wastes. The Aesop 2000, a robotic surgical arm made by California's Computer Motion Inc., allows doctors to operate on patients by using voice commands. *Integration technology* connects computers, telephones, satellites, television, cable systems, microwaves, and other electronic marvels, allowing us to meet, shop, sell, and monitor events from far away. Teleconferencing, perhaps the best example of integration technology, is already saving companies time and money, and it may eventually become a standard technology for the home. The Internet will be part of telephones and portable telephones. PictureTel's latest wrinkle is a dynamic speaker that can automatically home in on whoever's speaking, providing a tight framing shot without a camera operator. Technology will even make life a bit more interesting for couch potatoes. Over the next few years, cable companies will introduce devices that let fans choose the camera angles and order up replays.

One of the most promising trends in modern technology involves making things smaller and smaller. *Nanotechnology,* the manipulation of matter at the molecular level, opens the possibilities for creating whole new materials, forged atom by atom, with astounding properties. How about a fiber stronger than steel yet more elastic than a spider's web; or perhaps a one-molecule-thick coating, more slippery than glare ice, that virtually eliminates friction? These aren't just possibilities. They're realities. Nanotechnology promises superconducting materials, perfect lenses, frictionless bearings, and flawless diamonds. It may also offer the prospect of even smaller, more powerful computer chips. *Micromachines* are itsy-bitsy devices with gears, hinges, motors, and pumps the width of a human hair, small enough to work inside the human body to clean arteries, diagnose tumors, and dispense drugs. They can check for structural flaws in buried pipes and aircraft wings. One emerging use of micromachines: bug-sized devices that burrow into earthquake rubble to sense the heat of survivors' bodies.

Understanding the basic structure of matter makes it possible to improve on what is found in nature. *Materials science* is creating composites—alloys, ceramics, plastics, and fibers—that are lighter, stronger, better at withstanding heat or cold, and endowed with enhanced properties to conduct electricity or absorb noise. A thin layer of chemicals allows computer users to input commands by simply touching the screen. The benefits to consumers of materials science also include flame-retardant gloves impervious to the heat of a blow torch, lighter bicycles, and automobile finishes that resist dents and corrosion.

Outer space isn't so far from everyday life these days. Satellites are making instant global communications routine. The Iridium satellite system, introduced in late 1998, provides the next generation of mobile telephones. It works anywhere on the planet, from the middle of the Pacific Ocean to the Gobi Desert. With an upfront cost of $3,000 to $4,000 for equipment, Iridium will start out with a small market among globe-trotting corporate executives, but the system's price will eventually come down. *The Global Positioning System* already guides taxi drivers and keeps track of shipments on the nation's highways. Satellite-based navigational systems, which can direct drivers to any address in the country, became an option starting with some 1997 car models. They're likely to become standard equipment on vehicles in the next century, creating another automobile-related industry. The National Automated Highway Systems Consortium, led by General Motors, is experimenting with prototypes of self-navigating automobiles that will stay on track using information that comes from the heavens.

Medical advances are truly astounding. *Genomics*, the study of DNA structure, is leading to new vaccines and more accurate diagnoses. The Human Genome Project, whose aim is to map the location of 100,000 genes, is expected to be completed by 2003; it will allow doctors of the future to detect and treat diseases through DNA analysis. A fingertip-sized computer chip, developed by a researcher at the University of Texas Southwestern Medical School, can perform 64 separate DNA tests in a few seconds. Someday, genomics might lead to cures for cancers and treatments for baldness. *Bionics*, the merger of biology and mechanics, has already produced implants that pump insulin into a diabetics's body. Advanced Bionics Corp. produces a device, fitted within the ear canal, that permits the profoundly deaf to hear. The future of bionics holds out the promise of devices that help the blind to see.

Biotechnology gives us the capability of tinkering with plants and animals. Gene splicing produces tomatoes that won't die in a hard freeze. The University of Delaware's work with hydrophytes, plants that grow in water that has a high salt content, is developing useful species that can be harvested for edible oils and animal feed. The payoffs of biotechnology include increased crop yields and plants immune to disease and insects. The science is also opening the door to new disinfectants, fungicides, germicides, and herbicides. Biotechnology may lead to treatments for a number of diseases and the production of synthetic organs; it is already making possible clothing that kills germs, bugs that gobble up toxic waste, enzymes that soften blue jeans, and cholesterol-eating peanuts with a shelf life measured in years, not months. Companies are working on chewing gum that fights tooth decay. In late 1997, doctors at Boston's St. Elizabeth's Medical Center used gene therapy to make the body sprout new blood vessels around clogged arteries, relieving the need for amputation and opening the possibility that the heart will grow its own bypasses. A new technique uses a patient's own skin to clone collagen cells, which are injected into the skin to reduce wrinkles and scar tissue.

What other marvels may lie ahead? No one can predict. The American economy isn't in any danger of exhausting the fuel for the churn—for progress. We possess the potential of still-young industries on the brink of growth. Better yet, untapped technologies lie at our fingertips, ready to be molded into new goods and services. The only barrier is our imagination. Indeed, the next stage in economic evolution, the one after the Information Age, may well be the Imagination Age, where the limiting factor won't be technology per se but our ability to *imagine* what we can do with so many possibilities. A motherlode of new technologies is waiting to be mined as we shape our future, so there's every reason to believe progress will be faster than ever. Our economy isn't a rickety one, long past its prime. Quite to the contrary, it possesses untapped vitality. It's fully capable of delivering a richer lifestyle to the average American over the next quarter century and beyond. The potential for the United States—indeed, for the entire world—boggles the mind.

The Age of Human Capital

Technology isn't just about what we consume. It's also about how we work.

Work of the distant past made human beings little more than beasts of burden, masters mainly of muscle power. Farmers trudged behind their plows; pick-and-shovel laborers clawed at the earth; stevedores on loading docks slung cargo over their shoulders. As the economy advanced from being primarily agrarian to the Industrial Age, steam-driven devices, internal-combustion engines, and electric motors took over as the sources of raw power. Freed from the lifting and hauling, workers moved to other jobs, most of them as machine operators. They used tractors, backhoes, forklifts, cranes, lathes, metal stampers, and other labor-saving devices. Industrial Age tools were no longer driven primarily by muscle power. Workers used their motor skills in operating the machines. To accommodate the new tools, companies reduced jobs to small tasks. The new industrial order yielded big gains in output and wages but often put Americans to work on assembly lines, the ultimate expression of mankind's alliance with the machine. Surging productivity let companies shift workers from the factory floor to offices, creating jobs that engaged more of their mental faculties. Employees kept accounts, filled out forms, and rubber-stamped decisions. These tasks were, for the most part, the office equivalent of assembly-line work—repetitive, formulaic, sometimes mind-numbing. In the end, it was unsatisfying, tapping into only a small portion of human potential. The latest rounds of technological progress, coming in the past two decades, allowed machines to take on more of the routine chores. The signature invention of our times is the microprocessor, the tiny "brain" embedded in computers, industrial robots, and other tools. U.S. workplaces use literally billions of them. They crunch numbers faster than any human being, and they handle repetitive tasks with relentless precision (see Tables 8.2a and 8.2b).

Previous generations of tools shaped the physical world. Tractors, bulldozers, cranes, derricks, motors, gears, pulleys, presses, molds, looms, shears, metal-forming machines, conveyors—all ultimately had to do with transforming or transporting material goods. Modern tools are tools for the mind rather than muscle, producers of services rather than goods. They're used primarily for dealing with ideas. They create, transform, and move *information*. Tools for the mind will shape what Americans do on the job, today and in the future. Most of us will be freed from back-breaking and mind-numbing tasks. Work will be less work. We'll employ talents that are integral parts of human nature—intellect, imagination, personality, enthusiasm, and creativity.

To prepare for this future, we need to rethink our notions of capital. Traditionally, productive assets have been machinery, land, and structures—so-called physical capital. Over the past two centuries, the United States grew into the world's leading economic power by using its labor resources to build "hard" capital goods, largely making tangible products. In the emerging services- and technology-driven economy, physical capital won't be as dominant. The factor that will shape our economic destiny will be so-called human capital—a catchall phrase for all that workers know how to do, all our talents and abilities, innate as well as acquired. More than ever before, we're using the skills of the mind. One of these is the ability to teach, to create human, or "soft," capital, the output of which is largely services.

The Industrial Age required horsepower.

The Information Age requires brainpower.

The Imagination Age will require that—and more. Creating productive assets is no longer as straightforward as financing a new plant or office building. Human capital enters the production process differently, coming through the front door rather than the loading dock. It often involves direct contact with consumers, rather than production of a commodity that's shipped to market. Most important, human capital can't be separated from the employees that embody it. Human capital has to eat, and it has to sleep. It socializes. It has opinions. It makes choices. It cares about room temperature, lighting, and comfort of the workplace. It can motivate itself. It can shirk, sulk, and even destroy itself with drugs or alcohol.

TABLE 8.2a Tools of the Ages

Agrarian Age		Industrial Age		Information Age	
Invention	*Year*	*Invention*	*Year*	*Invention*	*Year*
Plow	4000 B.C.	Blast furnace	1300	Telescope	1608
Yoke	3000 B.C.	Ball bearings	1794	Stethoscope	1816
Aqueducts	600–500 B.C.	Lathe	1798	Camera	1826
Archimedes' screw	200 B.C.	Battery	1800	Telegraph	1843
Saddle	200	Steam engine	1800	Precision clocks	1850
Treadmill	200–300	Conveyor belt	1804	Typewriter	1867
Wheelbarrow	300–400	Circular saw	1810	Telephone	1876
Horse collar	500	Hydraulic jack	1812	Phonograph	1877
Windmill	870	Portland cement	1824	Slide rule	1881
Dredger	1540	Standard nuts and bolts	1825	X-ray machine	1895
Pressure cooker	1680	Sewing machine	1846	Radio	1906
Rifle	1730	Electric loom	1846	Cash register	1919
Threshing machine	1732	Bessemer steelmaking	1860	Television	1926
Swing plow	1780	Internal combustion engine	1860	Teletype machine	1931
Cotton gin	1793	Milling machine	1862	Radar	1934
All-iron plow	1808	Drive chain	1864	Tape recorder	1935
Reaper	1826	Dynamite	1866	Electron microscope	1939
Binder	1850	Two-stroke engine	1878	Computer	1946
Sheep shears	1868	Blow torch	1880	Xerography	1946
Barbed wire	1873	Ace welder	1886	Videotape recorder	1952
Milking machine	1878	Diesel engine	1892	Satellites	1958
		Electric motor (AC)	1892	Laser	1960
		Electric drill	1985	Floppy disk	1965
		Assembly line	1908	Microprocessor	1971

Rocket	1926
Jet engine	1939
Nuclear reactor	1942
Laser	1960
Industrial robots	1961
Personal computer	1975
Fiber-optic cables	1977
Facsimile machine	1981
Camcorder	1982
Cellular phone	1983
Compact disc	1983
World Wide Web	1991

Table 8.2b   *What's a person to do?*

Agrarian Age	*Industrial Age*	*Information Age*
Muscle power	Motor skills, formulaic intelligence	Analytic reasoning, creativity, humor, personal touch

Human capital emerges in a way that's far different from how physical capital is created. The cost of building tangible productive assets is typically borne by businesses. Firms borrow money to invest in new plants and equipment, hoping to benefit from lower costs, greater output, and higher profits. The burdens of creating human capital, however, fall to parents, taxpayers, employers, and individual employees. A productive worker emerges only after long years of nurturing, including schooling, work experience, and socializing. Even if others foot the bill for education and training, the rewards of investing in human capital go to the workers themselves in the form of fatter paychecks and to companies in the form of higher productivity and greater profits.

As technology advances, human beings won't become obsolete, not by a long shot. Whenever new tools take humans' jobs, workers and companies put other skills and talents to use. Freed from routine tasks, we'll create opportunities to use higher-level talents to accomplish what machines can't do or can't do well. A growing number of Americans will be designing hardware, developing software, and teaching cybernetics. They're creating entertainment and enjoyment. They're communicating, organizing, advising, marketing, researching, comforting, pampering, and catering. They're providing the helping hands and the human face. More often than ever before, what Americans do involves analytic reasoning, creativity, and a personal touch. More Americans will simply invent their own jobs. A computer, a few hundred dollars worth of software, and a laser printer can make almost any desktop computer a tiny publishing house. Some workers still put their backs into their jobs; some still run machines; some still spend their days on humdrum office tasks—but today's jobs are less likely to rely on the skills of the past: muscle power, motor skills, or repetitive mental processes.

Human capital includes training in the sciences, engineering, the professions, and the arts. Without doubt, traditional intelligence and schooling will retain their importance. Even so, the Information Age economy won't simply become a fast-track for technology whizzes. Opportunities will be available for those with little aptitude for math and scant interest in the inner workings of computers. A corollary to the traditional measure of intelligence, IQ, is emotional intelligence, abbreviated EQ. Although EQ sounds as though it must be something innate, it is subject to learning, and there's a need to hone EQ skills every bit as much as other job requirements. In the future, the economy will provide opportunities for both IQ and EQ. Those whose interests lie in biochemical engineering will find good jobs, but so will those who enjoy teaching, entertaining, and care-taking. Whether it's a matter of IQ or EQ, the age of human capital puts a premium on education. For generations, higher education has been the ticket to the highest-paying occupations. These occupations have for the most part involved services and technology: professionals, managers, engineers, technicians, nonretail sales. The average pay of jobs requiring a college degree exceeds the earnings in construction and factory work. In 1997, median weekly wages in occupations where 30 percent or more workers hold bachelor's degrees average nearly 60 percent more than job categories with less than 10 percent college graduates. Even in goods-producing sectors, advances in technology put a premium on education. The factory hands of tomorrow will have to be more computer-savvy, more analytical, and better at handling words and numbers than today's blue-collar worker. There are, of course, lower-paying service jobs that will stay with us, even as the economy moves forward. They include such occupations as dental assistants and flight attendants, plus handlers, helpers, cleaners, and laborers. More often than not, these jobs differ from services' top earners in one crucial respect—the level of education they require (see Table 8.3).

Education doesn't mean just sending our young people through 12 years of school and on to college. It's on-the-job training, vocational schools, career retraining, professional enrichment, and postgraduate work. It's learning from parents, grandparents, and friends; it's reading and studying independently. Even television, radio, newspapers, travel, and life's experiences can widen our horizons. Education isn't just studying hard. It's studying the right subjects, adapting the curriculum to meet the needs of business and industry, paying attention to market signals on what society values. Education isn't just accumulating knowledge and cognitive faculties. It includes developing personal skills and sensitivities to others' needs, learning how to give and take and embrace the idea of customer service.

Today, as in the past, progress depends on accumulating capital. In an economy increasingly dominated by technology and services, the resources that matter most will be the skills and talents of workers. In the age of human capital, the best way to prepare for the future involves investing in ourselves. Although billions of dollars flow into schools, some segments of society don't have access to the financial resources and schools needed to develop skills for today's jobs. As a result, too many Americans are underinvested in education. The cal-

TABLE 8.3 It's Not the Industry, It's the Education[a]

Percent with		Median Weekly Wages	Occupation	Primary Industry	Projected Growth, 1994–2005 (percent)
High School Diploma or Less	Bachelor's Degree or More				
6.5	76.2	$750	**Professional specialty:** engineers, architects, surveyors, scientists, physicians, nurses, pharmacists, professors, teachers, librarians, economists, psychologists, therapists, social workers, clergy, lawyers, writers, entertainers, athletes, photographers	Services	29.3
14.9	62.6	$725	**Executives, administrators, managers:** managers-marketing, advertising, purchasing, public relations, personnel, lodging, health, food serving, real estate; administrators-public sector, education, protective services; accountants and auditors, underwriters, financial officers, management analysts	Services	16.8
31.3	37.3	$584	**Sales (excluding retail):** insurance, real estate, advertising, financial securities and commodities salespersons; sales supervisors and proprietors	Services	19.5
21.4	30.5	$582	**Technicians and related support:** laboratory, radiology and health technicians; licensed practical nurses; electrical and electronic technicians; surveying technicians; biological and chemical technicians; airplane pilots and navigators; computer programmers; legal assistants	Services	19.7
64.0	6.9	$548	**Precision production, craft, repair:** mechanics-automobile, aircraft, industrial machinery, heating and refrigeration equipment repairers-electronic equipment, data-processing equipment, communications equipment; tool and die makers, machinists, plant operators, inspectors, carpenters, masons, electricians, painters, plumbers, roofers	Goods and services	5.9
72.0	5.3	$498	**Transportation and material moving:** truck drivers, bus drivers, taxicab drivers and chauffeurs; rail and water transportation workers; crane and tower operators; grader, dozer and excavating machine operators; industrial truck and tractor equipment operators.	Goods and services	10.1

45.2	$419	**Administrative support, including clerical:** secretaries, stenographers, typists, computer operators, clerks, travel agents, ticket agent, receptionists, telephone operators, mail carriers, messengers, dispatchers, meter readers, investigators and adjusters, bill collectors, bank tellers	Services	4.3
76.2	$390	**Machine operators, assemblers:** stamping-press machine operators; grinding, abrading and polishing press operators; sewing machine operators; launderers and dry cleaners; packing and filling machine operators; furnace, kiln, and oven operators; slicing and cutting machine operators; welders; assemblers; production inspectors, checkers, and testers	Goods	4.4
61.2	$328	**Service (excluding food service):** dental assistants, nursing and health aides, janitors and cleaners, household maids and servants, hairdressers and cosmetologists, child care workers, police and detectives, guards, correctional institution officers, firefighters, flight attendants	Services	16.1
74.9	$329	**Handlers, equipment cleaners, helpers, and laborers:** construction laborers, baggage handlers, machine feeders and bearers, service station attendants, car washers and equipment cleaners, hand packers and packagers	Services	9.8
68.0	$295	**Farming, forestry, fishing:** farmworkers, groundskeepers and gardeners, animal caretakers, timber cutting and logging	Goods	-3.0

ªEducation and wage data are for 1996, in 1997 dollars. Projections on job growth are as of November 1995.

iber of the country's intellectual capital varies widely, from world-class theoretical physicists to high-school dropouts unable to read and write. Americans with education can expect better wages, benefits, working conditions, and status. Those with the least education and the lowest skills will, more often than not, be forced to settle for the least desirable jobs, whether in the goods or services sector. A Third World education is going to command Third World wages, whether it's in North Korea or North Carolina.

Young Americans preparing for careers of the twenty-first century will succeed only if they're prepared to contribute to an economy dominated by services and technology. Job openings for financial planners and computer programmers aren't going to spell opportunity for crackerjack drill-press operators—at least not without retraining. To succeed, Americans must prepare for the jobs that will be, not for the jobs that were.

The question for America's future is not whether there will be any good jobs. It's whether our society will prepare workers to fill them.

With each new generation of tools, workers feared that technology would reduce the need for existing skills—and they were almost always right. The demand for yesterday's occupations is diminishing. That's why pay in low-skilled occupations isn't keeping up. That's why jobs are lost. It's an age-old story of economic forces at work, with few roles for heroes or villains. Since the dawn of time, a relentless churn has been making obsolete not just our jobs but our talents, too. The future will be very much like the past—only more so. There's every reason to believe that the pace of progress will accelerate in the next decade and beyond. Indeed, growth *should* be faster as markets expand and as society's bulging inventory of technology delivers new goods and services. As long as the country educates its workers for the jobs of the future, we can look forward without fear.

9 THE GREAT AMERICAN GROWTH MACHINE

OVER THE PAST QUARTER CENTURY, our economy has given Americans a great deal. Typical middle-class families possess material goods in an abundance that might make the wealthy of yesteryear envious. Compared with previous generations, we live in bigger, better-equipped houses, drive safer, more reliable cars, and earn enough to afford more of almost all goods and services. Innovations arrive on store shelves daily, adding to a long list of new products making life richer, easier, more fun. The quality and variety of nearly all goods and services is improving.

Many goods are cheaper in the currency that matters most—our time. We work shorter hours and take more paid vacations and holidays. We start our jobs later in life, retire earlier, do less work around the house, and spend more money than ever on recreation and entertainment. Working conditions have never been better. Incomes are rising for most Americans, including those on society's lower rungs. The country remains the world's economic powerhouse. Layoffs are a fact of life, but companies, big and small, new and old, have replaced lost jobs with tens of millions of new ones. A healthy share of those new jobs are higher-paying ones, including many in the much-misunderstood service sector. Best of all, we can expect these trends to continue. In the future as in the past, technology will shape our world: Inventiveness and entrepreneurial spirit abound in America, so there's little reason to doubt that the future will be as prosperous as the past quarter century. We'll see new products, new jobs, and higher living standards well into the twenty-first century.

All in all, it has been an extremely good period for most Americans. Free enterprise doesn't bestow its gifts willy-nilly. The ultimate guide to what the economy offers is *what we want*, indicated by how we're

179

willing to spend our hard-earned dollars. The miracle of our economic system involves aggregating the tastes and preferences of millions of people and translating them into goods, services, and benefits. Companies spend millions of dollars researching consumer tastes, but the final test will always be the market itself. If what's produced doesn't satisfy consumers, it won't sell. The same holds on the job. If companies don't offer competitive pay and working conditions, employees will pull out the help-wanted advertisements. We can count on it: The economy gives us what we want, whether it's a couple of extra rooms in a new house, a device that plays movies at home, a few hours of personal time during the workweek, or a better job.

What we want—more to the point, what we ask from the economy—doesn't stay the same over time. In a society growing wealthier, the evolution of consumption isn't haphazard. Quite the opposite, there's a well-ordered progression starting with relatively basic goods and services and expanding over time to include ever greater luxuries and even noneconomic concerns such as the environment. The best way to reveal the pattern is to make a list ranking what we want. Most us would start with fundamentals—food, clothing, and shelter. Once they're bought and paid for, we'd turn to other primary goods and services, such as tables, chairs, and appliances, maybe some means of transportation and communication. Safety and security might come next—visits to the doctor, insurance policies, saving for a rainy day. After that, we might opt for additional leisure time. Still further down the list, we'd fill the corners of our lives with various accents—fashionable clothes, dinners at nice restaurants, perfumes, wallpaper, pasta makers, artwork. Given enough money, many of us would free ourselves from daily drudgery by hiring out our cooking, cleaning, and other chores. We'd seek a safer, more secure work environment, one with less strenuous physical labor. At some point, most of us would opt for less tangible blessings—the personal fulfillment gained from doing a worthwhile job or the satisfaction of making the world a better place.

The details of this ranking would obviously vary from one person to another. Some of us might look for leisure even before we can afford three square meals a day, while others might neglect household needs in favor of a bright-red Mercedes convertible. What we want collectively, however, won't be distorted by such idiosyncrasies. Necessities come before luxuries. We serve physical concerns and creature comforts first, noneconomic needs later. The pattern of demand shouldn't come as much of a surprise. It mirrors the influential work of the American psychologist Abraham Maslow. Maslow's Pyramid, a staple of psychology, charts precisely this hierarchy of needs. At the most basic level are the physiological requirements, starting with food, clothing, and shelter. When those are met, we move on to increased safety, which might entail less dangerous working conditions and hedges against hard times. Next come social needs, such as recreation, leisure, and volunteer work. We then desire self-esteem, perhaps recognition at work or the social status that many of us get from the conspicuous consumption of luxuries. At the pinnacle of the pyramid, Maslow put self-actualization, the personal fulfillment that comes with meeting our physical, emotional, and spiritual needs (see Figure 9.1).

Economic progress involves moving up Maslow's hierarchy of needs. In poor societies, most people make do with the barest necessities, with regular meals, a few garments, a roof overhead, and an occasional holiday. As societies grow wealthier, most people can take basic consumption for granted. They use additional income to buy goods and services that meet social needs, bolster self-esteem, or make their lives more rewarding. That's exactly what the United States has been doing for the past 200 years, moving from an agrarian society with average annual income of a few hundred dollars to a nation awash in every conceivable variety of goods and services.

The list of what we want never ends because, although a few individuals may be satisfied with their lot in life, the human race never is. We never get enough. Many goods and services enter into our preferences in different ways, depending on how much we earn. High on anyone's wish list would be shelter from the elements—a basic dwelling. Given more money, most of us want a bigger house and then an even bigger one, perhaps with a stable for horses or a view of the ocean. Cheap cars get us from one place to another. More expensive ones also provide something extra, such as a plush interior or the ego boost of being behind the wheel of a luxury car. Consumers will always want something else—physical-fitness gurus, ecotourism, early retirement, home theaters, more expensive jewelry, private education, fine wines, gifts for friends and family. Even among the wealthy, there's the lure of another valuable artwork, a more exotic vacation, even more lavish entertaining, larger gifts to charity.

No catalogue of what we want exists. Consumption data, however, show that Americans' buying patterns are evolving in ways consistent with Maslow's Triangle. The changes are more pronounced over longer periods of time. A typical American at the turn of the century

FIGURE 9.1   Maslow's Hierarchy of Needs

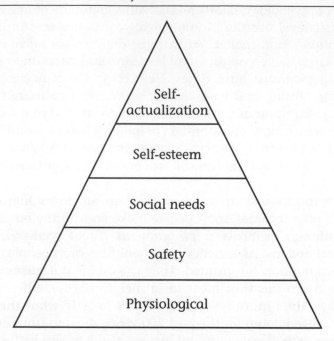

spent $76 out of every $100 on food, clothing, and shelter. By the 1990s, this portion had fallen to $37 of every $100. Even over a single generation, we can see the evolution of consumption. Food and beverages fell from 19.2 percent of spending in the 1970s to 15.2 percent in the 1990s. A Bureau of Labor Statistics (BLS) forecast projects that the figure will sink to 13.1 percent by 2005. Housing, utilities, and motor vehicles are taking smaller bites of our incomes, too. Among broad budgetary categories, we're spending relatively more on recreation, home furnishings, financial services, and contributions to religious and welfare activities. Overall, Americans' outlays on services and big-ticket goods are rising, while allocations to nondurable products, including food, are falling.

The pattern shows up in what Americans buy at different income levels. Among households with incomes below $15,000, food takes up 15 percent of the budget. For families over $50,000, it's down to 11 percent, and a larger portion of it is spent eating out. Once again, outlays for shelter and utilities go down as a percentage of spending for richer families. The shift from goods toward services shows up strongly at higher incomes. Below $15,000, households spend at least 53 percent of their income on goods. Above $70,000, the figure declines to just 41 percent. The wealthiest households spend relatively more on furniture and appliances, entertainment and hotels. The sharpest budget increases for high-income families come in insurance and pensions, a reflection of a desire to use additional income to reduce risks and prepare for a comfortable retirement. The rich also find time for good works. The percent of the population volunteering for church, civic, and cultural activities rises from 34 percent in households with incomes of less than $10,000 to 67.5 percent in families earning $100,000 or more.

The choices made by ever wealthier Americans underscore many of the progressions of our economy. We spend a dwindling portion of our incomes on goods because we can now afford more services, more convenience, and even a little pampering. Today's Americans don't work the long hours at the same kinds of jobs as their parents did because they're rich enough to indulge their preferences for greater leisure and jobs with better working conditions and self-fulfillment. The preferences of a richer nation might even shed some light on modern society's profusion of social and cultural events and political causes. Americans' consumption patterns are those of a rich nation—more amenities, more services, more leisure, more conveniences, more amusements, more luxuries, more personal fulfillment. We want more of just about everything, and we've been getting it.

Any social critic can find plenty to sneer at in the extravagances of higher incomes. Do we really need all the cosmetic surgery we've had in the past quarter century? Aren't private jets and sports stadiums' luxury suites the artifacts of a spoiled society? Hasn't the country gone too far when it allocates resources to straightening the teeth of show dogs? No doubt about it, we've got the luxury of having too much. The hallmark of a wealthy society is the proliferation of consumption that's further and further removed from fulfilling basic human needs.

Yet it's wrong to dismiss what we want as frivolous or even wasteful. Higher incomes allow most Americans to choose greater leisure. Few of us would contend that time spent vacationing or with our families isn't worthwhile. We're spending a lot more on health care, even though we're healthier and live longer than we did even a quarter century ago. Our desires aren't always self-indulgent. We're giving more of our time and money to charity. Society is moving down its list of wants, and this might even explain the prevalence of social causes in the United States. Only in wealthy nations, with the daily struggle for survival no longer at issue, can a large number of citizens spare the time and money for campaigns to save endangered species and preserve the environment. Better health and a cleaner environment are some of the unexpected gains from a quarter century of prosperity. Should we be surprised? Hardly. When we're better off, we pay more attention to quality of life, extending the market economy's bounty into areas that aren't typically regarded as economic.

The Mismeasured Economy

As we move down the list of what we want, a subtle change takes place in consumption. Meeting basic needs centers on physical goods, which for the most part can be measured fairly easily. It's a relatively simple matter to, say, count cars as they roll off the assembly line. The quality of ground beef may vary, but a pound of meat can be weighed, graded, and valued at market prices. A pound of sugar is a pound of sugar; a ton of steel is a ton of steel.

As we become wealthier, what we want becomes less tangible and harder to quantify. Services, leisure, and psychic rewards can't be counted as easily as cars, pounds of beef, sacks of sugar, or tons of steel. Difficulty in measuring the value of what we consume isn't an obstacle for individuals. Each of us possesses an intuitive feel for the value of just about all aspects of our lives—what economists call a "utility function." We make our buying decisions accordingly. The increasingly abstract nature of what we want creates obstacles in our ability to measure the overall economy and evaluate its performance. Simply put, it's getting harder to judge how well we're doing. The statistics on economic growth, output, income, inflation, and productivity are growing increasingly irrelevant in a modern economy where consumers allocate less of their resources to easily countable goods.

The problem lies in the tools economists use. In the late 1940s, the Department of Commerce developed the National Income and Product Accounts, designed to measure overall output by estimating the value of goods and services produced in the American economy. The procedure does a reasonably good job of measuring tangible products. Add up the money spent on everything, make adjustments for rising prices, and the result is the quarterly or annual economic output, expressed as real gross domestic product (GDP). This number is duly reported every three months as the broadest measure of the economy's performance. Once inscribed in the columns of statistical tables, real GDP is adapted for all kinds of uses—forecasts for businesses, projections of government revenues, elaborate studies of consumers' behavior, and the sales prospects for companies.

In real GDP, statisticians have created a measure of total economic output. What they can't create is a measure of well-being. At the time statisticians devised the National Accounts, more than half of U.S. output was manufacturing, mining, construction, and agriculture—countable, tangible goods. Today, the service sector makes up more than 70 percent of the American economy. More of our workers are earning their paychecks by counseling, consulting, entertaining, teaching, tending to customers' comfort, or even contemplating the next wave of economic changes. Counting the value of services presents problems. Those providing services get paid for them, a fact captured in our National Accounts. It's not as easy to say what their output is really worth. The steelworkers' product may be easy to calculate, but it's tricky to measure the economic worth of a singer, interior decorator, comedian, or financial adviser. What is a performance worth? How much does a well-appointed office add to a firm's productivity and profit? Is there a way to put a price on a laugh or smile? What's the worth of sound decision making?

A further complication is that some products' benefits are preventive. Statisticians can't measure goods unseen: Accidents that don't happen, people who don't get sick. Antilock brakes and air bags reduce collisions and injuries. Safety caps on pill bottles keep children from ingesting poisons. A vaccine might someday eliminate tooth decay. Dentists would be put out of work, but they could support themselves building houses or designing Internet web pages. Talented workers are rarely wasted for long. What the former dentists produce will get counted in GDP, but we've also gained the benefit of the cavities that aren't in people's teeth. What statistician can count this?

As Americans get richer, they are increasingly asking the economy to provide intangibles, such as more leisure, better working conditions, and a sense of self-worth. Our National Accounts don't even attempt to put a value on these aspects of everyday life—even though they're valuable to us, even though they're caught up in how we earn our paychecks and consume, even though they make us better off. What about variety? Americans are better off for being able to choose among different models and colors of automobiles. To the statisticians, every car is a white Chevrolet.

Statisticians keep track of cost, while the economy produces worth. These aren't always congruent. They diverge as new and better products allow the economy to deliver more worth at less cost. Adjustments for inflation only add to the static in statistics. The indexes of inflation are flawed because they can't keep up with increasingly rapid innovation, regular product redesign, and seemingly endless variety. Most experts conclude that measured inflation is at least one percentage point higher than actual inflation, an error that throws off every statistic that tries to account for rising prices (see Table 1.4).

By their very nature, the statistical weaknesses are hard to quantify. Attempts to get at the size of the inaccuracies are only educated guesses. With all the glitches, it's clear that the numbers that gauge our economy aren't giving us a fair reading. In almost every case, they make the economy appear less robust than it really is and understate gains in our living standards. Most important, the inaccuracies probably have grown worse over the past two decades. With consumption becoming more skewed toward services and other intangibles, the numbers are likely to drift further from reality as the economy moves into the twenty-first century. Our progress is becoming increasingly opaque to our statistical measurements.

Faulty measurement helps explain why so many of us aren't fully aware of how well the American economy has performed in the past quarter century. We no longer have accurate yardsticks to measure our progress. Worst of all, our statistics are probably going to fall wider and wider of the mark. It's ironic: Just when the economy is most successful—when it produces the most worth for the least cost— output is most likely to be undervalued. The economy gets the least credit when it's accomplishing the most. As we grow richer still in the years ahead, we can expect society to spend more of its time, energy, and income addressing needs that are further and further from the physiological. Pity the poor statistician who must keep track of our increasingly elusive gains.

The Triumph of Capitalism

The United States' success isn't an accident. It's not by mere chance that our forebears left isolated homesteads, centered on home production, to take better-paying jobs in an industrial economy. It's not by happenstance that a nation that once toiled with its hands and backs now earns its way chiefly with brainpower. It's surely not mere luck that Americans are 22 times richer now than they were when this country gained its independence. And it's not just hard work, either. To be sure, Americans have struggled mightily and labored diligently for generations. So have people in societies where profits flow to a few and progress arrives only in small dollops. Why has it all paid off so handsomely for the United States? Because U.S. citizens have been working hard within an economic system that gives individuals free reign to reap the rewards of their efforts, imaginations, talents, and good fortune.

The difference is the Great American Growth Machine.

In our prosperous era, we rarely take time to marvel at the system that's provided for us. Like water heaters or electric lights, the economy usually commands our attention only when something goes wrong—major job cuts, bad days on Wall Street, disappointing reports on inflation. Yet it's important to appreciate what drives America's $8.5 trillion behemoth, with its 130 million workers and 20 million enterprises. Although there's no central authority directing free enterprise, the system is well ordered and rational. The metaphor of the machine is apt in the sense that the economy consists of an immense number of individual parts, all working together to produce goods and services in abundance.

At the core of Great American Growth Machine are consumers and their endless list of needs, wants, conveniences, amusements, and luxuries. Unlimited wants clash with the fundamental fact of limited resources—that is, scarcity. We can't have everything we want, but we can satisfy more of our desires if we make better use of our resources. For employers and workers, stretching resources means boosting productivity, the driving force for higher wages. For consumers, it means shopping around for the best value. It all works because of competition: Companies vie for customers, making more money if they're able to reduce costs or increase market size while offering consumers a better deal (see Figure 9.2).

An economy with both existing and would-be competitors creates a constant drive to find new ways to meet consumers' needs—to innovate. Companies offer lower prices, better performance, new features, catchier styling, faster service, more convenient locations, higher status, more aggressive marketing, or more attractive packaging. Innovation comes in constant waves: inventions of new goods and services, improvements on existing products, and increases in efficiency for factory, farm, and office. The interplay of innovation and competition roils the status quo. New firms and industries emerge to take the market away from existing ones. Surviving firms reorganize production using more, newer, and better tools, making workers

FIGURE 9.2 How Progress Happens

Insatiable consumer wants, combined with the pursuit of self-interest, provide an endless fuel for economic growth. This diagram illustrates how the process works. Consumers will always want more than they have. The profit incentive, when allowed to operate, will continually power a quest for new ways to meet the needs of consumers. Innovation leads to the introduction of new and better products, which enhances consumption. New firms emerge to produce these products. In the process, they take business from old companies. The rising enterprises hire people for new and better jobs. Living standards rise. Even so, consumers still aren't satisfied and want more. 'Round and 'round it goes. The system slows if something—bad policies, for example—creates an impediment. The secrets of growth make it go faster.

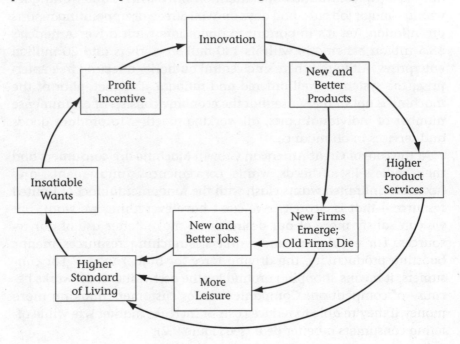

more productive. Consumers' tastes and expectations evolve. Companies that can no longer deliver what consumers want at reasonable prices simply don't survive.

In the process of innovation, the economy recycles labor, old jobs giving way to new ones. We harvest with combines, not by hand. We dig with heavy equipment, not picks and shovels. We build robots that build cars. We calculate with computers, not adding machines and slide rules. We diagnose with CAT scans and sonograms, not stethoscopes and tongue depressors. New technologies increase productivity. The payoff for employees is jobs with higher wages, better working conditions, and more time off. With fatter paychecks, workers head for the malls to buy more. Living standards rise. Yet there are still consumer needs and wants that remain satisfied. Possibilities for further innovation are never exhausted—better cars, more fun ways to spend our free time, safer travel, more convenient shopping, new medicines, greater choice of cuisine, and much more. The Great American Growth Machine doesn't stop.

America's economic history isn't just progress, it's a progression—a logical, orderly chain of development. Within this record lie the clues needed to predict which jobs will come and which will go, which businesses will flourish and fade, which skills will gain in value and which will lose value, what students should learn and where to invest. What's the ultimate secret? The answer is ironic: Americans make themselves richer by meeting the needs and wants of others. What makes the economy work is our pursuit of self-interest. The desire to improve one's life, however, wouldn't mean much without individual freedom. When people are free—able to choose what to do with their time, money, energy, and resources—their decisions matter. One person is free to make products; but another person is free to buy them—or not. Few of us doubt the innate drive to make ourselves better off. Yet we rarely acknowledge that the individual pursuit of gain raises the public good. Produce what benefits your fellow man, and you'll get rich! The Great American Growth Machine may be powered by self-interest, but it's guided by the needs of others.

Compared to the marketplace, government control is a feeble, inflexible mechanism. The state is necessary to maintain stability and order, to enact and enforce rules, but too much government is more apt to ruin economies, as illustrated by the collapse of the Soviet Bloc's central planning systems. It's not government that sets our alarm clocks so we wake early and get to work every morning. It's not by bureaucratic fiat that supermarkets stock more than 20,000 different items. It's not government policy that gave us drive-through service, instant mail, 24-hour automated-teller machines, home shopping networks, air-conditioned offices, and much, much more. It wasn't public decree that raised life expectancies by 30 years over the past century, or shortened our workweek by more than 20 hours. Over the past 200 years, we've progressed not by the grace of government but by the mechanism of the market. Of course, government contributed somewhat to our prosperity, especially infrastructure projects and funding for basic research. The most important element of America's success, however, has been the market—and it always will be.

By tradition and nature, Americans are optimistic. They expect their tomorrows—and their nation's tomorrows—to be bright. More often than not, this self-confidence has been rewarded. On the threshold of the twenty-first century, the country ought to anticipate even better days ahead. Most of what America needs for a prosperous future is already in place. The nation's bursting store of technology and entrepreneurial skill, combined with its dynamic marketplace, will no doubt deliver new industries and new job opportunities for decades to come. The United States will still run into the usual ups and downs of the business cycle, but overall the economy is raising our living standards faster than many people think, and may well do it faster still over the next quarter century.

Don't Mess with Success

The Great American Growth Machine provides a powerful mechanism to move society forward. Capitalism isn't fragile. It has weathered wars, financial panics, political crises, social upheavals, and ideological attack. Free enterprise is able to adjust to changing circumstances. Indeed, adaptability and resiliency are among its greatest strengths. Even so, our economic system isn't gremlin-proof. Americans who favor progress can't simply take it for granted that growth and prosperity will continue without interruption. Now that capitalism has triumphed over socialism in the great ideological war of the twentieth century, we must guard against damage from ill-advised tinkerers, many of whom profess enthusiasm for capitalism but fail to grasp how it works.

Here's what is important for keeping the American economic system humming:

Protect property rights. Private ownership of the means of production best serves economic progress. American entrepreneurs have done far more than all the commissars in Russia and all the potentates of Red China to improve the life of the common man and woman. Private ownership of the means of production allows Americans to reap the rewards of their talents and efforts. Incentives to increase yields, cut costs, satisfy consumers, and take advantage of new technology are greatest when they affect the pocketbook directly. Only when producers own their resources, invest in them, and profit from them will they be wholly energized to work year after year. It applies to entrepreneurs and workers alike. Public ownership won't make consumers' voices heard, but the free market does.

Avoid protecting existing jobs, industries, or businesses. As consumers' tastes change and as new technologies emerge, jobs come and go. Businesses flourish and fade. Whole industries grow and decline. An economy's natural evolution generates a continuous recycling of talents and resources. New products, new tools, and better methods of production and expanding markets all ignite changes that spawn even more changes. Free enterprise can never be stationary. Competition mobilizes. Protection immobilizes. It safeguards only the status quo, at the high cost of crimping and eventually strangling progress.

Keep taxes low and simple. Companies and workers will produce more if they can keep a larger share of what they earn, so lower income taxes spur the economy. Taxes that don't discourage work or investment—such as user fees or levies on consumption—are less harmful to the economy. Loopholes and special favors divert resources to less efficient uses. Taxes on capital gains and interest should be kept to a minimum, because they slow growth, making us worse off. Savings and investment act like an accelerator for economic growth by first requiring us to work and then enabling the work of others. Money saved by one household is money that can be borrowed to start businesses, expand production, and hire new employees. Taxes are necessary, of course, to pay for the legitimate activities of government, but we ought to choose our levies carefully, raising the revenues we need while doing the least harm to the economy.

Refrain from excessive regulation. Licenses, permits, fees, and other burdens on businesses impose the same disincentives as taxes. The justification for many rules is their benefit to consumers, workers, or society as a whole. The goals may be well intentioned. In most cases, though, businesses don't need government oversight to make sure they offer products that are safe, well made, properly labeled, and reasonably priced. Some abuses are inevitable, but regulation isn't foolproof either. Usually, it's costly to consumers. The prospect of losing customers—or defending lawsuits—provides a check on the corporate sector. It takes enough effort to design, test, finance, and market new products, secured only by the hopes that consumers will buy it. Having to fight government makes the task even more difficult, often unnecessarily so.

Create market-friendly institutions. There's something positive government can do—design institutions that help markets function. Capitalism flourishes in a climate of stability. At a minimum, institutions need to protect our lives and property rights. If the unscrupulous among us could plunder the fruits of others' labor, few would bother to work. In addition to enforcing property rights, government can bolster competition through antitrust laws. A well-conceived system of patent laws encourages innovation and nurtures growth. In short, the best system society can have is not one in which government is totally absent, but one in which it creates and supports those essential institutions that foster citizens' rights to live, work, and prosper.

Focus unemployment outlays on retraining. Producing more goods for less work is what raises living standards. Doing it entails figuring out easier ways to produce. Society progresses when it devises new and improved production methods and puts them into place. A properly functioning economy creates new jobs and destroys old ones, sometimes leaving workers unemployed. If government is going to help workers when they are unemployed, then it should do so by helping them get back to work, rather than giving them an excuse not to. Unemployment programs should prepare displaced workers for new jobs and provide incentives to work. Some minimum unemployment benefits may be needed to help workers for a short period of adjustment, but society's most humane response lies in encouraging workers to regain the dignity and pride of caring for themselves. A hand up, not a hand-out, is the best way to keep the wheels of the economy turning.

Nurture business credit. Capitalism without capital is just another idle *ism*. The free-market system grinds to a halt if deprived of credit. Those who start businesses usually don't have money to finance them, and they must borrow to start or expand their ventures. Even large, established firms require regular infusions of outside money to keep themselves moving forward. It's important to ensure that the public retains confidence in the financial system. Credit creation is the financial complement to innovation. In many other economies, the lack of developed credit markets holds back growth. Borrowing is harder and more expensive than it needs to be. The world's most sophiscated system of credit exists in the United States. The banking system, venture capital firms, stock markets, and commercial bond and credit markets all help grease the mechanism of free enterprise. It's best when credit flows toward business. That's how the economy creates jobs and paychecks. Consumer credit helps maintain demand, but it competes with businesses for available funds. Government borrowing should be limited only to that necessary to build infrastructure.

Make education a priority. America's wealth once flowed from abundant natural resources and productive capital. They are still important, but today more of our well-being flows from human capital. Today's assets are mental not physical, built in schools, not factories. Education isn't an option in the Information Age—it's a necessity. In the future even more than in the past, progress will depend on how well we can tailor education to the economy's needs. Are most of today's students getting the training they need to develop their talents? Are most of today's businesses finding students prepared with the skills they need? Probably not. The solution may lie in making competition work for our schools the way it works for our economy. Competition has proved it can deliver the goods. Yet, we don't apply it to produce the most important "good" in today's knowledge-based world—education. School choice ought to help improve the quality of America's education. We could do more. We might treat educational expenses as investment under the tax code. It's productive, expensive to acquire, and depreciates. Why should the break-room microwave in an automobile plant qualify for a tax deduction but not money spent on learning? We have Iron Age tax policies in an Information Age world.

Promote free trade. Government can promote society's welfare by promoting free trade. We need to keep trade barriers low, which means avoiding tariffs, quotas, and other restrictions to the free import and export of goods internationally. Specialization and trade are the primary sources of a nation's wealth. We're better off if we make goods as cheaply as possible and trade them for what others can produce. Exceptions to free trade offer an opening for special interests of companies and workers to limit competition. Any breaches must be narrow. They might include provisions that uphold property rights and support innovation. Patent laws, for example, take precedence over free trade, simply because potential gains from encouraging research and development outweigh what might be lost by giving some companies exclusive rights.

Invest in infrastructure. In the free-market system, companies and individuals provide most of what they need to produce the goods and services they intend to sell. They invest in physical capital, such as factories and machines, and they invest in human capital, including education and skills. For some economic needs, however, it is best to turn to government. Where benefits are spread broadly, collective action ensures that society doesn't underinvest in vital projects. Traditionally, public goods include roads, bridges, harbors, water projects, and education. If infrastructure investment is done wisely, then society will be amply paid back by the dividends from faster growth.

Maintain stable prices.   Money is one of society's most useful inventions. Without it, we are reduced to barter, a cumbersome practice that retards improvements in living standards. The existence of money whose value we can trust allows us to accept payment for our own products and hold on to the proceeds until we're ready to buy others' goods and services. The key lies in our willingness to trust money's value, usually a function of stable prices. The primary job of a nation's central bank is regulating the value of money. By controlling money's supply in a way to keep prices stable, monetary authorities can help the economy avoid gyrations that interfere with production and employment. Inflationary policies hinder growth, so governments must avoid the temptation to turn to the printing press to pay for excessive spending. Central-bank independence—placing the central bank at arm's length from those who budget and finance public spending—provides the best guarantee against reckless monetary policy.

The first admonishment to doctors is "do no harm." The same should apply to policy makers and regulators. There are many ways in which meddling can scuttle an economy's future. Indeed, modern history offers cautionary tales of well-endowed economies taken down by ill-advised policies. So far, the United States hasn't succumbed to such a fate. Although America isn't perfect, our economy doesn't need radical adjustments. In all we do, we should strive to make free enterprise flourish, not just for ourselves but for the generations that will come after us.

Putting the Myths to Rest

It works.

If there's a simple message in this book, it's just that. Our economic system works, and it works well.

Over the past decade or so, economic pessimists have invested a great deal of time and effort in trying to show that something has gone wrong, that the U.S. economy is failing us. In the end, though, it is the critics who fail. Their assessment of America's economy turns out to be a series of clunkers. The record of America refutes all of it. Abundant facts and figures prove that our free-enterprise system continues to deliver. The myths presented at the outset can now be restated to reflect what's true:

1. Americans' living standards rose over the past quarter century, just as they have during most of the nation's 200 years.
2. The rich are getting richer, but the poor are getting richer, too. Most of us are still getting ahead.
3. For the nation as a whole, life has never been easier: We're working less than ever, both on the job and at home, and there's more time for us to enjoy life.
4. Both adults have always worked to maintain a family's standard of living, but these days more of us are taking advantage of market opportunities, hiring others to perform household chores.
5. The United States is still the Land of Opportunity, where hard work, education, and entrepreneurial spirit pay off in a better life for most families.
6. Women and minorities are making great strides in nearly all economic measures, including better jobs, higher incomes, and increased business ownership.
7. The United States still ranks as the world's preeminent economic power, more dominant than ever as what we want shifts toward more sophisticated goods and services.
8. Good jobs are routinely destroyed in response to new products, higher productivity, and shifts in consumer demand—but more and better jobs are being created as companies expand into new markets.
9. American workers in nearly all industries are more productive than ever, largely because companies are investing in computers and other new technologies.
10. The growth of the service sector isn't new and it isn't condemning the United States to becoming a nation of "hamburger flippers," because the majority of service jobs require high-level skills and are well paying.

11. The nation's rich endowment of technology bodes well for jobs and growth in the future, so it's virtually certain that the current generation of children won't be the first in history not to live as well as their parents.

12. America can still compete in the technology-driven world of the future because the country is a leader in nearly all the technologies that will shape the next quarter century.

All of this is good news. None of it denies potential difficulties that lie ahead, nor the occasional hardships we'll encounter. Companies and families will go bankrupt. Workers will lose their jobs and struggle to make ends meet. Despite an overall improvement in living standards, the poor still number in the millions. Not all of our workers have the skills to match the jobs being created. Even with a balanced budget in 1998, the nation's finances remain deeply in debt. These flaws are real, and they shouldn't be glossed over. Our faults, however, should not be given so much weight that we're blind to the fundamental truth of the nation's success. It's here that a proper understanding of how the system works becomes important. A lot of the nation's so-called economic problems are just part of the price of progress. We cannot move forward to higher living standards and better jobs if we fail to accept this proposition: We have to take the bad with the good. For the past generation, the good has overwhelmed the bad—and this is quite likely to continue for the rest of our lives and for generations to come.

Epilogue

Apocalypse Not Now!

Some part of human nature connects with the apocalyptic. Time and again, the pessimists among us have envisioned the world going straight to hell. Never mind that it hasn't: A lot of us braced for the worst. Whether the source is the Bible or Nostradamus, Thomas Malthus, or the Club of Rome, predictions of calamities yet to come aren't easily ignored, no matter how many times we wake up the morning after the world was supposed to end.

So it is with the pessimists' view of an economy careening downhill toward a future of declining living standards, dead-end jobs, and increasing insecurity. Many Americans, even those with bullish expectations for themselves and their families, accept this view, overlooking all the evidence of progress and prosperity, not just in their own lives but in the economy as a whole. In accepting diminished expectations, we lose touch with America's tradition of optimism. We fail to see the world as it really is: All the relevant facts and figures—a good many of them presented in this book—prove that we've never had it so good.

So why do we feel so bad?

By virtually any objective standard, Americans should be, if not happy, at least hopeful as they approach the twenty-first century. Yet angst abounds. If the 1980s were the "me" decade, the 1990s might be characterized as the "woe is me" decade. We worry about making ends meet. We dread the day we'll lose our jobs. We fret about having to work too hard. We fear being overwhelmed by debt or foreign competition. We fuss over the solvency of Social Security, the country's failure to save, our kids' job prospects.

And these are just the jitters over economic matters!

Making sense of the appeal of negativism in today's world takes us beyond the precision of economic principles or the data in the *Statis-*

197

tical Abstract of the United States, put out by the U.S. Census Bureau. The collective psyche of 270 million Americans doesn't lend itself to being weighed and measured in the same way as household possessions, prices, incomes, working conditions, and jobs. Even so, it's probably worthwhile to conclude our survey of the U.S. economy with a few stabs at explaining why so many Americans are picking up on the bad news and missing out on the good news.

Part of it may simply lie in the way we're wired. In many of us, no doubt, there's a tendency to believe good times can't last. Perhaps it's just anxiety about an impending payback—a feeling that the other shoe could drop at any time. After a generation or two of good times, the better part of valor might lie in not tempting fate by appearing too cavalier about the future. We know bad things do happen to good people. Most workers may be reasonably secure in their employment, but when pollsters come around they respond that, yes indeed, they're concerned about losing their jobs. In a healthy economy, the actual probability of getting laid off might be low. Displaced workers might find new work without too much trouble. Most of us go about our business without dwelling on job losses. No matter. The surveys give the impression of a labor force quaking in anticipation of the pink slip. The pollsters aren't making it up, of course. Many Americans do lose their jobs. Newspapers and television report the facts any day that a major company decides to trim 10,000 jobs. The 130 million Americans who didn't lose their jobs that day weren't news. A string of layoffs within a few weeks establishes a trend—and an occasion for another batch of downcast reports on an economy in trouble.

It's hard to fault Americans for failing to grasp the economy's strengths. When they say the economy isn't performing well, or that new jobs aren't good ones, they're merely repeating what they're hearing. Much of it isn't positive, even in flush times. Although pessimistic reports, books, and campaigns don't reflect the economic reality presented in this book, they certainly come off as more dramatic, more compelling. It's simply a fact of life that bad news sells better than good news. We live in a society deluged by information. The sensational, the extreme, and the garish compete for attention. Anyone wanting to rise above the information clutter, or advance a career or cause, succeeds through rhetorical inflation—by presenting the worst possible case. A report on workers' diminished prospects, or some disconcerting analysis of ebbing U.S. competitiveness, makes the front page of the *New York Times.* A problem doesn't make the six o'clock news unless it carries the weight of a full-blown crisis. When Asian or Latin American nations tumble into currency or credit problems, warnings sound about a possible recession in the U.S. economy. A book titled *The Great Depression of 1990* can sound an alarm, even though kids graduating from high school haven't seen more than a few months of recession. We're a rich society, one that can afford legions of professional fault finders. Advocacy groups focus on the country's problems, not its strengths. Their policy papers usually present a nation or generation at risk. Our political discourse only adds to the air of negativity. In a highly charged partisan atmosphere, one side or the other is always spouting bad news and trumping every problem into a crisis. Those out of office bewail the status quo: "Life is bad! The country is in trouble! Vote for me and I'll help." Incumbents of course take the opposite tack. When campaigning, they spread the word about how well the economy is doing. If it's not here yet, prosperity is just around the corner.

If society gives money and attention to bad news, the enterprising among us will respond to the incentive to produce more of it. Some among us benefit from churning bad news. They profit from book sales. A proposal to investigate some great failing might win its authors grant money, public or private. The notoriety of trashing the economy might open a path to promotion or employment. Like it or not, some folks get rich making others worry. The perks of pessimism aren't all monetary. A doubting Thomas, spinning tales of economic calamity, can grab a bit of celebrity with appearances on television and quotes in national publications.

In at least some cases, the urge to find fault with the economy may come from ignorance or ideology. Some critics just don't understand how the economy works. They fail to appreciate that many of today's unpleasant transitions are nothing new, ominous, or unexpected. For example, jobs always have been routinely created and destroyed. No society moves forward unless the jobs of the past give way to the jobs of the future. The churn can be unsettling, but it's what makes free-market economies succeed. New technology destroys most jobs, but many economic critics prefer to rage against imports, an easy target. Then there are those who simply loathe capitalism. Their motives are obscure, their scholarship often biased, but they play up the failures of the economy. They diminish the evidence of progress and play up the black marks, such as declining real wages. More important, they impose upon our economic system obligations that aren't realistic. We've delivered unrivaled prosperity to the great American masses, yet there are those among us who condemn the system because the poverty rate still hangs at 13 percent. We've produced 30 million jobs in a decade, yet there are those among us who wonder why every working-age adult in America doesn't have a well-paying job.

Another human bias involves looking back in a hazy glow of good feelings. Many of us fail to remember the turbulence of the past—the wars, the recessions, the scandals, the crimes, and the human failings that afflict the human race in every era. In the 1990s, there's nostalgia for the 1950s and 1960s as more peaceful and more prosperous times. Yet those eras had their own horrors—the threat of nuclear annihilation, an unpopular war in Vietnam, racial strike that erupted into rioting, assassinations, political hanky-panky, and higher rates of poverty than we had in the 1990s. Many of us think we grew up in a country where workers could take a job and expect to keep it until retirement. Not so. Employment has always been subject to the churn's relentless forces. The travails of the past are at a safe distance. By contrast, today's troubles are confirmed by daily trials and tribulations at home and at work, or the latest reports of layoffs and bankruptcies. The present almost always pales when measured against the "good old days."

When were those good old days? It depends on whom you ask. People typically regard as the best of times the decade when they were in their late teens and early twenties. Those now in their seventies or eighties might wax nostalgic for the 1930s and 1940s, even with the hardships of the Great Depression and World War II. Those in their forties and fifties might yearn for the 1960s and 1970s. The reason seems obvious. For most of us, youth is a relatively carefree time of growth and discovery. In middle age, we shoulder the greatest burdens, providing for children, maintaining living standards, saving for retirement, and sometimes even caring for parents.

Members of the Baby Boom generation, that bulge in population that sways cultural and social trends, entered their middle years in the past two decades. It's a time of life when few of us ever have enough time or enough money. As with just about everything about the Boomers, their midlife experience has become society's dominant theme. Over the next decade or two, this generation will move into a less hectic time of life as their children leave home and workers settle into retirement. Upcoming generations can look forward to greater prosperity. Perhaps then, the negativism will begin to fade.

In trying to explain why Americans are uneasy, it's impossible to ignore the stresses of our times. Under the country's intense competition and rapid-fire innovation, the economic landscape is shifting under our very feet. The Industrial Age has given way to the Information Age, bringing sweeping changes in the way we live and work. At the same time, there's an unsettling shift from a national economy to an international one. Skills, technologies, and product lines can fall by the wayside in just a few years. The churn is shifting into overdrive, making changes in jobs more frequent. Change makes people jittery—always has, always will. The arrival of the Industrial Revolution in the late 1800s upset societies accustomed to the pace of agrarian life. The leap from a local to a national economy in the early twentieth century created upheavals as the Main Street merchant came into competition with Sears, Roebuck. Over time, though, people get used to a new environment, making what adjustments they have to, finally forgetting how people lived in the previous age. We can't stifle the economic forces changing our world, but we can learn to understand them. If we do, there will be less reason to fear what's going on around us. We might even find ways to take advantage of it.

Free enterprise has been good to us—so good, in fact, that it has given rise to expectations that may well be too high. We can't reasonably anticipate total elimination of poverty, unemployment, dead-end jobs, or bankruptcies. These hardships—and others—will always be with us. They're part of the economic landscape, and other systems have worse faults. Americans ought to accept the world as it is. As good as it gets, capitalism will never be perfect. What's more, Americans expect more than ever before out of life. They now know it's possible to get fresh fruit in the wintertime, air conditioning in their cars, the complete array of household appliances. They don't want their children embarrassed by crooked smiles, and so don't feel well-off until they slap braces on their kids' teeth. This is a society of rising expectations. We take for granted devices that didn't even exist for our parents and grandparents. What were once luxuries are now viewed as necessities, made reasonably affordable by the forward march of our economic system.

We live in a complex, contradictory world. Not in this era, nor in any other, should we expect the country to get better by every measure. The general gains in heath are clouded by the AIDS epidemic. Air and water may be getting cleaner overall, but they still aren't pristine. Environmentalists warn of global warming, deforestation, hazardous-waste dumping, and the loss of endangered species. We are alarmed by the increasing incidence of crime and violence. In many surveys, crime ranks first among Americans' worries, even though it isn't a sudden jolt to an otherwise peaceful society. Crime remains high, but there hasn't really been a big surge in the past 20 years. Statistically, the increase in reported offenses came earlier—from 1960 to the mid-1970s. In fact, overall crime has declined in the 1990s. Disease, pollution, and crime are but a few of the threats in the modern world. We ought to take all reasonable measures to deal with them, but we shouldn't let a few aspects of life overshadow two decades—no, two centuries—of progress in our living standards.

The prevailing pessimism seems somewhat out of place. The United States is, after all, as renowned for optimism as it is for opportunity. Many of us are upbeat about our personal lives. We love our families. We enjoy our jobs. We even approve of our congressmen. Life in these United States isn't by any means grim, at least not for most Americans. That's especially true for the material side of life. We've experienced splendid economic progress over the past quarter century, and we're likely to continue to see our living standards and jobs improve. Instead of fixating on the warts, we should give thanks for the blessings of free enterprise. Instead of worrying about potential glitches, we should have faith that capitalism will continue to deliver benefits for nearly all Americans.

The best is yet to come.

Notes

The *Statistical Abstract of the United States* (referred to throughout these notes as *Statistical Abstract*) and Current Population Reports (various individual titles) are compiled by the U.S. Bureau of the Census, which is part of the Department of Commerce. The Census Bureau also compiled *Historical Statistics of the United States: Colonial Times to 1970* (referred to as *Historical Statistics*), published in a Bicentennial Edition (Washington, D.C.: U.S. Government Printing Office, 1975).

Works cited in the notes that are published by the Bureau of Labor Statistics (BLS), which is part of the Department of Labor, include the multi-volume work *Employment, Hours, and Earnings, United States, 1909–94*, and the periodicals *Monthly Labor Review* and *Employment and Earnings*.

The Economic Report of the President is put out yearly by the Council of Economic Advisers and, like most government publications, is published by the U.S. Government Printing Office (GPO) in Washington, D.C.

As noted, all monetary figures are expressed in (constant) 1997 dollars and all monetary comparisons are on a real (inflation-adjusted) basis. Monetary figures expressed in current dollars are not inflation adjusted and pertain to the specific years noted. Whenever possible, data used are the latest available, unless other comparisons are called for in a specific analysis.

Preface

xvii   Mark Twain's observation: "TCPN Quotation Center," at The People's Cyber Nation (TCPN) Website, http://www.cyber-nation.com/victory/quotations, accessed September 18, 1998.

xviii   Misery index: *Economic Report of the President, February 1998*, pp. 331, 353. 1998 data are taken from the U.S. Bureau of Labor Statistics Website, http://www.bls.gov.

xviii   Consumer confidence: The Conference Board, press release no. 4400, February 24, 1998, "Consumer Confidence Soars to 30-Year High in February."

Chapter 1
Waking Up to Good Times

3   James Sharlow story: "The Downsizing of America," *New York Times*, March 5, 1996, p. 1.

3   Rene Brown and Steven Holthausen stories: Ibid.

4   Average hourly wages from 1953 to 1996 (and Figure 1.1): Real-wage figures are calculated by dividing the average hourly earnings of production or nonsupervisory workers by the Consumer Price Index for all urban consumers (CPI-U). Wage data are from *Employment, Hours, and Earnings, United States, 1909–94*, vol. 1, p. 4, and for later years, *Employment and Earnings*, May 1998, p. 47. Data on CPI-U are from the *Economic Report of the President, February 1998*, p. 349.

5   Gasoline prices: Average of 1970 retail gasoline prices for 47 selected U.S. cities was 35.7 cents per gallon. *Basic Petroleum Data Book*, July 1995, section 6, table 12.

8   Homebuilding and housing amenities (and Figure 1.2): U.S. Department of Housing and Urban Development, *Characteristics of New Housing*, series C25; *Statistical Abstract*, "Characteristics of New Privately Owned One-Family Houses Completed," table, various years.

8   Average energy consumption: *Statistical Abstract: 1996*, table 921, "Residential Energy Consumption and Expenditures, by Type of Fuel and Selected Household Characteristics," p. 583.

8   Housing data: U.S. Department of Housing and Urban Development, *Characteristics of New Housing*, series C25, various issues.

8   Median price of a new home: Ibid.; *Statistical Abstract*, "Median Sales Price of New Privately Owned One-Family Houses Sold," table, various years. Figures are in current dollars.

8   Income: U.S. Bureau of the Census, Historical Income Tables—Families, table F-5, "Race and Hispanic Origin of Householder—Families by Median and Mean Income: 1947 to 1996," at the Census Bureau Website, http://www.census.gov/hhes/income/histinc/f05.html, accessed September 18, 1998. Figures are in current dollars.

8   Mortgage interest rates: *Statistical Abstract: 1993*, "Money Market Interest Rates and Mortgage Rates: 1970 to 1992," p. 520; Board of Governors of the Federal Reserve System, "1.53 Mortgage Markets," *Federal Reserve Bulletin*, July 1998, p. A34.

8   Home-ownership rates: U.S. Bureau of the Census, "Housing Vacancy Survey: Historical Tables," as reported at the Census Bureau Website, http://www.census.gov/hhes/www/housing/hvs/historic/histt14.html, and "Housing Vacancies and Home Ownership, First Quarter 1998," at the Census Bureau Website, http://www.census.gov/hhes/www/housing/hvs/q198prss.html.

9   Average age at which Americans first buy a home: *Statistical Abstract: 1997*, table 1212, "Recent Home Buyers—General Characteristics: 1976 to 1996," p. 730.

9   Median age at the time of first marriage: U.S. Bureau of the Census, "Estimated Median Age at First Marriage, by Sex: 1890 to Present" and "Marital Status and Living Arrangements," as reported at the Census Bureau Websites, http://www.census.gov/population/socdemo/ms-la/95his06.tx., and http://www.census.gov/population/www/socdemo/ms-la.html.

9   Percent who never marry: *Statistical Abstract: 1996*, table 58, "Marital Status of the Population, by Sex, Race, and Hispanic Origin: 1970 to 1995," p. 54.

9   Number of children per family: U.S. Bureau of the Census, "Average Number of Own Children Under 18 per Family, by Type of Family: 1955 to the Present," as reported at the Census Bureau Website, http://www. census.gov/population/socdemo/hh-fam/95his09.txt.

10   Family ownership of various appliances: See sources to table 1.1, p. 7.

10   Appliances manufactured in 1996: Association of Home Appliance Manufacturers, "Industry Statistics," at the association's Website, http://www.aham.org/mfrs/stats/port1996.htm.

Sources for Table 1.1 begin here

10   Average size of a new home, new homes with central heat and air, and new homes with a garage: U.S. Department of Housing and Urban Development, *Characteristics of New Housing*, series C25; *Statistical Abstract*, "Characteristics of New Privately Owned One-Family Houses Completed," various years.

10   Average household size: U.S. Bureau of the Census Web site http://www.census.gov/population/socdemo/hh-fam/htabHH-4.txt.

10   Average square feet per person in the household: Calculated as the average size of a new home divided by average household size.

10   Housing units lacking complete plumbing and homes lacking a telephone: *Statistical Abstract: 1996*, table 1189, "Housing Units—Historical Trends for Selected Characteristics: 1950 to 1993," p. 719. *Statistical Abstract: 1997*, table 1196, "Housing Units—Historical Trends for Selected Characteristics: 1991 to 1995," p. 722.

10   Households with computers: Robert Famighetti, ed., *World Almanac and Book of Facts 1998*, (Mahwah, N.J.: K-III Reference Corp., 1998), "U.S. Computer Sales and Ownership, 1984–97," p. 650.

10   Households with no vehicle, two or more vehicles, and vehicles per 100 persons aged 16+: The 1970 data are interpolated using data for 1969 and 1977 as reported in *Statistical Abstract: 1996*, table 1008, p. 626. The 1969 figure for households with no vehicle is 20.6 percent and the figure for households with two or more vehicles is

31.0 percent. Data for 1995 from Federal Highway Administration, *Nationwide Personal Transportation Survey*, Our Nation's Travel 1995 NPTS Early Result Report, Data Appendix.

10   Households with color TV and households with two or more TVs:Television Bureau of Advertising, "Television Households" and "Multi-Set & Color TV Households," at the TBA Website, http://www.tvb.org/researchreports/trends_tv/.

10   Households with cable TV: *Statistical Abstract: 1997*, table 888, "Utilization of Selected Media: 1970 to 1995," p. 566.

10   Households with answering machine, cordless phone, computer printer, camcorder, cellular phone, CD player, VCR: Consumer Electronics Manufacturers Association.

10   Households with clothes washer and households with clothes dryer: 1970 data from *Statistical Abstract:1975*, table 1235, "Selected Electrical Appliances—Number and Percent of Homes with Appliances: 1960 to 1974," p. 723. Later data are from *Beyond Poverty, Extended Measures of Well-Being: 1992*, Current Population Reports, P70-50RV, November 1995, Household Economic Studies, U.S. Department of Commerce, Bureau of the Census, calculated as a weighted average of the percent access to consumer durables of poor and non-poor households, and treating 13.3 percent of persons in families as poor in 1992, according to *Poverty in the United States: 1995*, Table C-1 Poverty Status of Persons by Family Relationship, Race, and Hispanic Origin: 1959 to 1995, p. C-2.

10   Households with a microwave, and households with dishwasher: The Conference Board, *Special Consumer Survey Report*, November 1996, "Household Inventory." 1970 dishwasher: *Statistical Abstract:1975*, table 1235, "Selected Electrical Appliances—Number and Percent of Homes with Appliances: 1960 to 1974," p. 723.

10   Households with coffeemaker and households with vacuum cleaner: *Statistical Abstract:1975*, table 1235, "Selected Electrical Appliances—Number and Percent of Homes with Appliances: 1960 to 1974," and various later issues.

10   Households with frost-free refrigerator and households with outdoor gas grill: *Housing Characteristics, 1993*, Energy Information Administration, table 3.16b, "Appliances by Census Region and Climate Zone, Percent of U.S. Households, 1993," pp. 93, 95; Energy Information Administration, table 3.29b, "Appliances by Census Region, Percent of U.S. Households, 1997-Preliminary," at EIA Website, http://www.eia.doe.gov/emeu/recs/recs97_hc/tbl3_29b.html, accessed October 19, 1998.

10   Mean household ownership of furniture, mean household ownership of appliances, mean household ownership of video and audio prod-

ucts, mean household ownership of jewelry and watches, mean household ownership of books and maps, mean household ownership of sports equipment: U.S. Department of Commerce, Bureau of Economic Analysis, *Survey of Current Business*, January 1992, table 20, "Constant Cost Net Stock of Durable Goods Owned by Consumers, by Type, 1925–90," p. 135 and ibid., September 1997, table 24, "Chain-Type Quantity Indexes for Net Stock of Durable Goods Owned by Consumers, by Type, 1986–97," p. 47. Figures here and in all constant dollar calculations are expressed in 1997 dollars.

10   Mean household net worth and median household net worth: "Survey of Consumer Finances, 1983: A Second Report," *Federal Reserve Bulletin*, Board of Governors of the Federal Reserve System, December 1984, pp. 857–68, (particularly, p. 862), and "Family Finances in the U.S.: Recent Evidence from the Survey of Consumer Finances," *Federal Reserve Bulletin*, Board of Governors of the Federal Reserve System, January 1997, pp. 1–24 (particularly, p. 6). Figures are in 1997 dollars.

10   Work time to buy gas for a 100-mile trip: Calculated as average retail price per gallon of gasoline divided by the average number of miles per gallon then divided by the average hourly wage of production and non-supervisory employees. Source for average price per gallon is American Petroleum Institute, *Basic Petroleum Data Book*, Petroleum Industry Statistics, Volume XV, Number 2, July 1995, Section VI, table 12, "Average United States Retail Gasoline Prices for Selected Cities." Source for average miles per gallon is *Statistical Abstract: 1996*, table 1019, "Domestic Motor Fuel Consumption, by Type of Vehicle: 1970 to 1994," p. 632. Source for average hourly wage is Bureau of Labor Statistics, *Employment, Hours, and Earnings, United States, 1909–94, Volume I*, pp. 3–4, and for later years *Employment and Earnings*, various issues.

10   Annual visits to the doctor: *Statistical Abstract: 1996*, table 182, "Physician and Dental Contacts, by Patient Characteristics: 1970 to 1994," p. 124.

10   Per capita consumption of bottled water: International Bottled Water Association.

10   Americans taking cruises: Cruise Lines International Association, *The Cruise Industry: An Overview*, marketing edition, January 1997, p. 2, and ibid., "News About Cruises," no. 104881.

10   Air miles traveled per capita: Data are U.S. air transportation scheduled revenue passenger miles flown per capita on both domestic and international flights as reported in *Historical Statistics*, series Q 585, "Scheduled Air Transportation, Domestic and International: 1926 to 1970," p. 769; *Statistical Abstract: 1996*, table 1039, "U.S. Scheduled Airline Industry—Summary: 1985–1994," p. 645; Current Popula-

tion Reports, series P25, *Population Estimates and Projections;* Air Transport Association, "Load Factor-US Scheduled Airlines," ATA Website, http://www.air-transport.org/data/loadfctr.htm.

10   Per capita spending on sporting goods: *Statistical Abstract: 1976,* table 1364, "Retail Trade Sales, by Broad Merchandise Lines: 1967 and 1972," p. 806; ibid., *1993,* table 413, "Sporting Goods Sales, by Broad Product Category: 1980 to 1992," p. 255; ibid., *1997,* table 421, "Sporting Goods Sales, by Product Category: 1987 to 1996," p. 261.

10   Recreational boats per 1,000 people: *Statistical Abstract: 1993,* table 411, "Selected Recreational Activities," p. 253; ibid., *1997,* table 418, "Selected Recreational Activities," p. 258.

10   Manufacturers' shipments of RVs: *Statistical Abstract: 1996,* table 1006, "Recreational Vehicles—Number and Retail Value of shipments: 1970 to 1993," p. 624; ibid., *1997,* table 1013, "Recreational Vehicles-Number and Retail Value of shipments: 1980 to 1995," p. 628.

Sources for Table 1.1 end here

12   Spending on overseas travel and tourism: Per capita expenditures abroad by U.S. travelers in 1997 dollars averaged $102 in 1970 and $275 in 1994. Data are inflation-adjusted using the urban-weighted Consumer Price Index (CPI-U-X1). *Statistical Abstract: 1996,* table 427, "International Travelers and Expenditures, with Projections: 1970 to 1995," p. 265; *Economic Report of the President, 1997,* table B-32, "Population by Age Group, 1929–96," p. 337; U.S. Bureau of Labor Statistics (CPI-U-X1).

12   Number of stores: *Statistical Abstract: 1996,* table 1253, "Retail Trade—Summary: 1963 to 1992," p. 761.

12   Use of credit cards: *Statistical Abstract: 1975,* table 772, "Percent of Families Using Credit Cards, by Income: 1970," p. 475; ibid., *1996,* table 792, "Usage of General Purpose Credit Cards by Families: 1989 and 1992," p. 516.

12   Household median and average net worth, net financial assets, and consumer debt: Board of Governors of the Federal Reserve, "Survey of Consumer Finances, 1983: A Second Report," *Federal Reserve Bulletin,* December 1984, pp. 857–868, especially p. 862; ibid., "Family Finances in the U.S.: Recent Evidence from the Survey of Consumer Finances," *Federal Reserve Bulletin,* January 1997, pp. 1–24, especially p. 6. Figures are in 1997 dollars.

13   Household investment in mutual funds: Board of Governors of the Federal Reserve System, *Flow of Funds Account of the United States,* June 11, 1998, Z.1, "Statistical Release," tables F.100 and L.100, "Households and Nonprofit Organizations." Figures in current dollars.

14   Poverty rate: U.S. Bureau of the Census, Historical Poverty Tables—Persons, table 2, "Poverty Status of Persons, by Family Relationship,

Race, and Hispanic Origin, 1960–1995, " at the Census Bureau Website, http://www.census.gov/hhes/poverty/histpov/hstpov2.html; *Poverty in the United States: 1996,* table A, p. vii.

14   Poverty thresholds: In 1996, poverty thresholds for families of three and four persons were $12,516 and $16,036, respectively, and average family size was 3.2. The implied poverty threshold for an averaged-sized family is roughly $13,220. Figures in current dollars; U.S. Bureau of the Census, "Poverty Thresholds: 1996," at Census Bureau Website, http://www.census.gov/hhes/poverty/threshld/thresh96.html.

14   Home ownership among poor families: Maya Federman et al., "What Does It Mean to Be Poor in America?" *Monthly Labor Review,* May 1996, pp. 3–17, and table 3, "Housing Characteristics in 1992 and 1993," p. 8; U.S. Bureau of Labor Statistics, *Consumer Expenditure Survey Series: Interview Survey, 1972 and 1973,* table 1a, "Selected Family Characteristics and Annual Expenditures by Family Income Before Taxes," p. 4; U.S. Bureau of the Census, "Weighted Average Poverty Thresholds for Families of Specified Size, Historical Poverty Tables," table 1 at the Census Bureau Website, http://www.census.gov/hhes/poverty/histpov/hstpov1.html.

14–15 Access to consumer durables by poor households (and Table 1.2): Current Population Reports, P70–50RV, *Beyond Poverty, Extended Measures of Well-Being: 1992,* Household Economic Studies (November 1995); *Statistical Abstract:* various issues; Current Population Reports, series P-65, no. 33, *Consumer Buying Indicators; Residential Energy Consumption Survey, Housing Characteristics 1984,* table 25, "Fuel Use by Family Income, as of November 1984," p. 55, and table 39, "Appliance Use by Family Income as of November 1984," p. 92; Current Population Reports, series P-70, no. 26, *Extended Measures of Well-Being: Selected Data from the 1984 Survey of Income and Program Participation,* table 7-B, "Selected Housing Conditions and Consumer Durables by Household Income-to-Poverty Ratio," p. 48. The government didn't collect a broad set of data on ownership patterns by low-income households in the 1970s, so the only comparison that can be made is with 1984. However, data for the consumption of all households in 1971, as shown in Table 1.2, rule out the possibility that poor households owned more in the early 1970s than they did in 1994.

15   Access to credit cards by poor households: *Statistical Abstract: 1975,* table 772, "Percent of Families Using Credit Cards, by Income: 1970," p. 475; ibid., *1996,* table 792, "Usage of General Purpose Credit Cards by Families: 1989 and 1992," p. 516.

15   Outlays for food, clothing, and shelter by poor households: Evan Jacobs and Stephanie Shipp, "How Family Spending Has Changed in the U.S.," *Monthly Labor Review,* March 1990, pp. 20–27, particularly

table 2, "Consumption Expenditures of Urban Wage Earner and Clerical Consumer Units, 1901 to 1986–87"; U.S. Bureau of Labor Statistics, "Average Annual Expenditures and Characteristics of All Consumer Units, 1984–95," *Consumer Expenditure Survey,* 1995, obtained at the BLS Website, ftp://ftp.bls.gov/pub/special.requests/ce/standard/y8495.txt.

15   Income and consumption of low-income households in 1995 (and Table 1.3): U.S. Bureau of Labor Statistics, *Consumer Expenditure Survey, 1995,* table 1, "By Quintiles of Income Before Taxes: Average Annual Expenditures and Characteristics of All Consumer Units," as reported at the BLS Website, gopher://hopi2.bls.gov:70/00/Special%20Requests/ce/standard/1995/quintile.prn. Figures in current dollars.

16   Ownership of $300,000 homes: U.S. Department of Housing and Urban Development, U.S. Department of the Commerce, and U.S. Census Bureau, Current Housing Reports, series H150/93, *American Housing Survey for the United States in 1993,* table 2-20, "Income of Families and Primary Individuals by Selected Characteristics—Occupied Units," pp. 6–7. Figures in current dollars.

16   The poverty rate as measured by consumption: Daniel T. Slesnick, "Gaining Ground: Poverty in the Postwar United States," *Journal of Political Economy,* February 1993, pp. 1–38.

16   Consumption per person in rich and poor households: U.S. Bureau of Labor Statistics, *Consumer Expenditure Survey, 1995,* table 1, "By Quintiles of Income Before Taxes: Average Annual Expenditures and Characteristics of all Consumer Units," as reported at the BLS Website, gopher://hopi2.bls.gov:70/00/Special%20Requests/ce/standard/1995/quintile.prn. Figures in current dollars.

18   Per capita real income (and Figure 1.4): National income figures deflated using CPI-U-X1 (the urban-weighted Consumer Price Index). Department of Commerce, Bureau of Economic Analysis (BEA), *Survey of Current Business,* May 1997, table 4, "National Income and Disposition of Personal Income," p. 26; for 1997 figure, see the BEA Website, http://www.bea.doc.gov/bea/dn/pitbl.htm, accessed September 18, 1998; *Economic Report of the President,* table B-32, "Population by Age Group, 1929–96," p. 337; U.S. Bureau of Labor Statistics (CPI-U-X1).

18   Employee benefits as a percentage of payroll: U.S. Chamber of Commerce, *Employee Benefits Historical Data: 1951–1979,* table 4, "Employee Benefits as Percent of Payroll, by Type of Benefit, 1951–79," p. 11; ibid., *Employee Benefits Report,* table 6, "Employee Benefits as Percent of Payroll, by Type of Benefit and Industry Groups, 1980–1997."

18   Total compensation (and Figure 1.4): Board of Governors of the Federal Reserve System.

19   Construction of the Consumer Price Index: U.S. Bureau of Labor Statistics, "Consumer Price Indexes: Addendum to Frequently Asked Questions," from the BLS Website, http://www.bls.gov/cpiadd.htm.

19   Treatment of new goods and services by the CPI and overstatement of inflation (and Table 1.4): Senate Advisory Committee to Study the Consumer Price Index, *Toward a More Accurate Measure of the Cost of Living: Final Report to the Senate Finance Committee,* December 4, 1996; Brent R. Moulton, "Bias in the Consumer Price Index: What Is the Evidence?" *Journal of Economic Perspectives,* Fall 1996, pp. 159–177; U.S. Bureau of Labor Statistics, table 1, "The Experimental CPI Using Geometric Means, All Urban Consumers (CPI-U-XG), December 1990–Present," at the BLS Website: http://www.bls.gov/cpigmtab.htm. If one uses the Boskin Commission's (common name for the "Advisory Committee to Study the Consumer Price Index") estimates of inflationary bias, per capita personal income grew at an average annual rate of 2.6 percent since 1973, very close to the 2.8 percent from 1950 to 1973. Under the conventional inflation measure, productivity growth slumps 1.1 percent after 1973, compared with 2.3 percent from 1950 to 1973. With the Boskin correction, productivity growth posts an increase from 2.1 to 2.6 percent a year since 1973, identical to the long-term trend from 1870 to 1973. In 1997, the Department of Labor began to test an alternative CPI that corrects some of the flaws in the index. Initial readings show slightly tamer inflation. For the period December 1990 to December 1997, the new index pegged inflation at 2.3 percent a year, compared with 2.7 percent for the old measure.

20   Videocassette recorder prices: *Radio Electronics,* July 1971; *Consumer Reports,* September 1978; Sears, Roebuck catalogue, September 1990; average price of models in 1997 Sears, Roebuck and J.C. Penney catalogues.

20   Automobile tire prices: F. Lee Moore, "Index Mischief: Price Versus Cost," *Electric Perspectives,* 1978, no. 5, pp. 8–27.

20   The price of light: William D. Nordhaus, "Do Real Output and Real Wage Measures Capture Reality? The History of Light Suggests Not," Yale Cowles Foundation Discussion Paper no. 1078, September 1994.

Chapter 2
New and Improved!

23   Cost of new single-family home: National Association of Homebuilders, at NAHB Website, http://www.nahb.com/nhp.html, accessed November 11, 1998.

23   First transcontinental automobile trip: "From Ocean to Ocean by Auto in 51 Days," in *Chronicle of the 20th Century* (Liberty, Mo.: JL International Publishing, 1992 edition), p. 55.

23–24   First television broadcast: "Scot Shows Something Called Television," in *Chronicle of the 20th Century*, p. 332.

24   First commercial air travel: Kenneth Hudson, *Air Travel: A Social History* (Totowa, N.J.: Rowman and Littlefield, 1972), p. 31.

24   First open-heart bypass surgery: *The World Book Encyclopedia*, 1994, vol. 9, p. 145, s.v. "Entry 'Heart'."

24   Invention of penicillin: Peter North, *The Wall Chart of Science and Invention* (New York: Dorset Press, 1991).

24   First sales of aspirin: David Wallechinsky and Irving Wallace, *The People's Almanac #2* (New York: Bantam Books), p. 817.

25   First hand-held calculator: Texas Instruments, Inc.

25   Blockbuster Entertainment Inc.'s customers and stores: Blockbuster Entertainment Inc.

26   Top-rated TV shows October 1970–April 1972: David Wallechinsky and Irving Wallace, *The People's Almanac #3* (New York: William Morrow, 1981), p. 413.

27   Use of computers in 1996: U.S. Bureau of the Census, "Table B: Use of Computers at Home, School, and Work by Persons 18 Years and Older: October 1993" (unpublished data), at the Census Bureau Website, http://www.census.gov/population/socdemo/computer/compuseb.txt, accessed July 24, 1998.

27   Computers in American schools: *Statistical Abstract: 1997*, table 263, "Computers for Student Instruction in Elementary and Secondary Schools: 1985 and 1997," p. 171.

27   Software titles in 1998: CNET, Inc., http://www.shareware.com, accessed November 11, 1998.

27   On-line investing accounts: Stanton-Crenshaw Communications, "New On-Line Trading Service Offers Fastest Confirmation, Lowest Rates," at the Website, http://www.newsbureau.com/archives/sept97/webstreet.htm, accessed 27 July 27, 1998.

28   Videotelephone: Intel Corp.

28–29   Cellphone subscribers: Cellular Telecommunications Industry Association, press release, March 3, 1997, "The Wireless Revolution Continues: 10.2 Million Subscribers in 1996; $23.6 Billion in Revenue; 16,000 New Employees"; WOW-COM, http://www.wow-com.com/professional/pmain.cfm, accessed November 11, 1998.

29   First Federal Express overnight delivery: FedEx.

29   First satellite dishes: "Satellite Technology," http://www.satellitetech.com/basics.html, accessed July 27, 1998.

30   Organ transplants: *Statistical Abstract: 1996*, table 200, "Organ Transplants and Grafts: 1981 to 1995," p. 134; United Network for Organ Sharing, "Organ: Heart, Number of Transplants Performed

1968–1987" (unpublished data); "Numbers of U.S. Transplants—1988–1996," at the Website, http://www.unos.org/sta_tran.htm, accessed July 7, 1997; "Number of Transplants Performed from January to December 1997," at the Website, 207.87.26.13/Newsroom/critdata_main.htm, accessed July 27, 1998.

30 Average life expectancy at birth: *Statistical Abstract: 1997*, table 117, "Expectation of Life at Birth, 1970 to 1995, and Projections: 1995 to 2010."

30 Americans' ratings of their health: U.S. Department of Health and Human Services, *Health—United States—1982*, table 27, "Self-Assessment of Health and Limitation of Activity, According to Selected Characteristics: United States, 1975 and 1980," p. 80; ibid., *Health—United States—1995*, table 62, "Respondent-Assessed Health Status, According to Selected Characteristics: United States, 1987–94," p. 172.

30 Infant mortality rates: *Statistical Abstract: 1997*, table 123, "Infant, Maternal, and Neonatal Mortality Rates and Fetal Mortality Ratios, by Race: 1980 to 1994," p. 92.

30 Death rate from natural causes: U.S. Department of Health and Human Services, *Health—United States—1992*, table 28, "Age-Adjusted Death Rates for Selected Causes of Death, According to Sex and Race: United States, Selected Years 1950–90," p. 45.

31 Patient injections of own collagen: Dermatology Associates of Dallas.

31 Computing power in automobiles: Jon Bigness, "Forget Horsepower," *Dallas Morning News*, September 29, 1997, p. D2; Roger Rosenblatt, "To Be or Not to Be . . . Whatever," *Time*, December 30, 1996.

32 Vehicle miles per gallon: *Statistical Abstract: 1996*, table 1019, "Domestic Motor Fuel Consumption, by Type of Vehicle: 1970 to 1994," p. 632.

32 Ownership and development of radar detectors: Michael Van Boven, "Electronic Countermeasures on the Interstate: A Study in Variety," unpublished paper, Southern Methodist University, April 30, 1996.

32 Automobile navigating devices: *Advanced Transportation Technology News*, June 1996, http://www.itsonline.com/attn/msg00003.htm, accessed July 9, 1997.

32 Consumer assessment of overall auto quality: J. D. Power and Associates, press release, April 30, 1997, "J. D. Power and Associates Reports Dramatic Improvements in Initial Vehicle Quality," http://www.jdpower.com/70430car.htm, accessed July 9, 1997.

33 Microprocessor speed: G. Christian Hill, "Bringing It Home," *Wall Street Journal,* June 16, 1997, pp. R1, R4 (see tables "Driving Technology" and "The Technology Culture").

34   Modem speed: "Computer Deal to Raise Speed on Internet," *Dallas Morning News*, January 20, 1998, p. 1A.

34   Household television sets: TVB Resource Center, "Trends in Television," at the TVB Website, http://www.tvb.org/researchreports/trends_tv/televisionsets.htm, accessed December 6, 1997.

34   Radio and television repair shops: U.S. Bureau of the Census, *County Business Patterns 1970* (1971), table 1B, "United States, by Industry: 1970"; ibid., *County Business Patterns 1995* (1997), table 1b, "United States—Establishments, Employees, and Payroll, by Industry and Employment-Size Class: 1995," p. 67.

34   Appliance electricity usage: Association of Home Appliance Manufacturers, unpublished data on energy efficiency and consumption trends, http://www.aham.org/mfrs/stats/egy_wash.htm, http://www.aham.org/mfrs/stats/egy_ref.htm, http://www.aham.org/mfrs/stats/egy_dish.htm, http://www.aham.org/mfrs/stats/egy_rac.htm, accessed December 1, 1997.

35   Cadillac night vision: "Cadillac to Offer Night Vision Option in Year 2000 Model," *Dallas Morning News*, August 20, 1998.

36   Consumers create their own compact discs: Jennifer Steinhauer, "Custom-Made CD's on Demand at Kiosks," *New York Times*, August 24, 1998.

37   Variety of carbonated soft drinks: Ira U. Cobleigh, "Soft Drink Stocks," *The Commercial and Financial Chronicle*, January 7, 1971; Eric Sfiligoj, "Ladies and Gentlemen, and Beverages of All Ages," *Beverage World*, April 1994; Greg W. Prince, "Soft Drink All-Star Review," *Beverage World,* March 1995.

37   Variety of breakfast cereals: Jerry A. Hausman, "Valuation of New Goods Under Perfect and Imperfect Competition," in T. Bresnahan and R. J. Gordon, eds., *The Economics of New Goods* (Chicago: University of Chicago Press for NBER, 1996), pp. 209–247; Nielsen North America, "Volume, Share, and Change Ranking Report, Kroger Dallas KMS T.A., 52 Weeks Ending 12/30/95, TTL RTE Cereal" (unpublished data), March 21, 1996.

37   Variety of chips and snacks foods: Frito-Lay Co.

37   Variety of automobile styles: *CPI Value Guide to CARS of Particular Interest*, July–September 1998, CPI, Laurel, Md.

37   Variety of sport-utility vehicles: *PC Carbook,* 1998, wysiwyg://4/http://www.dealernet.com/bin/tex.html, accessed June 25, 1998.

37   Choice of television screen sizes: "'73 Solid-State and Hybrid Color TVs: What They're Like," *Popular Science*, August 1972, p. 92.

37–38 History of cable television and cable access: National Cable Television Association (NCTA), "The History of Cable Television," at the NCTA Website, http://www.ncta.com/history.html, accessed July 28, 1998; *Statistical Abstract: 1997*, table 888, "Utilization of Selected Media: 1970 to 1995," p. 566.

38 Variety of television channels: DirectTV, Inc., Los Angeles.

38 Radio stations over the Internet: AudioNet, information from their Website, http://www.audionet.com.

38 Number of new books and editions: *Statistical Abstract: 1975*, table 873, "New Books and New Editions Published, by Subject: 1960 to 1974," p. 525; ibid., *1997*, table 910, "New Books and New Editions Published and Imports, by Subject: 1990 to 1995," p. 574.

38 Retail space: International Council of Shopping Centers, National Research Bureau Shopping Center Database and Statistical Model 1997, "Shopping Center Statistics: Number of Centers and Gross Leasable Area in the U.S. by Year."

39 Consumer products entering the U.S. market in 1996: *Statistical Abstract: 1997*, table 864, "New Product Introductions of Consumer Packaged Products: 1980 to 1996," p. 552.

39 Price of a 1970 Ford Galaxie 500 and 1997 Ford Taurus: Robert Lichty, *Standard Catalog of Ford 1903–1995* (Iola, Wis.: Krause Publications, 1995), pp. 224–226; Yahoo! "New Car Guide," at the Yahoo! Website, http://autos.yahoo.com/ppage/autosaic1997fortaurus-g-f4sdn-.html, accessed August 31, 1997. Prices in current dollars.

39 Price of a McDonald's hamburger and Big Mac: McDonald's Corp.; John Love, *McDonald's: Behind the Golden Arches* (New York: Bantam Books, 1986). Prices in 1998 dollars.

39 Consumer Price Index: U.S. Bureau of Labor Statistics, "Consumer Price Index: All Urban Consumers," series ID CUUR0000SA0, data extracted from BLS website September 21, 1998.

40 Thoreau quote: Henry David Thoreau, *Walden*, chapter 1, "Economy."

40 Wage data: The hourly wage used in these calculations is that of a typical manufacturing worker, called a "production and non-supervisory worker" by the U.S. Department of Labor. In 1970, it stood at $3.35 an hour. By 1997, the hourly wage had hit an all-time high of $13.18, a livable wage but nothing worthy of *The Lifestyles of the Rich and Famous*. What's most important about these earnings is that they're representative of the great middle of American society. In calculating work prices, we ignored taxes but we also omitted fringe benefits. Today's workers take more of their compensation as health insurance, vacation, holidays, retirement plans, and other nonwage income. The extras rose from being worth an additional 19 percent of wages in 1953 to 44 percent today. Including these benefits would make today's goods and services even cheaper in work time. Data for taxes and benefits aren't available before 1950, which makes long-term comparisons impossible. What's most important, however, is that adjustments for benefits would outweigh those for taxes—so we'd find that modern consumers are better off. Moreover, American consumers are presumably getting something for their tax dollars, even if not the

dollar-for-dollar value they would like. Actually, an hour of work isn't without its vagaries—at least if we try to measure the effort and discomfort involved in doing our jobs. The majority of today's workers, sitting at computers in well-lighted offices, are sacrificing less of their energy and well-being to the accomplishment of their work than yesterday's cotton picker, coal miner, or barge hand. *Employment, Hours, and Earnings, United States, 1909–84*, vol. 1, p. 57; *Employment and Earnings*, April 1996, table B-2, p. 46; U.S. Bureau of Labor Statistics, series ID EES30000006, "Average Hourly Earnings of Production Workers," available at the BLS Website, http://www.bls.gov, accessed March 9, 1998; Whitney Coombs, *The Wages of Unskilled Labor in the Manufacturing Industries of the United States, 1890–1924* (New York: AMS, 1926), p. 162.

40　Prices of bacon, coffee, milk, ground beef, chicken, oranges, and other market-basket grocery items (and Figure 2.1): U.S. Bureau of Labor Statistics, unpublished data. Prices in current dollars.

42　New single-family home prices, square feet, and amenities: U.S. Department of Housing and Urban Development, *Characteristics of New Housing*, series C25; *Statistical Abstract*, various years. Prices in current dollars.

42　Household size: U.S. Bureau of the Census, "Households by Size, 1960 to Present, HH-4," Internet release date, May 28, 1998, at the Census Bureau Website, http://www.census.gov/population/socdemo/hh-fam/htabHH–4.txt. Average household size fell from 3.14 persons in 1970 to 2.65 in 1996. Smaller households mean that the time at work required to buy 500 square feet of new-home space *per person* fell from 3.8 years in the first half of the 1970s to under 3.6 in the early 1990s.

42　Price of a kitchen stove, clothes washer, clothes dryer: Carnegie Library of Pittsburgh, Science and Technology Department; General Electric ad "The Dollar Makes a Comeback," *Life*, June 26, 1970, pp. 18–19; Dallas area retailer, personal communication. Prices in current dollars.

42　Price of a dishwasher: Friday Historical Business Archives; *Life*, June 26, 1970; Dallas area retailer. Prices in current dollars.

42　Price of a vacuum cleaner and lawn mower: Sears, Roebuck catalogue, various years. Prices in current dollars.

42　Price of a refrigerator: Frigidaire Home Products; Sears, Roebuck catalogue. Prices in 1998 dollars.

42　Price of a mattress and box springs: Simmons Company; *Life*, July 24, 1970; Dallas area retailer. Prices in current dollars.

42　Price of a room air conditioner: *Life*, June 26, 1970; Dallas area retailer. Prices in current dollars.

42　Price of a portable radio: General Electric advertisement, *Life*, June 26, 1970; Dallas area retailer. Prices in current dollars.

42 Price of 100 kilowatt hours of electricity: *Historical Statistics,* series S 108–119, "Growth of Residential Service, and Average Prices for Electric Energy: 1902 to 1970," p. 827; U.S. Department of Energy, Energy Information Administration, *Annual Energy Review 1995,* table 8.11, "Retail Prices of Electricity Sold by Electric Utilities, 1960–1995," p. 251. Prices in current dollars.

42 Price of a Ford automobile: Lichty, *Standard Catalog of Ford 1903–1995.*

42 Price of a gallon of gasoline: American Petroleum Institute, *Basic Petroleum Factbook—Petroleum Industry Statistics* (Washington, D.C.: American Petroleum Institute, published yearly), various issues. Prices in current dollars.

44 Average miles per gallon: *Statistical Abstract: 1996,* table 1019, "Domestic Motor Fuel Consumption, by Type of Vehicle: 1970 to 1994," p. 632.

44 Price of auto rental: *Life,* July 24, 1970; Hertz Corp. Prices in current dollars.

44 Price of a movie: Motion Picture Association of America. Prices in current dollars.

44 Price of 100 miles of air travel: Air Transport Association of America; *Statistical Abstract: 1978,* table 1134, "Scheduled Air Carriers—Summary of Operations: 1950 to 1977," p. 671. Prices in current dollars.

44 Price of a seven-day Caribbean cruise: Carnival Cruise Lines. Prices in current dollars.

44 Price of dry cleaning a dress: International Fabricare Institute. Prices in current dollars.

44 Price of a man's suit: History Channel, a biography on Charles Lindbergh; Hart Marx; Dallas retailer. Prices in current dollars.

44 Price of soft contact lenses: "Soft Contact Lenses," *Consumer Reports,* May 1972, p. 272; Lens Express, Inc. Prices in current dollars.

44 Price of a large pepperoni pizza: Pizza Hut Totally New pizzas. Prices in current dollars.

44 Price of a Coca-Cola: Coca-Cola Company. Prices in current dollars.

44 Price of potato chips: Frito-Lay, Inc. Prices in current dollars.

44 Price of a McDonald's hamburger and Big Mac: McDonald's Corp.; Love, *McDonald's: Behind the Golden Arches.*

44 Price of a hand-held calculator: Texas Instruments, Inc. Prices in current dollars.

44 Price of a slide rule: Sphere Research Corporation. Prices in current dollars.

44–45 Price of a color TV: Friday Historical Business Archives; Dallas area retailer. Prices in current dollars.

45 Price of a VCR: *Radio Electronics,* July 1971; *Consumer Reports,* September 1978; Sears, Roebuck catalogue, September 1990; Sears, Roebuck catalogue average; J.C. Penney catalogue average.

45   Price of a cellular telephone: Motorola Inc. Prices in current dollars.

45   Price of a camcorder: Ritz Collectibles; Friday Historical Business Archives; Thomson Consumer Electronics, Inc. Prices in current dollars.

45   Price of a microwave oven: Amana Appliances. Prices in current dollars.

45   Price of computing power of one MIPS: International Business Machines Corporation. Prices in current dollars.

46   Price of a three-minute coast-to-coast call: *Historical Statistics*, series R 13–16, "Telephone Toll Rates Between New York City and Selected Cities: 1902 to 1970," p. 784; Federal Communications Commission, *Statistics of Communication Common Carriers,* 1993–94 edition, table 7.1, "AT&T Historical Rates at Year End, 1950 through 1993, Interstate Message Toll Telephone Rates (Five and Ten Minute Calls)," p. 255; AT&T basic long-distance rates, business day, New York–San Francisco, AT&T Corporate Archives (unpublished data). Prices in current dollars. (Some of these sources also used for Table 2.2).

46   Price of high-density TV sets: Jennifer Files, "High-Definition TVs Make Debut at Show," *Dallas Morning News,* January 8, 1998, p. 10D. Prices in current dollars.

47   Arrival of products to the marketplace: Lorraine Glennon, ed., *Our Times* (New York: Century Books, 1995); Paul Dickson, *Timelines* (Reading, Mass.: Addison-Wesley, 1991).

48   Cost of a frontal crash test and prototyping a part: Ford Motor Company, *1996 Annual Report,* pp. 7, 11. Prices in current dollars.

48   Number of car manufacturers in 1920: Tad Burnes, *Cars of the Early Twenties* (Philadelphia: Chilton Book Company, 1968), pp. 1–13; Beverly Kimes, *Standard Catalog of American Cars, 1805–1942* (Iola, Wis.: Krause Publications, 1996).

48   Output per hour: U.S. Bureau of Labor Statistics, "Major Sector Productivity and Costs Index," series ID PRS30006093, data extracted from BLS website August 23, 1998. The calculation uses the government's standard productivity statistics. It uses a conventional inflation index, not corrected for the errors of about 1 percentage point a year (see Chapter 1). If anything, it understates the gains in productivity.

49   Schumpeter quote: Joseph A. Schumpeter, *Capitalism, Socialism and Democracy* (New York: Harper & Brothers, 1950), p. 67.

49   Cost of three-minute coast-to-coast call: *Historical Statistics*, Series R 13–16, "Telephone Toll Rates Between New York City and Selected Cities: 1902 to 1970," p. 784; Federal Communications Commission, *Statistics of Communication Common Carriers,* 1993–94, table 7.1, "AT&T Historical Rates at Year End, 1950 through 1993, Interstate Message Toll Telephone Rates (Five and Ten Minute Calls)," p. 255; AT&T basic long-distance rates, business day, New York–San Fran-

cisco, AT&T Corporate Archives (unpublished data). Prices in current dollars.

49 Wages of factory workers: *Employment, Hours, and Earnings, United States, 1909–94*, vol. 1, p. 57; *Employment and Earnings*, April 1996, table B-2, p. 46; U.S. Bureau of Labor Statistics, series ID EES30000006, "Average Hourly Earnings of Production Workers," http://www.bls.gov, accessed March 9, 1998.

50–51 Price of a Hershey chocolate bar: Hershey Foods Corp. Prices in current dollars.

51 Price of a five-stick pack of Wrigley's chewing gum: Wm. Wrigley Jr. Company. Prices in current dollars.

51 Price of a pair of Levi's: Levi Strauss & Co. Prices in current dollars

51 Tuition and fees at public colleges: National Center for Education Statistics, table 312, "Average Undergraduate Tuition and Fees and Room and Board Rates Paid by Students in Institutions of Higher Education, by Type and Control of Institution: 1964–65 to 1996–97." Prices in current dollars.

51 The earnings premium for a bachelor's degree: U.S. Bureau of Labor Statistics, *Current Population Survey, March 1997,* table P-16, "Years of School Completed—Persons 25 Years Old and Over by Mean Income and Sex: 1967 to 1990," and table P-23, "Educational Attainment—Persons 25 Years Old and Over Working Year Round, Full Time by Mean Earnings and Sex: 1991 to 1996." Comparisons in constant dollars.

Chapter 3
Time for Symphonies and Softball

53 Increase in two-income families: Current Population Reports, series P60, no. 80, *Income in 1970 of Families and Persons in the United States*, table 12, "Fifths of Families Ranked by Size of Money Income, by Selected Characteristics: 1950, 1960, and 1970," p. 25; ibid., no. 193, *Money Income in the United States: 1995*, table 4, "Median Income of Families by Selected Characteristics, Race, and Hispanic Origin of Householder: 1995, 1994, and 1993," p. 13.

53 Two-income families, where both husband and wife hold jobs: Bureau of the Census, *Money Income in the United States: 1997*, table 4, "Median Income of Families by Selected Characteristics, Race, and Hispanic Origin of Householder: 1997, 1996 and 1995," p. 13.

54 1996 NBC-*Wall Street Journal* poll: Ellen Graham and Cynthia Crossen, "The Overloaded American: Too Many Things to Do, Too Little Time to Do Them," *Wall Street Journal*, March 8, 1996.

54–55 Length of the workday and workweek (and Tables 3.1 and 3.2): Jeremy Atack and Fred Bateman, "How Long Was the Average Workday in 1880?" *Journal of Economic History*, March 1992, pp. 129–160; Edward F. Denison, *Why Growth Rates Differ* (1967), p. 363; Theresa

Dis Greis, *The Decline of Annual Hours Worked in the United States Since 1947*, Manpower and Human Resources Studies, no. 10, The Wharton School (Philadelphia: University of Pennsylvania Press, 1984); *Employment, Hours, and Earnings, United States, 1909–94*, vol. 1, pp. 3–4; *Employment and Earnings*, various years; Angus Maddison, *Dynamic Forces in Capitalist Development* (New York: Oxford University Press, 1991), p. 270; ibid., *Economic Growth in the West*, p. 228; *Worldbook Encyclopedia*, 1993, vol. 12, p. 11, s.v. "Entry 'Labor Movement.'" The Department of Labor measures the workweek by the unambiguous standard of hours employers pay for, not what workers say they work. Time-diary studies suggest the typical worker puts in even less time than the official statistics show.

55 Vacations, holidays, and other absenteeism (and Tables 3.1 and 3.2): Jane Hatch, *The American Book of Days* (New York: H. Wilson, 1978), pp. 8, 502–503, 621–622, 818–819, 1012, 1059, 1146; John E. Buckley, "Variations in Holidays, Vacations, and Area Pay Levels," *Monthly Labor Review*, February 1989, pp. 24–30; *Employment and Earnings*, January 1997, p. 215, table 44, "Absences from Work of Employed Full-Time Wage and Salary Workers by Age and Sex"; see also *Employment and Earnings*; Janice Neipert Hedges, "Absence from Work—Measuring the Hours Lost," *Monthly Labor Review*, October 1977, pp. 16–23; *Worldbook Encyclopedia*, vol. 10, p. 107.

55 1997 *U.S. News & World Report* poll: Amy Saltzman, "When Less Is More," *U.S. News & World Report*, October 27, 1997.

55–56 Average daily time devoted to household chores (and Table 3.2): Robert Eisner, *The Total Incomes System of Accounts* (University of Chicago Press, 1989), p. 65.

56 Average age at which people begin work (and Table 3.2): *Statistical Abstract: 1996*, table 271, "High School Dropouts by Age, Race, and Hispanic Origin: 1970 to 1994"; table 273, "Employment Status of High School Graduates and School Dropouts: 1980 to 1993"; table 279, "College Enrollment of Recent High School Graduates: 1960 to 1994"; table 283, "College Population by Selected Characteristics: 1987 and 1994"; and table 299, "Time Spent Earning Bachelor's Degree, by Selected Characteristics: 1993."

56 Proportion of high-school graduates who continue their education (and Table 3.2): *Statistical Abstract: 1996*, table 279, "College Enrollment of Recent High School Graduates: 1960 to 1994," p. 180; ibid., *1978*, table 259, "High School Graduates and College Enrollment of Persons 20–24 Years Old, by Sex and Race: 1960 to 1977," p. 160.

56 Median number of years to graduate from college (and Table 3.2): *Statistical Abstract: 1996*, table 299, "Time Spent Earning Bachelor's Degree, by Selected Characteristic: 1993," p. 191.

56 Retirement age (and Table 3.2): Murray Gendell and Jacob S. Siegel, "Trends in Retirement Age by Sex, 1950–2005," *Monthly Labor Review,* July 1992, pp. 22–28.

56–57 Life expectancy (and Table 3.2): *Historical Statistics,* series B 116–125, "Expectation of Life at Specified Ages, by Sex and Race: 1900 to 1970," and series B 126–135, "Expectation of Life at Specified Ages, Sex, for Massachusetts: 1850 to 1949–51;" *Statistical Abstract 1997,* table 118, "Selected Life Table Values: 1979 to 1994," p. 88; National Center for Health Statistics, *Monthly Vital Statistics Report,* September 11, 1997, table 16, "Expectation of Life by Age, Race and Sex: United States, final 1995 and preliminary 1996," p. 31.

57 Proportion of high-school graduates who continue their education up from 25.4 percent in 1970: *Statistical Abstract: 1996,* table 279, "College Enrollment of Recent High School Graduates: 1960 to 1994," p. 180; ibid., *1978,* table 259, "High School Graduates and College Enrollment of Persons 20–24 Years Old, by Sex and Race: 1960 to 1977," p. 160.

57 Average net worth of retirement-age Americans: Board of Governors of the Federal Reserve System, "Survey of Consumer Finances, 1983: A Second Report," *Federal Reserve Bulletin,* December 1984, pp. 857–868 (see especially p. 862), and "Family Finances in the U.S.: ibid., "Recent Evidence from the Survey of Consumer Finances," *Federal Reserve Bulletin,* January 1997, pp. 1–24 (see especially p. 6). Figures in constant (1997) dollars.

57 Exercise among the elderly: *Statistical Abstract: 1996,* table 414, "Participation in Selected Sports Activities: 1994," p. 259.

57 Entertainment and reading among older Americans: Ibid., table 402, "Expenditures per Consumer Unit for Entertainment and Reading: 1985 to 1994," p. 253.

57 Workweek of women who don't work outside the home: Eisner, *Total Incomes System of Accounts,* p. 65.; *Employment, Hours, and Earnings, United States, 1909–94,* vol. 1, pp. 3–4; for figures for later years, see *Employment and Earnings.*

58 Net effect on the overall workforce: *Statistical Abstract: 1996,* table 616, "Employment Status of the Civilian Population: 1960 to 1995," p. 395, and table 619, "Civilian Labor Force—Percent Distribution, by Sex and Age: 1960 to 1995," p. 396.

58 Moonlighting: John F. Stinson, Jr., "Multiple Jobholding Up Sharply in the 1980s," *Monthly Labor Review,* July 1990, pp. 3–10; *Employment and Earnings,* June 1996, table A-35, "Multiple Jobholders by Selected Demographic and Economic Characteristics," p. 63; John F. Stinson, Jr., "New Data on Multiple Jobholding Available from the CPS," *Monthly Labor Review,* March 1997, pp. 3–8; Thomas Amirault, "Char-

acteristics of Multiple Jobholders, 1995," *Monthly Labor Review*, March 1997, pp. 9–15.

58–59   University of Maryland time-diary surveys: John p. Robinson and Geoffrey Godbey, *Time for Life* (University Park: Pennsylvania State University Press, 1997).

59   Per capita recreational and amusement spending: *Statistical Abstract: 1996*, table 401, "Personal Consumption Expenditures for Recreation Expenditures in Real (1992) Dollars: 1970 to 1994," p. 252; Current Population Reports, series P60–193, *Money Income in the United States: 1995,* table B-1, "Annual Average Consumer Price Index (CPI-U): 1947 to 1995," 1996, p. B-2. Figures in constant (1997) dollars.

59   Money allocated to fun and games: *Statistical Abstract: 1993*, table 699, "Personal Consumption Expenditures, by Type of Expenditure, in Current and Constant (1987) Dollars: 1970 to 1991," p. 44; ibid., *1996,* table 695, "Personal Consumption Expenditures in Current and Real (1992) Dollars, by Type, 1980 to 1994," p. 450.

59–60,   Americans who play golf or bowl, the number of adult softball
61   teams, and movie attendance: *Statistical Abstract: 1987*, table 376, "Selected Recreational Activities: 1970 to 1985," p. 217; ibid., *1996*, table 413, "Selected Recreational Activities: 1975 to 1994," p. 258.

60   Number of golf courses: *Statistical Abstract: 1987*, table 376, "Selected Recreational Activities: 1970 to 1985," p. 217; unpublished data, National Golf Foundation.

60   Attendance at big-league sports events: *Statistical Abstract: 1986,* table 392, "Selected Spectator Sports: 1970 to 1984," p. 229; ibid., *1996,* table 412, "Selected Spectator Sports: 1985 to 1994," p. 257.

60   Average ticket prices at big-league sports: Annual survey conducted by Team Marketing Support in Chicago, Illinois. Prices in current dollars.

60   NASCAR's Winston Cup customers: NASCAR Headquarters, Daytona Beach, Florida.

60   Television contracts for football, basketball, and baseball: *Dallas Morning News*, August 26, 1998, p. B1. Figures in current dollars.

60   Attendance at symphonies and orchestras: *Statistical Abstract: 1993*, table 416, "Performing Arts—Selected Data: 1970 to 1991," p. 256; ibid., *1996,* table 421, "Performing Arts—Selected Data: 1980 to 1994," p. 263.

60   Number of books sold: Book Industry Study Group, Inc. (BISG), press release, "21st Edition of Book Industry TRENDS 1998: Study Calls Online Bookselling the Issue for the Year," at the BISG Website, http://www.bookwire.com/bisg/trends–98.html, accessed September 23, 1998; *Books in Print* database, R. R. Bowker.

61 Time spent watching television: *Statistical Abstract: 1989,* table 900, "Utilization of Selected Media: 1960 to 1988," p. 544; ibid., *1996,* table 878, "Media Usage and Consumer Spending: 1989 to 1999," p. 562; John p. Robinson and Geoffrey Godbey, *Time for Life,* p. 145; TVB Resource Center, "Time Spent Viewing," at the TVB Website, http://www.tvb/org/researchreports/trends_tv/timespent.html, accessed July 18, 1998.

61 Number of stores and malls: *Statistical Abstract: 1996,* table 1254, "Retail Trade Establishments—Number, Sales, Payroll, and Employees, by Kind of Business: 1987 and 1992," p. 763, and table 1270, "Shopping Centers—Number, Gross Leasable Area, and Retail Sales, by Gross Leasable Area: 1990 to 1994," p. 772.

61 Number of pleasure trips: *Statistical Abstract: 1976,* table 367, "Volume and Characteristics of Travel: 1972," p. 222; ibid., *1997,* table 430, "Characteristics of Business Trips and Pleasure Trips: 1985 to 1995," p. 265.

61 Visits to national parks, monuments, seashores, and recreational areas: *Statistical Abstract: 1997,* table 402, "National Park System— Summary: 1985 to 1995," p. 250; ibid., *1976,* table 351, "National Park System—Summary: 1950 to 1975," p. 214.

61 Volunteer work: *Statistical Abstract: 1996,* table 608, "Percent of Adult Population Doing Volunteer Work: 1993," p. 387.

62 Wives who work outside the home: *Statistical Abstract: 1975,* "Married Women (Husband Present) in the Labor Force, by Age and Presence of Children: 1950 to 1974," p. 347; ibid., *1996,* table 625, "Marital Status of Women in the Civilian Labor Force: 1960 to 1995," p. 399. In 1970, there were 12,795,500 women aged 20 to 39 at work. Today, they would make up the 45-to-64-year-old group, and there are 16,221,500 of them at work, an increase of 3,426,000 in a total labor force of 132,304,000.

62 Average workweek of yesterday's housewife: Eisner, *Total Incomes System of Accounts,* p. 65.

63 Spending on food at restaurants: Evan Jacobs and Stephanie Shipp, "How Family Spending Has Changed in the U.S.," *Monthly Labor Review,* March 1990, pp. 20–27, especially chart 1, "Percent Distribution of the Family Food Budget Between Food at Home and Away, 1909 to 1986–87," p. 23; U.S. Bureau of Labor Statistics, *Consumer Expenditure Survey,* table 2, "By Income Before Taxes: Average Annual Expenditures and Characteristics of All Consumer Units," as reported at the BLS Website, 1995gopher://hopi2.bls.gov:70/00/ Special%20Requests/ce/standard/1995/income.prn; National Restaurant Association (NRA), *1997 Restaurant Industry Pocket Factbook,* available at the NRA Website, http://www.restaurant.org/research/ pocket/index.htm.

63   Demand for take-out food: National Restaurant Association, "'Tis the Season to Eat Out—Holiday-Dining Update, Fast Food Figures," available at the NRA Website, http://www.restaurant.org/RUSA/.

63   Home production as a share of market GDP: Eisner, *Total Incomes System of Accounts,* p. 73.

64   The income contribution of working women: *Statistical Abstract: 1975,* table 603, "Median Annual Earnings of Full-Time Workers, by Sex and Occupation: 1962 to 1973," p. 370; ibid., *1996,* table 668, "Workers Paid Hourly Rates, by Selected Characteristics: 1995," p. 429.

64   1996 Gallup Poll on job satisfaction: Gallup Organization, Inc., "Gallup Poll Shows Unexpected Job Satisfaction," at the Website, http://www.inc.com/beyondthemag/between_the_pp./gallup.html.

65   Work-related deaths: National Safety Council, *Accident Facts,* 1996, pp. 36–37; *Employment and Earnings*, January 1997, table 1, "Employment Status of the Civilian Noninstitutional Population, 1933 to Date," p. 158.

65   Work-related accidents: Bureau of Labor Statistics, Health and Safety Statistics, table 4, "Occupational Injury and Illness Incidence Rates per 100 Full-Time Workers, 1973–95," at the BLS Website, http://stats.bls.gov:80/news.release/osh.t04.htm.

65   The most dangerous industries and their share of total employment: *Statistical Abstract: 1995*, table 613, "Recordable Occupational Injury and Illness Rates, by Industry: 1972 and 1974," p. 376; Bureau of Labor Statistics, Health and Safety Statistics, table 1, "Nonfatal Occupational Injury and Illness Incidence Rates per 100 Full-Time Workers, (1) by Industry Division, 1995," at the BLS Website, http://stats.bls.gov:80/news.release/osh.t01.htm; *Statistical Abstract: 1996*, table 641, "Employment, by Industry: 1970 to 1994," p. 410; *Accident Facts, 1971,* p. 23.

65   Workers with unemployment insurance: Social Security Administration, *Annual Statistical Supplement, 1996, to the Social Security Bulletin*, table 3.B2, "Total Earnings and Wages and Salaries in Employment Covered by Selected Social Insurance Programs, 1946–94," p. 161.

65   Workers with employer-paid health care: Figures refer to medical coverage. *Statistical Abstract: 1974*, table 459, "Public and Private Employee Benefit Plans-Summary: 1950 to 1970," p. 289; Ann Foster, "Employee Benefits in the United States, 1993–94," *Compensation and Working Conditions* (Bureau of Labor Statistics), Spring 1997.

65   Employees' out-of-pocket payments for health-care costs: *Statistical Abstract: 1996*, table 154, "National Health Expenditures: 1960 to 1994," p. 111.

65   Workers covered by employee-sponsored retirement plans: *Statistical Abstract: 1975*, table 471, "Employee-Benefit Plans—Summary:

1950 to 1973," p. 294; ibid., *1996*, table 671, "Employee Benefits in Private Establishments: 1993 and 1994," p. 431.

65 Fringe benefits as a proportion of total wages: U.S. Chamber of Commerce, *Employee Benefits Historical Data: 1951–1979*, table 4, "Employee Benefits as Percent of Payroll, by Type of Benefit, 1951–79," p. 11; ibid., *Employee Benefits Report*, table 6, "Employee Benefits as Percent of Payroll, by Type of Benefit and Industry Groups."

65 Length of time the average worker has been on the job: Bureau of Labor Statistics, table 1, "Median Years of Tenure with Current Employer for Employed Wage and Salary Workers by Age and Sex, Selected Years, 1983–96," at the BLS Website, http://stats.bls.gov/news.release/tenure.t01.htm.

66 Fraction of the labor force unemployed for 15 weeks or more: Labor force statistics from the *Current Population Survey*, series ID LFU224001800000, "Number Unemployed for 15 weeks Over," and series ID LFU40000000, "Civilian Labor Force Level," at the BLS Website, 146.142.4.24/cgi-bin/surveymost accessed September 22, 1998 .

66 Probability of holding a job for a full decade: Francis X. Diebold, David Neumark, and Daniel Polsky, "Job Stability in the United States," NBER Working Paper no. 4859, September 1994.

66 Jobs taken away versus jobs created: "Worker Displacement During the Mid-1990s," *News* (Bureau of Labor Statistics), August 22, 1996.

66 Workers covered by maternity leave, paternity leave, and child care: Bureau of Labor Statistics, "Employee Benefits Survey," at the BLS Website, http://stats.bls.gov:80/cgi-bin/surveymost.

66 Time at which Americans travel to work: U.S. Bureau of the Census, "Time Leaving Home to Go to Work for the United States: 1990 Census," table at the Census Bureau Website, http://www.census.gov/population/socdemo/journey/usdeptim.txt.

66 Hewitt Associates survey on flexible hours, job sharing, four-day scheduling, and working at home: Hewitt Associates, press release, July 22, 1998, "Hewitt Study Shows Increase in Work and Family Benefits," September 22, 1998, at the Hewitt Website, http://www.hewitt.com/news/pressrel/1998/07–22–98w.htm; "Changing Times: Compressed Week Winning Followers in Workforce," *Dallas Morning News*, September 28, 1998, p. 1D.

66 The ranks of telecommuters: JALA International, Inc., at the JALA Website, http://www.well.com/user/jala/qanda.htm.

67 Time-diary studies on leisure pursuits on the job: John P. Robinson and Ann Bostrom, "The Overestimated Workweek? What Time Diary Measures Suggest," *Monthly Labor Review*, August 1994, pp. 11–23; James Patterson and Peter Kim, *The Day America Told the*

Truth, 1991, chapter 22, "American Workers Get to Tell the Truth," p. 155.

Chapter 4
By Our Own Bootstraps

69   Executive compensation at the nation's largest 350 companies: Joann S. Lublin, "Pay for No Performance," *Wall Street Journal*, April 9, 1998, pp. R1–R4. Figures in 1998 dollars.

70   Distribution of income by quintiles in 1996 (and Figure 4.1): Bureau of the Census, series P60–197, *Money Income in the United States: 1997 (With Separate Data on Valuation of Noncash Benefits)* (Washington, D.C.: GPO, 1997), table B, "Selected Measures of Household Income Dispersion: 1967 to 1997," p. xi.

70–71   Allotment of income since 1975 (and Figure 4.2): ibid., and table B-1, "Annual Average Consumer Price Index (CPI-U): 1947 to 1996," p. B-2, and table B-3, "Share of Aggregate Income Received by Each Fifth and Top 5 Percent of Households by Race and Hispanic Origin of Householder: 1967 to 1996," p. B-6.

72–73   University of Michigan's Panel Survey on Income Dynamics and research on income mobility (also Tables 4.1–4.3 and Figure 4.3): *A Panel Study of Income Dynamics* (Ann Arbor: University of Michigan, Institute for Social Research); "By Our Own Bootstraps: Economic Opportunity and the Dynamics of Income Distribution," Federal Reserve Bank of Dallas, *1995 Annual Report,* pp. 2–23. The conclusions come from a sample of 3,725 respondents to the University of Michigan survey from 1975 to 1991. This may seem small, but most social science relies on similar-sized, or even smaller, slices of the population. Even the Census Bureau's studies of income distribution rely on a relatively few people, rather than the entire country. Not all respondents are suitable for testing income mobility. The focus is on the employed, the unemployed, students, and retirees. Those at home maintaining a family aren't included, largely because the decision is a personal one, saying little about the economy's opportunities. Also left out are minors, prisoners, the military, the permanently disabled, and the mentally ill. Respondents couldn't be included unless they reported their income every year over a long period of time. Using the standard government definition, income includes wages, investment earnings, pensions, government transfers such as Social Security benefits, unemployment benefits, and welfare. The University of Michigan's income data before 1975 aren't compatible with later observations. Figures reported are in constant (1997) dollars.

74   Median duration of poverty spells and the long-term poverty rate: Current Population Reports, series P70–45, Martina Shea, *Dynamics*

of Economic Well-Being: Poverty, 1991 to 1993, table D, "Poverty Status, by Employment and Disability Status: 1991 and 1992," p. 6.

76–77   Treasury Department income mobility study (and Figure 4.4): "Household Income Changes Over Time: Some Basic Questions and Facts," *Tax Notes* (U.S. Department of the Treasury, Office of Tax Analysis), August 24, 1992, pp. 1065–1073.

79   Average income of blacks compared to whites: Current Population Reports, series P60–197, *Money Income in the United States: 1996,* table 8, "Selected Characteristics of Persons—Total Money Income in 1996 of Persons 15 Years Old and Over by Work Experience in 1996 and Sex," pp. 30–33; ibid., series P60–97, *Money Income in 1973 of Families and Persons in the United States* (Washington, D.C.: GPO, 1975), table 60, "Work Experience and Total Money Income in 1973—Civilians 14 Years Old and Over, by Race and Sex," pp. 131–132.

79   Proportion of African-American families earning more than $75,000 annually: Current Population Reports, series P60–197, *Money Income in the United States: 1996,* table B-4, "Families by Total Money Income, Race, and Hispanic Origin of Householder: 1967 to 1996," p. B-10. Figures based on current dollars.

79   Number of black-owned and Hispanic-owned businesses: Census Bureau, table B "Comparison of Number of Firms and Business Receipts of Minority-Owned Firms to Total Business Activity," based on data from IRS statistics of income for 1967; ibid, "Minority-Owned Firms Compared to All U.S. Firms by State: 1992," "Black-Owned Firms Compared to All U.S. Firms by State: 1992," "Hispanic-Owned Firms Compared to All U.S. Firms by State: 1992," "Women-Owned Firms Compared to All U.S. Firms by State: 1992," from Census Bureau Website, accessed November 13, 1998; Bureau of Economic Advisors, *Survey of Current Business,* August 1998, table 3, "Price Indexes and the Gross Domestic Product and Gross Domestic Purchases Implicit Price Deflators," p. 159.

79   African-American companies with revenues of $100 million or more: Ronald J. Alsop, ed., *The Wall Street Journal Almanac, 1998* (New York: Ballantine Books, 1997), p. 235. Calculations based on current dollars.

79   College enrollment among African-Americans and Hispanics: *Statistical Abstract: 1993,* table 272, "College Enrollment, by Sex, Age, Race, and Hispanic Origin: 1972 to 1991," p. 174; ibid., *1997,* table 300, "College Population, by Selected Characteristics: 1987 and 1995," p. 190.

79   Blacks' representation in high-paying professions: Alsop, *Wall Street Journal Almanac, 1998,* p. 319.

79   Layoff rate for blacks: Robert Fairlie and Lori G. Kletzer, "Race and the Shifting Burden of Job Displacement: 1982–93," *Monthly Labor Review*, September 1996, p. 15.

79–80   Hispanics' median weekly earnings: *Statistical Abstract: 1997,* table 666, "Full-Time Wage and Salary Workers—Number and Median Weekly Earnings, by Selected Characteristics: 1983 to 1987," p. 406; *Employment and Earnings,* January 1997, table 37, "Median Weekly Earnings of Full-Time Wage and Salary Workers by Selected Characteristics," p. 204.

80   Rate at which women are starting businesses and number of female executive vice presidents: "Women's Figures," *Wall Street Journal,* January 1, 1997, p. A14.

80   Women-owned businesses in the United States: Diana Furchtgott-Roth and Christine Stolba, *Women's Figures* (Arlington, Va.: Independent Women's Forum, 1996), p. xii; *Statistical Abstract: 1977,* table 897, "Women-Owned Firms—Number and Receipts, by Industry: 1972," p. 552; U.S. Census Bureau, "Women-Owned Firms Compared to All U.S. Firms by State: 1992," at the Census Bureau Website, http://www.census.gov/agfs/smobe/view/w_pr.txt, accessed May 4, 1998.

80   Top management positions held by women at major corporations: "Room at the Top for Women," *American Demographics*, July 1996, pp. 28–37.

80   Business traveling by women, and women Porsche buyers: *Advertising Age,* November 10, 1997, p. 24.

80   Women managers and professionals, professors, lawyers, police officers, and detectives: Barbara H. Wooton, "Gender Differences in Occupational Employment," *Monthly Labor Review*, April 1997, pp. 16–17.

80   College enrollment of females versus males: *Statistical Abstract: 1997,* table 298, "College Freshmen—Summary Characteristics: 1970 to 1996," p. 189; ibid., *1996,* table 300, "Earned Degrees Conferred, by Level and Sex, with Projections: 1950 to 2006," p. 191.

80   Women earning Ph.D.s, and law, dental, and medical degrees: Furchtgott-Roth and Stolba, *Women's Figures,* pp. 18–20.

81   Number of women on-line: Find/SVP, "Gender Gap Narrows in Internet Use," July 1997; ZD Internet MegaSite-CyberStats, July 1997 statistics, at the Website, wysiwyg://203/http://search.zdnet.com/zdimag/cyberstats/1997/07/gap.html, accessed May 5, 1998.

81   Earnings of women relative to men for full-time wage and salary workers and by age: Bureau of Labor Statistics, table A-1, "Usual Weekly Earnings of Employed Full-Time Wage and Salary Workers by Age, Sex, Race, and Hispanic Origin, 1996, Annual Averages" (unpublished data).

81   Proportion of working wives who earn more than their husbands: Bureau of Labor Statistics, *Current Population Survey, March 1988–96,* "Wives Who Earn More Than Their Husbands, 1987–95."

81   Earnings of women aged 27 to 33 who have never had children relative to men of the same age: Furchtgott-Roth and Stolba, *Women's Figures,* p. vi.

81   Percentage of women versus men who aspire to be chief executive: Ibid., p. 7.

81   Median number of years women leave the labor force: Joyce P. Jacobsen and Laurence M. Levin, "Effects of Intermittent Labor Force Attachment on Women's Earnings," *Monthly Labor Review,* September 1995, pp. 14–19.

81–82   Marital status and earnings of women who work at home: Linda N. Edwards and Elizabeth Field-Hendrey, "Home-Based Workers: Data from the 1990 Census of Population," *Monthly Labor Review,* November 1996, pp. 26–34.

81   Earnings comparisons adjusted for differences in education: Current Population Reports, series P60–184, *Money Income of Households, Families, and Persons in the United States: 1992* (Washington, D.C.: GPO, 1993), table 29, "Educational Attainment—Total Money Earnings in 1992 of Persons 25 Years Old and Over, by Age, Race, Hispanic Origin, Sex, and Work Experience in 1992," p. 120.

83   Earnings of men in 1951, 1973, and 1993 by age (and Figure 4.5): U.S. Bureau of Labor Statistics, *Current Population Survey,* table P-4, "Age—Persons 15 Years Old and Over, by Median and Mean Income, and Sex: 1947 to 1993" (unpublished data). The figures are for men only. Data for women in 1951 are incomplete.

85   College graduation and high school dropouts among the top and bottom fifths of income earners: Current Population Reports, series P60–184, *Money Income of Households, Families, and Persons in the United States: 1992,* table 15, "Percent Distribution of Families, by Selected Characteristics Within Income Quintile and Top 5 Percent in 1992," p. 46; *Statistical Abstract: 1997,* table 726, "Money Income of Families—Percent Distribution, by Income Quintile and Top 5 Percent: 1995," p. 470.

85–86   Median household income by education: Current Population Reports, series P60–197, *Money Income in the United States: 1996,* table 2, "Selected Characteristics—Households by Total Money Income in 1996," p. 6.

86   Annual weeks worked by income quintile: Current Population Reports, series P60–184, *Money Income of Households, Families, and Persons in the United States: 1992,* table 3, "Percent Distribution of Households, by Selected Characteristics Within Income Quintile and Top 5 Percent in 1992," p. 7.

86 Percent of part-time workers seeking full-time work: U.S. Department of Labor, *Employment and Earnings*, March 1998, table A-7, "Employed Persons by Marital Status, Occupation, Class of Worker, and Part-Time Status, Seasonally Adjusted," p. 13.

86 Minimum wage of $5.15 an hour: *Federal Register*, February 24, 1998, pp. 9235–9238.

86 Median assets of households by income quintile: Current Population Reports, series P70–47, T. J. Eller and Wallace Fraser, *Asset Ownership of Households: 1993* (Washington, D.C.: GPO, 1995), table C, "Percent of Households Owning Assets and Median Value of Holdings by Monthly Household Income Quintile for Selected Asset Types: 1993 and 1991." Figures in 1997 dollars.

86 Sources of income for the elderly by income quintile: Employee Benefit Research Institute, *Baby Boomers in Retirement: What Are Their Prospects?* SR–23, Issue Brief no. 151, July 1994, table 6, "Sources of Income of the U.S. Population Aged 65 and Over by Income Quintile, Selected Years 1974–1992," p. 12.

86 Prevalence of nonfamily households by income quintile: *Statistical Abstract: 1997,* table 721, "Money Income of Households—Percent Distribution, by Income Quintile and Top 5 Percent: 1995," p. 467.

86 Unemployment rates by city: Bureau of Labor Statistics, table 1, "Civilian Labor Force and Unemployment by State and Metropolitan Area" (unpublished data), available at the BLS Website, http://www.bls.gov/news. release/metro.t01.htm, accessed May 7, 1998.

87 Hourly wage rates by occupation: *Employment and Earnings*, March 1998, table B-15, "Average Hours and Earnings of Production or Nonsupervisory Workers on Private Nonfarm Payrolls by Detailed Industry," pp. 98–117.

87 Wage premium for knowing how to operate a computer: Alan B. Krueger, "How Computers Have Changed the Wage Structure: Evidence from Microdata, 1984–1989," *Quarterly Journal of Economics*, February 1993, pp. 33–60.

87 Income by age: Current Population Reports, series P60–197, *Money Income in the United States: 1996*, table 2, "Selected Characteristics—Households by Total Money Income in 1996," p. 5. Figures in 1997 dollars.

88 Experimental economy of unemployed Canadians in 1970: Raymond C. Battalio, John H. Kagel, and Morgan O. Reynolds, "Income Distribution in Two Experimental Economies," *Journal of Political Economy*, vol. 85, no. 6, 1977, pp. 1259–1271.

Chapter 5
Still on Top of the World

91 First prototype VCR: Steve Schoenherr, "Recording Technology History," February 22, 1998, at the Website, http://ac.acusd.edu/History/ recording/notes.html, accessed May 8, 1998.

92–93   America's economic growth compared to Japan's: Organisation for Economic Co-operation and Development, Website, http://www.oecd.org/std/gdp.htm, accessed May 7, 1998.

93   Goods and services where the United States still ranks as the top producer: Ralph T. King, "High-Tech Edge Gives U.S. Firms Global Lead in Computer Networks," *Wall Street Journal*, September 9, 1994, p. A1.

93   U.S. and foreign semiconductor production: Semiconductor Industry Association, "Chip Industry Statistics," at their Website, http://www.semichips.org/indstats/shares.htm, accessed May 8, 1998.

93   Share of world auto output produced by Detroit's Big Three: "World Auto Production Led by US Companies," *IGN Newsletter*, August 1996, at the IGN Website, http://www.pangaea.net/IGN/NEWS0016.HTM, accessed November 22, 1997.

93   GDP by country: Department of Commerce, Bureau of Economic Analysis, news release on gross domestic product, table 3, "Real Gross Domestic Product and Prices: Change from Preceding Period," at Website, http://www.bea.doc.gov/bea/dn/niptbl-d.htm, accessed May 7, 1998.

93   United States and foreign income and job creation (and Table 5.1): Organisation for Economic Co-operation and Development (OECD), "GDP per Capita in US dollars, in 1996," at the OECD Website, http://www.oecd.org/std/gdpperca.htm, accessed May 9, 1998; U.S. Bureau of Labor Statistics, "Comparative Civilian Labor Force Statistics, Ten Countries, 1959–1997," at the BLS Website, ftp://146.142.4.23/pub/special.requests/foreignLabor/flslforc.txt, accessed May 7, 1998.

93   The 15 most profitable companies worldwide: "The Fortune Global 5 Hundred," *Fortune*, August 4, 1997, pp. F-1–F-11.

93   Productivity among major industrial nations: Bureau of Labor Statistics, table 3, "Real GDP per Employed Person 1993 Benchmark EKS PPPs/1 (1996 U.S. Dollars)" (unpublished data), published at the BLS Website, ftp://146.142.4.23/pub/special.requests/ForeignLabor/flsgdp.txt, accessed May 8, 1998.

93–94   The world's fastest computer: John Markoff, "U.S. Regains Top Spot as Maker of Fastest Supercomputers," *New York Times*, Internet edition, November 17, 1997.

94   U.S. share of world computing power: International Institute for Management Development, *The World Competitiveness Yearbook 1997* (Lausanne, Switzerland: IMD, 1997).

94   Exports, by nation: *Statistical Abstract: 1997*, table 1384, "Foreign Trade—Source of Imports and Destination of Exports, by Country: 1994," p. 857. The United States makes up 24 percent of the work economy and Japan 12 percent. Each can sell in its home market, of course, but these goods are not counted as exports. Thus, the United States has only 76 percent of the world economy to export to, compared to Japan's 88 percent.

94   Overall economic performance as evaluated by the World Economic Forum: International Institute for Management Development, *The World Competitiveness Yearbook 1997*, table on p. 19, "The World Competitiveness Scoreboard." Japan was at the top of the World Economic Forum rankings for much of the 1980s and early 1990s. In 1996, it ranked ninth and the United States ranked first. Coming after the United States are Singapore, Hong Kong, Finland, Norway, the Netherlands, Switzerland, and Denmark.

94   Hourly compensation of U.S. and Japanese manufacturing workers: Bureau of Labor Statistics, table 2, "Hourly Compensation Costs in U.S. Dollars," at the BLS Website, http://stats.bls.gov/news.release/ichcc.t02.htm, accessed September 24, 1998. Wage comparisons in current dollars.

95   Dollar's value relative to the yen from 1985 to 1995: International Monetary Fund, *International Financial Statistics*, June 1998.

95   Japan's per capita income in 1995 in current dollars and current exchange rates: Organisation for Economic Co-operation and Development, *OECD National Accounts, Main Aggregates, Volume 1*, March 1997.

95   U.S. and Japanese per capita income based on purchasing power parities and constant (1997) dollars: Organisation for Economic Co-operation and Development, "GDP per Capita in US dollars, in 1996," at the OECD Website, http://www.oecd.org/std/ gdpperca.htm, accessed May 9, 1998.

Sources for Table 5.2 begin here

95   Appliance ownership: Current Population Reports, Kathleen Short and Martina Shea, "Beyond Poverty, Extended Measures of Well-Being: 1992," November 1995; *Japan Almanac 1993–Ashahi Shimbum*; *Statistical Abstract: 1996*, table 1339, "Percent of Households Owning Selected Appliances, by Country: 1990–1991," p. 838.

95   TV, phone, and cell phone ownership: *Statistical Abstract: 1997*, table 1354, "Telephones, Newspapers, Television, and Radio, by Country," p. 842.

96   Computer ownership: International Institute for Management Development, *The World Competitiveness Yearbook 1997*, "Technological Infrastructure 5.12. Computers per Capita 1996," p. 409.

96   Auto ownership: Ibid., table 1340, "Motor Vehicle Registrations, by Country: 1993," p. 838, and table 1341, "Motor Vehicle Miles of Travel for Selected Countries," p. 838; *Statistical Abstract: 1993*, table 1374, "Population, by Country, 1980, 1990, and 1993, and Projections, 2000," pp. 840–841.

96   Competitiveness ranking: International Institute for Management Development (IMD), "World Competitiveness On-Line: The World

Competitiveness Scoreboard, Rankings as of April 19, 1998," at the IMD Website, http://www.imd.ch/wcy/factors/overall.html, accessed May 11, 1998.

96 Unemployment rate: Organisation for Economic Co-operation and Development, press release, April 15, 1997, "Standardised Unemployment Rates."

96 Long-term unemployment rate: Ibid., *The OECD Jobs Study: Part 1, Evidence and Explanations* (Paris: OECD, 1994), table 1, "The Profile of OECD Unemployment," p. 14.

96 Job growth: Bureau of Labor Statistics, "Comparative Civilian Labor Force Statistics, Ten Countries, 1959–1996" (prepared September 1997), table 2, "Civilian Labor Force, Employment, and Unemployment, 1959–1996."

96 GDP per capita: Organisation for Economic Co-operation and Development, *OECD National Accounts, Main Aggregates, Volume 1*, January 1998, "GDP per Capita in US dollars, in 1996."

96 Life expectancy, crude death rate, and suicide rate: *Statistical Abstract: 1997*, table 1336, "Vital Statistics, by Country: 1997 and 2000," pp. 832–833, and table 1339, "Death Rates, by Cause and Country," p. 834.

96 College-educated population: Organisation for Economic Co-operation and Development, *The Condition of Education in 1997*, International Indicators Project, supplemental table 23-1, "Percentage of the Population Who Had Completed Secondary and Higher Education, by Sex, Country, and Age: 1994," at U.S. National Center for Education Statistics Website, nces.ed.gov/pubs/ce/c9723d01.html, accessed May 12, 1998.

96 High-tech employment, R&D scientists, old-age dependency ratio, and earnings of women relative to men: Organisation for Economic Co-operation and Development, *The OECD Jobs Study: Part 1, Evidence and Explanations* (Paris: OECD, 1994), table 4.13, "Employment in High-Technology Manufacturing Industries," p. 150; table 4.18, "R&D Scientists and Engineers," p. 156; table 1.13, "Ageing of the Population and Future Labour Force Trends," p. 24; table 1.10, "Earnings Differentials by Education, Age, and Gender," p. 20.

96 Tax rate for social security: *Statistical Abstract: 1997*, table 1357, "Employee-Employer Payroll Tax Rates for Social Security Programs, by Country: 1981 to 1996," p. 843.

96 American and foreign net financial wealth per capita: Organisation for Economic Co-operation and Development, *Financial Accounts of OECD Countries, United States 1955–1996*, p. 127; *Italy 1989–1996*, p. 34; *Spain 1981–1996*, p. 59; *Sweden 1980–1995*, p. 57; *Germany 1981–1996*, p. 41; *France 1981–1996*, p. 59; *Belgium 1980–1995*, p. 49; *Japan 1981–1996*, p. 43; table 33B, "Outstanding

Financial Assets and Liabilities of Sectors N.E.I."; *Statistical Abstract: 1997*, table 1385, "Foreign Exchange Rates: 1996," p. 858; ibid., *1996*, table 1325, "Population, by Country: 1980 to 2000," pp. 827–829; Organisation for Economic Co-operation and Development, OECD Main Economic Indicators, "Purchasing Power Parities," obtained at the OECD Website, http://www.oecd.org, accessed October 3, 1998. Figures are net financial wealth for 1996, except for the figures for Sweden and Belgium, which are for 1995. Data for Switzerland, Denmark, the Netherlands, and the United Kingdom are unavailable. Figures are in 1997 dollars and on a "purchasing-power parity" basis.

96 Occupational injury rate and injury death rate: International Labour Office (ILO), *1996 Yearbook of Labour Statistics* (Geneva: ILO, 1996), table 8A, "Occupational Injuries: Persons Injured, by Economic Activity."

96 Big Mac price in minutes of work: "McCurrencies: Where's the Beef?" *The Economist*, April 27 1996, p. 82, and Bureau of Labor Statistics, table 6, "Hourly Direct Pay in National Currency for Production Workers in Manufacturing, 29 Countries or Areas, 1975–1996," data compiled January 1998.

96 Student-to-teacher ratio: National Center for Education Statistics, *The Digest of Education Statistics 1996*, table 390, "Pupils per Teacher in Public and Private Elementary and Secondary Schools, by Level of Education: Selected Countries, 1985 to 1992."

96 Student-to-computer ratio: *Statistical Abstract: 1997*, table 263, "Computers for Student Instruction in Elementary and Secondary Schools: 1985 and 1997," p. 171; National Center for Education Statistics, *Education Indicators: An International Perspective*, table 29, "Percentage of Schools Using Computers for Instructional Purposes and Median Student/Computer Ratio, by Level of Education and by Country: 1989."

96 Pace of life: Robert Levine, "The Pace of Life in 31 Countries," *American Demographics*, November 1997.

96 Nobel Prizes: International Institute for Management Development, *The World Competitiveness Yearbook 1997*, "Scientific Environment table 2.27 Nobel Prizes, 1996."

Sources for Table 5.2 end here

96 U.S. share of world GDP in 1950 and the 1990s: Angus Maddison, *Dynamic Forces in Capitalist Development* (New York: Oxford University Press, 1991), p. 198; *Statistical Abstract: 1997*, table 1347, "Gross National Product, by Country: 1985 to 1995," p. 838.

96 Size of the American economy in 1950 and 1995: U.S. Department of Commerce, Bureau of Economic Analysis, *Survey of Current Business*, August 1997, table 2A, "Real Gross Domestic Product," p. 152.

99 U.S. merchandise trade, services trade, and capital flows (and table 5.3): *Statistical Abstract: 1996,* table 1283, "U.S. International Transactions, by Type of Transaction: 1980 to 1995," pp. 784–785; U.S. Department of Commerce, Bureau of Economic Analysis (BEA), "U.S. International Transactions (Millions of Dollars, Seasonally Adjusted)," at the BEA Website, http://www.bea.doc.gov/bea/di/trans1.htm, accessed May 12, 1998. In 1997, the U.S. trade deficit was 2.5 percent of gross national product. In that sense, it's not a world record. Other countries, with much smaller economies, have racked up even larger deficits as a portion of total output. Figures in current dollars.

99 Japan's merchandise trade surplus with the United States: U.S. Bureau of the Census, "U.S. Trade with Japan," at the Census Bureau Website, http://www.census.gov/foreign-trade/sitc1/1997/c5880.htm, accessed May 12, 1998. Figures in current dollars.

99 China's merchandise trade surplus with the U.S.: U.S. Bureau of the Census, "U.S. Trade with China," at the Census Bureau Website, http://www.census.gov/foreign-trade/sitc1/1997/c5700.htm, accessed May 12, 1998. Figures in current dollars.

101 Direct investment in the United States from foreign countries during the mid-1990s: International Institute for Management Development, *The World Competitiveness Yearbook 1997,* "Foreign Direct Investments 2.27. Direct Investments Stocks Inward." Figures in current dollars.

102 Ricardo's theory of comparative advantage: John Eatwell, Murray Milgate, and Peter Newman, eds., *The New Palgrave: A Dictionary of Economics* (London: Macmillan, 1987), vol. 4, pp. 183, 194, s.v.

103–104 The U.S. trade deficit and economic performance, 1980–1987: Daniel T. Griswold, "America's Maligned and Misunderstood Trade Deficit," CATO Institute Center for Trade Policy Analysis, no. 2, Washington, D.C., April 24, 1998.

104 Commerce Department study on wages in export industries, and average U.S. tariff rate: "If Free-Trade Opponents Win This Week, You Lose," *USA Today,* November 4, 1998, p. 23A.

106 Smoot-Hawley tariff: Jude Wanniski, *The Way the World Works* (New York: Simon & Schuster, 1978), table 7, "The Stock Market and the Wedge," pp. 116–148.

106 Growth in per capita income in the United States and Japan (and Figure 5.1): U.S. Bureau of Economic Analysis, *Survey of Current Business,* August 1997, p. 160, table 3, "Price Indexes and the Gross Domestic Product and Gross Domestic Purchases Implicit Price Deflators"; Organisation for Economic Co-operation and Development, *National Accounts, Main Aggregates, Volume 1, 1960–1995,* (Paris: OECD, 1997), p. 153, table 2, "GDP per Capita."

106 Growth rates of Asian nations: World Bank, *The State in a Changing World: World Development Report 1997* (New York: Oxford University Press, 1997), pp. 234–235, table 11, "Growth of the Economy."

106 Per capita GDP in China: International Institute for Management Development, *The World Competitiveness Yearbook 1997*, "Value Added 1.09, GNP Per Capita (PPP) 1995." Figures in 1997 dollars.

107 Japanese and U.S. economic growth in the 1960s, 1970s, 1980s, and 1990s: Maddison, *Dynamic Forces in Capitalist Development*, table A.8, "Movement in GDP, 1950–1989," pp. 218–219, and table B.4, "Mid-Year Population, Annual Data, 1950–1989," pp. 238–239; Bureau of Labor Statistics, table 1, "Real GDP per Capita" (unpublished data), at the BLS Website, ftp://146.142.4.23/pub/special. requests/ForeignLabor/flsgdp.txt, accessed May 13, 1998.

Chapter 6
The Upside of Downsizing

112 Jobs cut at General Motors, IBM, Sears, AT&T: Allen Sloan, "The Hit Men," *Newsweek*, February 26, 1996, pp. 44–46. The numbers represent the layoffs as announced in the extensive newspaper and television coverage, not the total number of jobs companies cut in the 1990s. At General Motors, for example, employment fell from 761,400 in 1990 to 647,000 in 1996. The actual declines in employment: 133,000 at IBM, 125,000 at Sears, and 143,000 at AT&T, a company adjusting to competition after its breakup in 1984. The reports at the time, although trying to be apocalyptic, actually underestimated the job cutting at many big companies.

112 U.S. Department of Labor survey on workers dismissed, 1990–1995: "Worker Displacement During the Mid-1990's," *News* (Bureau of Labor Statistics), August 22, 1996.

112 Unemployment rate lowest since 1969: Bureau of Labor Statistics, "Economy at a Glance" (unpublished data), at the BLS Website, http://www.bls.gov/eag.table.html, accessed June 22, 1998; *Economic Report of the President, 1997*, p. 330, table B-42, "Civilian Unemployment Rate, 1950–97."

112–113 Labor force reductions at Eastman Kodak, AT&T, Woolworth's, Citicorp, International Paper, Raytheon, and Levi Strauss: Challenger Gray and Christmas, "Why Layoffs are Getting Lighter," *Fortune*, March 2, 1998, p. 224; John J. Keller, "AT&T's Armstrong Is Expected to Cut as Much as 15% of Staff," *Wall Street Journal*, January 22, 1998, p. A3; Associated Press, "Report: Raytheon to Cut 10,000 Jobs," *New York Times*, January 20, 1998.

113 Job cuts involving 50 or more workers: Bureau of Labor Statistics, table 1, "Mass Layoff Events and Initial Claimants for Unemploy-

ment Insurance, October 1996 to March 1998" (unpublished data), at the BLS Website, http://www.bls.gov/news.release/mmls.t01.htm, accessed June 23, 1998.

113 Jobs gained at Wal-Mart, Home Depot, Circuit City, Office Depot, EDS, Microsoft, Hewlett-Packard, Sun Microsystems, Compaq, Silicon Graphics, Dell, Gateway 2000, MCI, Sprint, Airtouch Communications, 360 Communications, and Nextel Communications (and Table 6.1): Standard & Poor's Compustat. A national roster of employment by company doesn't exist. The best proxy is a database of publicly held companies, which provide annual reports on the number of workers. Although observations are available for 9,400 companies, the data miss an even larger number of smaller units. There's every reason to believe that privately held firms also had a lot of job cutting and creation.

113 Employment in the cellular business: Cellular Telecommunications Industry Association, "The Cellular Telecommunications Industry Association's Annualized Wireless Industry Data Survey Results," at the association's Website, http://www.wow-com.com/professional/reference/graphs/gdtable.cfm, accessed June 27, 1998.

113 Domestic employment in automotive companies: Bureau of Labor Statistics, "EMPL. LEVEL Motor vehicles & mtr. veh. equip.," labor force statistics from the *Current Population Survey,* series ID LFU11121900000, at the BLS Website, http://146.142.4.24/cgi-bin/dsrv, accessed June 23, 1998.

113 Americans working at Japanese auto dealerships: Japan Automobile Manufacturers Association, press release, September 29, 1997, "Nearly Seventy Percent of Japanese Vehicles Sold in US are Built in America—JAMA Report Outlines Results of $14 Billion Commitment Over Two Decades," at Website, http://www.japanauto.com/library/press/pr_1997/pr_093097.htm, accessed June 26, 1998.

115 Job growth by company size (and Table 6.2): Cognetics, Inc., Cambridge, Massachusetts.

115 Jobs created in the United States from 1982 to 1997: U.S. Bureau of Labor Statistics, *Current Population Survey,* series ID LFU11000000, "EMPL.LEVEL—Civilian Labor Force," at the BLS Website, http://146.142.4.24/cgi-bin/surveymost, accessed September 25, 1998. From 1964 to 1979, the country created 30 million jobs, the next biggest employment burst. The 48 percent increase coincided with the Baby Boom's arrival in the labor force en masse, a factor that in and of itself stimulated growth.

116 Schumpeter quote: Joseph Schumpeter, *Capitalism, Socialism, and Democracy*, 3rd ed. (New York: Harper & Brothers, 1950), p. 83.

117 Employment by occupation, 1900 to 1997 (and Tables 6.3, 6.4, and 6.7): *Employment and Earnings*, January 1998, table 11, "Employed

Persons by Detailed Occupation, Sex, Race, and Hispanic Origin," pp. 174–179 (see also this table number in various other issues); *Historical Statistics*, series D 233–682, "Detailed Occupation of the Economically Active Population: 1900 to 1970," pp. 140–145.

117 Employment and wages of Webmasters: "Webmaster gaining credibility as a career," *The Record*, November 3, 1997, p. H10; "Backlash Against Title of Webmaster," *WebWeek*, September 15, 1997; Kathy Chin Leong, "Web Skills @ a Premium," *Communications Week*, November 25, 1996, p. 75.

117–118 Total employment in America: U.S. Bureau of Labor Statistics, *Current Population Survey*, "EMPL.LEVEL—Civilian Labor Force," labor force statistics from the series ID LFU11000000, at the BLS Website, http://146.142.4.24/cgi-bin/surveymost, accessed September 25, 1998.

121 Department of Labor projections on job growth, 1994 to 2005: George T. Silvestri, "Occupational Employment to 2005," *Monthly Labor Review*, November, 1995, pp. 60–84.

123 Company "churn," 1917 to 1997 (and Table 6.5): Standard & Poor's Compustat.

123 Robert Fulton's *Clermont* and the first viable steam locomotive: Franklin Folsom, *Impatient Armies of the Poor* (Niwot: University Press of Colorado, 1991), p. 5; Isaac Asimov, *Asimov's Chronology of Science and Discovery* (New York: Harper & Row, 1989), pp. 260, 283.

124 Americans employed in water transport: U.S. Bureau of the Census, *Special Reports: Occupations at the Twelfth Census* (Washington, D.C.: GPO, 1904), table 5, "Number of Persons Credited to the Various Occupation Designations Used at the Censuses of 1850 and 1860, Arranged According to the Classification of Occupations in 1900," p. 1v.

124 Carriage and harness makers in 1900: U.S. Bureau of the Census, *Census of Manufacturers 1914* (Washington, D.C.: GPO, 1919), table 2, p. 755, and table 80, p. 713.

124 Blacksmiths in 1910: *Historical Statistics: Colonial Times to 1970, Bicentennial Edition* (Washington, D.C.: GPO, 1975), series D 233–682, "Detailed Occupation of the Economically Active Population: 1900 to 1970," p. 142.

124 Number of Americans working on the railroads (and Figure 6.1): *Historical Statistics*, series Q 398–409, "Railroad Employment and Wages, and Accidents and Fatalities: 1890 to 1970," pp. 739–740; U.S. Bureau of Labor Statistics, "National Employment, Hours and Earnings," series ID EEU41401101, "Class I Railroads, All Employees," at the BLS Web Site, accessed July 2, 1998.

124–125 Employment in automobile-related industries and in aviation: U.S. Bureau of the Census, *County Business Patterns 1995* (Washington, D.C.: GPO, 1997); *Employment and Earnings*, January 1998, table 14,

"Employed Persons by Detailed Industry, Sex, Race, and Hispanic Origin," pp. 187–191.

125 Pony Express, telegraph, transcontinental railroads, and telephone service: Robert Famighetti, ed., *The World Almanac and Book of Facts 1997* (Mahwah, N.J.: K-III Reference Corp., 1996), pp. 500–501.

125 Airmail: R. E. G. Davies, *Airlines of the United States Since 1914* (Washington, D.C.: Smithsonian Institution Press, 1972), pp. 38–39.

125–126 Overnight delivery: Gerald Gunderson, *The Wealth Creators* (New York: Truman Talley Books, 1989), pp. 250–251.

126 Fax machines: Peter North, *The Wall Chart of Science and Invention* (New York: Dorset Press, 1991).

126 Employment at America Online: America Online "Careers," http://www-db.aol.com/corp/careers/, accessed July 5, 1998.

128 Agricultural workers as a share of total employment: *Historical Statistics*, series D 167–181, "Labor Force and Employment, by Industry: 1800 to 1960," p. 139; *Employment and Earnings*, January 1998, table 11, "Employed Persons by Detailed Occupation, Sex, Race, and Hispanic Origin," pp. 174–179.

128–129 Volume of long-distance phone calls and long-distance rates (and Table 6.7): *Historical Statistics*, series R 1–12, "Telephones and Average Daily Conversations (Bell and Independent Companies): 1876–1970," p. 783; Federal Communications Commission, *Statistics of Communications Common Carriers*, 1995–96 ed., table 2.6, "Telephone Calls and Minutes for Reporting Local Exchange Carriers—Year Ended December 31, 1996," p. 26; ibid., table 7.1, "AT&T Historical Rates at Year End, 1950 through 1994," p. 289; U.S. Bureau of Labor Statistics, data from "National Employment, Hours, and Earnings," series ID EEU30000006, "Average Hourly Earnings of Production Workers," at the BLS Website, accessed June 27, 1998. The calculation is based on the work time required for a typical manufacturing employee to pay for a five-minute daytime residential call from New York to Los Angeles. The call cost 40.3 minutes of pay in 1970, and 7 minutes in 1994. Under some bargain plans available in 1997, the cost of the call dropped to as little as 3 minutes.

129–130 Employment and output in textiles and apparel, steel, coal mining, railroad transport, manufacturing (and Table 6.8): U.S. Bureau of Labor Statistics, data from National Employment, Hours, and Earnings, series IDs EEU32230001, EEU32220001, EEU31331001, EEU10120001, EEU41400001, EEU30000001, "Major Sector Multifactor Productivity Index," series ID MPU312304, MPU312204, MPU300004, PIUL42503, PIUL01703, PIUL72603, data extracted from the BLS Website on June 27, 1998; Office of Productivity and Technology, Data from Industry Productivity Database, at the BLS

Websites, ftp://ftp.bls.gov/pub/special.requests/opt/dipts/outhiin.txt and ftp://ftp.bls.gov/pub/ special.requests/opt/dipts/outaiin.txt, accessed September 26, 1998.

129–130 Agriculture: Employment data is from U.S. Bureau of Labor Statistics, Current Population Survey, series LFU11102000000, extracted from BLS Website on June 27, 1998. Output data calculated from *Statistical Abstract: 1978,* table 721, "National Income Without Capital Consumption Adjustments, by Industrial Origin: 1960 to 1977," p. 446; Bureau of Economic Advisors, *Survey of Current Business,* August 1997, table 2A, "Real Gross Domestic Product," p. 152, and Sherlene Lum and Robert Yuskavage, "Gross Product by Industry, 1947–96," Bureau of Economic Advisors, *Survey of Current Business,* November 1997, table 11, "Gross Domestic Product by Industry Group in Current Dollars, 1947–96," and table 12, "Real Gross Domestic Product by Industry Group, 1977–96," p. 32.

130–132 Employment, sales, and stock prices of ten downsized companies in the 1990s (and Table 6.9): Standard & Poor's Compustat; Dow Jones News Retrieval Service. Productivity in this study is calculated as output per worker, rather than the usual output per hour. The financial gains would be larger with dividends. At 3.13 percent, the dividend yield for the 10 stocks outperformed the S&P 500's 2.88 percent for the same period. After reinvesting all dividends, a $100 investment at year-end 1990, spread evenly across all 10 firms, would have grown to $269.16 (average annual rate of 21.9 percent), compared with $214.95 (16 percent per year) for the S&P 500. The $58,000 potential output gain per rehired worker comes from dividing GDP by employment. It assumes, of course, that companies invest in the capital equipment necessary to make these employees as productive as those already employed.

133–134 Letter from Martin Van Buren to President Andrew Jackson (and Figure 6.2): Sylvia Simmons, *How to Be the Life of the Podium* (New York: Amacom, 1991), p. 78. It has been widely debated whether Martin Van Buren actually wrote such a letter to Andrew Jackson. Robert J. McCloskey, "Bogus Letter," *The Washington Post,* October 7, 1983, p. A22. Regardless of the letter's authenticity, the lesson is the same.

136 Minimum wages in Europe: Organisation for Economic Co-operation and Development, "*The OECD Jobs Study: Part II, The Adjustment Potential of the Labour Market*" (Paris: OECD, 1994), pp. 1–61. Figures in current dollars.

136 Jobs added in the United States and Europe since 1990: U.S. Bureau of Labor Statistics, *Current Population Survey,* series ID LFU1100000, "EMPL. LEVEL-Civilian Labor Force," at the BLS Website, accessed June 27, 1998; Organisation for Economic Co-operation and Devel-

opment, *OECD Economic Outlook* (Paris: OECD, 1997), annex table 23, "Labour Force, Employment and Unemployment," p. A26.

136 Unemployment rates in the United States and the European Community: Organisation for Economic Co-operation and Development, *OECD Economic Outlook*, annex table 22, "Standardised Unemployment Rates," p. A25.

136 Long-term unemployment in the United States and, European Community: Organisation for Economic Co-operation and Development, *The OECD Jobs Study: Evidence and Explanations* (Paris: OECD, 1994), table 1, "The Profile of OECD Unemployment," p. 14.

Chapter 7
Somebody Always Flipped Hamburgers

140–141 The categorization of goods versus services: Office of Management and Budget, *Standard Industrial Classification Manual 1987* (Springfield, Va.: National Technical Information Service, 1987).

141 Employment in agriculture, mining, manufacturing, construction, and services, 1800 to 1997 (and Figure 7.1): *Historical Statistics*, series D 11–25, "Labor Force Status of the Population: 1870 to 1970," p. 127; series D 127–141, "Employees on Nonagricultural Payrolls, by Major Industry Divisions: 1900 to 1970," p. 137; series D 152–166, "Industrial Distribution of Gainful Workers: 1820–1940," p. 138; and series D 167–181, "Labor Force and Employment, by Industry: 1800 to 1960," p. 139; Bureau of the Census, *Historical Statistics: 1789–1945* (Washington, D.C.: GPO, 1949), series D 47–61, "Labor Force—Industrial Distribution of Gainful Workers (NBER): 1820 to 1940," p. 64; series D 62–76, "Labor Force—Industrial Distribution of Employed (NICB): 1900 to 1945," p. 65; *Employment and Earnings*, March 1998, table A-1, "Employment Status of the Civilian Noninstitutional Population 16 Years and Over, 1964 to Date," p. 6, and table B-1, "Employees on Nonfarm Payrolls by Major Industry, 1947 to Date," p. 45.

141 Output in services industries as a share of total GDP: U.S. Bureau of Economic Analysis, *Survey of Current Business*, November 1997, table 12, "Real Gross Domestic Product by Industry Group, 1977–96," p. 32.

143 Occupations by industry, 1972 and 1997 (and Table 7.1): *Employment and Earnings*, September 1982, table B-17, "Employed Persons by Industry and Occupation, 1972–81," p. 632; ibid., June 1998, table A-21, "Employed Persons by Industry and Occupation."

143 Number and size of service-producing establishments: U.S. Bureau of the Census, *County Business Patterns 1995* (Washington, D.C.: GPO, 1997), table 1b, "United States—Establishments, Employees, and Payroll, by Industry and Employment-Size Class: 1995."

143 Wages of NBA players: *U.S. News &,World Report*, July 13, 1998, p. 42. Figures in current dollars.

144–145 Wages in various service occupations: John W. Wright, *The American Almanac of Jobs and Salaries*, 1997–98 edition (New York: Avon Books, 1996); Helen S. Fisher, *American Salaries and Wages Survey*, 4th ed. (Detroit: Gale, 1997). Figures in current dollars.

145 Average weekly hours and hourly wages by industry (and Figure 7.3): *Employment and Earnings*, March 1998, table B-2, "Average Hours and Earnings of Production or Nonsupervisory Workers on Private Nonfarm Payrolls by Major Industry, 1964 to Date," pp. 46–48, and table B-12, "Employees on Nonfarm Payrolls by Detailed Industry," pp. 66–77. Wage figures in current dollars.

145 Unemployment rates in the service sector: *Employment and Earnings*, March 1998, table A-29, "Unemployed Persons by Occupation and Sex," p. 36.

145 Union membership in service industries: *Statistical Abstract: 1997*, table 691, "Union Members, by Selected Characteristics: 1983 and 1996," p. 442.

146 Employment in fast-food establishments: U.S. Bureau of the Census, *County Business Patterns 1995* (Washington, D.C.: GPO, 1997), table 1b, "United States—Establishments, Employees, and Payroll, by Industry and Employment-Size Class: 1995," p. 56; ibid., *1992 Census of Retail Trade* (Washington, D.C.: GPO, 1995), table 1, "Sales Size of Establishments: 1992."

146–147 Wages, employee age, average workweek, and employee tenure in fast-food restaurants: Robert W. Van Giezen, "Occupational Wages in the Fast-Food Restaurant Industry," *Monthly Labor Review*, August 1994, pp. 24–30. Figures in current dollars.

147 First jobs at McDonald's: John Love, *McDonald's: Behind the Golden Arches* (New York: Bantam Books, 1986).

148–149 Household consumption of goods versus services by income (and Figure 7.4): U.S. Bureau of Labor Statistics, *Consumer Expenditure Survey, 1995,* table 2, "By Income Before Taxes: Average Annual Expenditures and Characteristics of All Consumer Units." Figures in 1997 dollars.

149 Per capita spending on goods versus services, 1947–97 (and Figure 7.4): *Economic Report of the President, 1997,* table B-16, "Personal Consumption Expenditures, 1959–97." Figures in 1997 dollars.

149 Spending on goods versus services by country (and Figure 7.4): United Nations, *National Accounts Statistics: Main Aggregates and Detailed Tables, 1991* (New York: United Nations, 1993), pp. 878–879, 1228, 1539, 1675, 1843; Organisation for Economic Co-operation and Development, *National Accounts, Detailed Tables, Volume 2, 1975–1987.* pp. 9, 33, 61, 163, 183, 211, 265, 403, 501. Figures in 1997 dollars.

149 Engel's Law: John Eatwell, Murray Milgate, and Peter Newman, eds., *The New Palgrave: A Dictionary of Economics* (New York: Stockton Press, 1987), s.v. "Engel, Ernst," pp. 142–144.

149 Price of services relative to goods (and Figure 7.5): U.S. Department of Commerce, Bureau of Economic Analysis, *Survey of Current Business*, August 1998, table 1, "Gross Domestic Product," and table 3, "Price Indexes and the Gross Domestic Product and Gross Domestic Purchases Implicit Price Deflators."

153–155 Employment in household, personal, and information services (and Figure 7.6): Author's own categories, based on data from *Employment and Earnings*, March 1998, table B.12, "Employees on Nonfarm Payrolls by Detailed Industry," pp. 66–77. See also the same table in earlier issues.

153–154 Persons ages 16 and over per household: Figures based on total population aged 16 and over and labor force participation rate, and total households. *Economic Report of the President, 1997*, table B-34, "Population, Employment, Wages, and Productivity," p. 321, and table B-39, "Civilian Labor Force Participation Rate and Employment/Population Ratio, 1950–97," p. 327; Current Population Reports, series P20–509, HH-1. "Household and Family Characteristics: March 1997" and "Households by Type: 1940 to Present," at the Census Bureau Website, http://www.census.gov/population/socdemo/hh-fam/htabHH-i.txt, accessed August 16, 1998.

Chapter 8
The Economy at Light Speed

159 Top 10 inventions and discoveries of modern times (and Table 8.1): Authors' own appraisal based on the extent of technology spillovers to other industries and products.

160 Telegraph operators: *Historical Statistics*, series D 233–682, "Detailed Occupation of the Economically Active Population: 1900 to 1970," p. 141.

160 First powered flight: Isaac Asimov, *Asimov's Chronology of Science and Discovery* (New York: Harper & Row, 1989), p. 426.

161 Diffusion of personal computers (and Figure 8.1): Robert Famighetti, ed., *The World Almanac and Book of Facts 1998* (Mahwah, N.J.: K-III Reference Corp., 1997), p. 650, "U.S. Computer Sales and Ownership, 1984–1997" (figures from Electronic Industries Association, Arlington, Virginia).

161 Diffusion of cellular phones (and Figure 8.1): Cellular Telephone Industry Association.

161 First mass-produced autos, horses versus cars in the 1920s, and auto diffusion (and Figure 8.1): *Historical Statistics*, series K 564–582, "Livestock—Number, Value per Head, Production and Price:

1867–1970," p. 519; series Q 148–162, "Motor Vehicle Factory Sales and Registrations, and Motor Vehicle Usage: 1900–1970," p. 716; and series Q 175–186, "Percent Distribution of Automobile Ownership, and Financing: 1947–1970," p. 717.

161 Diffusion of telephone service (and Figure 8.1): Ibid., series R 1–12, "Telephones and Average Daily Conversations: 1826 to 1970," p. 783.

161 Diffusion of electric power (and Figure 8.1): Ibid., series S 108–119, "Growth of Residential Service, and Average Prices for Electric Energy: 1902 to 1970," p. 827.

161 Diffussion of television (and Figure 8.1): Ibid., series R 93–105, "Radio and Television Stations, Sets Produced, and Households with Sets: 1921 to 1970," p. 796.

161 Diffusion of other products (and Figure 8.1): W. Michael Cox and Richard Alm, "The Economy at Light Speed: Technology and Growth in the Information Age and Beyond," Federal Reserve Bank of Dallas, *1996 Annual Report;* "Time Well Spent: The Declining *Real Cost of Living in America*," Federal Reserve Bank of Dallas, *1997 Annual Report.*

162 Jacquard's loom: Otto Johnson, ed., *Information Please Almanac* (Boston: Houghton Mifflin, 1994), pp. 552–553.

162 Invention of the typewriter and electric lighting: Asimov, *Asimov's Chronology of Science and Discovery*, pp. 351, 369.

162 Invention of the television: Peter North, *The Wall Chart of Science and Invention* (New York: Dorset Press, 1991).

162 Invention of the microprocessor: Famighetti, *The World Almanac and Book of Facts 1998,* p. 638; Dean Takahashi, "Yet Another 'Father' of the Microprocessor Wants Recognition," *Wall Street Journal,* September 22, 1998, p. B6.

163 Biologists identification of new proteins: J. Willett, "Memorandum Regarding Outcome of Molecular Biosciences and Technology Institute External Insights Meeting, 12/4/95," meeting held at Micro Biosciences and Technology Institute, George Mason University; memo at university Website, http://mbti.gmu.edu/DEC14MTG.html, accessed January 13, 1997.

163 Work time required to buy a PC: International Business Machines Corp.

164 The 400 richest Americans and how they got that way: "Vision's the Thing," *Forbes,* October 17, 1994.

165 Nobel Prize winners: International Institute for Management Development, *The World Competitiveness Yearbook 1997* (Lausanne, Switzerland: IMD, 1997), "Scientific Environment 7.12, Nobel Prizes, 1996."

166 Uses of lasers: U.S. National Ignition Facility, "All About Lasers," at Website, http://lasers.llnl.gov/lasers/about.html, accessed January

13, 1997; Coherent Medical Group, "Aesthetic Surgery," at Website, http://www.cohr.com/cmg/cmg_aesth.html, accessed January 8, 1997; Doug Abrahams, "Radiance Dreams of Cleaning Up with Laser Technology," *Washington Times*, September 29, 1997.

166 Use of optics technology: W. Wayt Gibbs, "Bandwidth, Unlimited," *Scientific American*, January 1997, p. 41; Nick Doran and Ian Bennion, "Optical Networks to Span the Globe," *Physics World*, November 1996, pp. 35–39; Michael Meyer, "Why Size Doesn't Matter," *Newsweek*, August 10, 1998, p. 44.

166 Use of holography: *Holography News* (published by Reconnaissance Holographics Ltd.); "Discover Awards 1996 Finalists," *Discover*, April 1996; at *Discover* Website, http://www.dc.enews.com/magazines/discover/a96st.html, accessed January 15, 1997; "Holograms on Your Hard Drive?" *Business Week*, April 15, 1996, p. 77.

166 Uses of photonics: Ingrid Wickelgren, "Sunup at last for Solar?" *Business Week*, July 24, 1995, p. 84.

166 Artificial intelligence: "Sandia deploys intelligent agents," *Intelligent Manufacturing*, February 1996; Steve Lohr, "I.B.M. Opens the Doors of Its Research Labs to Surprising Results," *New York Times*, July 13, 1998.

167 General Electric: Geanne Rosenberg, "A Lawyer Minus the Briefcase," *New York Times*, November 10, 1997.

167 Body scans: Ann Eisenberg, "If the Shoe Fits, Click It," *Wall Street Journal*, August 13, 1998, p. D1.

167 Recognition technology: "New Technique Checks Signatures," *Dallas Morning News*, March 25, 1996; "ATM Makes an Eyes-Only Security Check," *Dallas Morning News*, May 28, 1996; Ginger Orr, "New Voice Software Gives Students a Helping Hand," *Chicago Tribune*, March 23, 1998.

167 Virtual reality: John Toon, "High-Tech Therapy," *Research Horizons* (Georgia Institute of Technology), Spring 1995.

167 Noise-reduction technology: "Headsets to Hush the Hospital Noise," *Business Week*, October 7, 1996, p. 159.

167 Robotics: "Robotic Arm Shortens Operative Times, Reduces Costs," *Minimally Invasive Surgical Nursing*, Summer 1996, and Computer Motion, Inc.

167 Integration technology: "PictureTel Receives Patent for Its Dynamic Speaker-Locating Technology," *Business Wire*, August 17, 1998.

168 Nanotechnology: John Carey, "Science's New Nano Frontier," *Business Week*, July 1, 1996, pp. 101–102. Neil Gross and Otis Port, "The Next Wave," *Business Week*, August 31, 1998.

168 Micromachines: Kaigham Gabriel, "Engineering Microscopic Machines," *Scientific American*, September 1995, p. 150; Bill Andrews, "Getting the Bugs Out," *Challenge Magazine* (UCLA), 1996.

168 Materials science: "Ceramic in Wonderland," *The Economist*, April 27, 1996, p. 88; Joseph Weber, "This Compound Can Take the Heat," *Business Week*, June 10, 1996, p. 109.

168 Iridium's satellite phone service: Kevin Maney, "3,000 Gadget Might Be Globe-Trotters' Best Friend," *USA Today*, September 17, 1998, p. B1.

168 *Global Positioning System:* John Carey, "Tilling the Soil by Satellite," *Business Week*, December 11, 1995, p. 112; Phil Scott, "Never Get Lost Again," *Reader's Digest*, August 1996, pp. 55–59; Otis Port, "Look Ma, No Hands," *Business Week*, August 14, 1995, pp. 80–81.

169 Human Genome Project: Michael Gruber, "Map the Genome, Hack the Genome," *Wired*, October 1997, pp. 152–156, 194–198; National Institutes of Health, *The Human Genome Project: New Tools for Tomorrow's Health Research*, NIH, Washington, D.C., September 1992; "Mapping Genes: Government Project Plans to Finish Its Work by 2003," *Chicago Tribune*, September 22, 1998.

169 Bionics: Victoria Griffith, "A Helping Hand," *Financial Times*, September 30, 1997, p. 20

169 Biotechnology: Neil Gross, "Extreme Enzymes," *Business Week*, April 1, 1996, pp. 84–86; Ruth Sorelle, "Explorer for Artery Research," *Houston Chronicle*, July 31, 1998, p. 33.

170–171 Generations of tools (and Table 8.2a, b): Edward De Bono, *Eureka! An Illustrated History of Inventions from the Wheel to the Computer* (New York: Holt, Reinhart & Winston, 1974); *Information Please Almanac 1994* (Boston: Houghton Mifflin, 1994); North, *Wall Chart of Science and Invention*; Abbott Payson Usher, *A History of Mechanical Inventions* (New York: McGraw Hill, 1988).

174–175 Emotional intelligence: Daniel P. Goleman, *Emotional Intelligence: Why It Can Matter More Than IQ* (New York: Bantam Books, 1997).

175 Median weekly wages, education, and projected job growth, by occupation (and Table 8.3): George T. Silvestri, "Occupational Employment to 2005," *Monthly Labor Review*, November 1995, pp. 60–84; *Employment and Earnings,* January 1998, table 39, "Median Weekly Earnings of Full-Time Wage and Salary Workers by Detailed Occupation and Sex," pp. 209–214; U.S. Bureau of Labor Statistics, "Industry and Occupation Tables," table 10, "Employed Persons by Occupation, Years of School Completed, Sex, Race, and Hispanic Origin (25 to 64 Years), Annual Average 1997 (based on CPS)" (unpublished data).

Chapter 9
The Great American Growth Machine

181 Maslow's hierarchy of needs and wants: Bryan Adam, "Looking for a Purpose in a Paycheck," *New York Times*, June 21, 1998, section 4, p. 1.

181–182 Portion of household budget spent on food, clothing, and shelter: Evan Jacobs and Stephanie Shipp, "How Family Spending Has

Changed in the U.S.," *Monthly Labor Review*, March 1990, pp. 20–27, especially table 2, "Consumption Expenditures of Urban Wage Earner and Clerical Consumer units, 1901 to 1986–87"; U.S. Bureau of Labor Statistics, *Consumer Expenditure Survey 1995*, "Average Annual Expenditures and Characteristics of All Consumer Units, 1984–95," at the BLS Website, ftp://ftp.bls.gov/pub/special.requests/ce/standard/y8495.txt.

182 BLS forecast of household budget outlays: Norman C. Saunders, "The U.S. Economy to 2005," *Monthly Labor Review*, November 1995, pp. 10–28, particularly table 3, "Personal Consumption Expenditures, 1983, 1993, and Projected to 2005."

182–183 Household spending, by income level: U.S. Bureau of Labor Statistics, *Consumer Expenditure Survey, 1995,* table 2, "By Income Before Taxes: Average Annual Expenditures and Characteristics of All Consumer Units," at the BLS Website, ftp://ftp.bls.gov/pub/special.requests/ce/standard/1995/income.txt, accessed September 26, 1998. Income figures in 1997 dollars.

183 Volunteering, by income level: *Statistical Abstract: 1997,* table 613, "Percent of Adult Population Doing Volunteer Work: 1995," p. 391.

185 Size of the service sector: *Employment and Earnings,* January 1998, table 14, "Employed Persons by Detailed Industry, Sex, Race, and Hispanic Origin," p. 187–191.

186 Overestimate of inflation: Senate Advisory Committee to Study the Consumer Price Index, *Toward a More Accurate Measure of the Cost of Living: Final Report to the Senate Finance Committee,* December 4, 1996; Brent R. Moulton, "Bias in the Consumer Price Index: What Is the Evidence?" *Journal of Economic Perspectives,* Fall 1996, pp. 159–177.

186 Per capita GDP in 1997 and 1776: Alan C. Stockman, *Macroeconomics* (Harcourt Brace/The Dryden Press), table 9.2, "Per Capita Real GDP in 1994 Dollars," p. 227; U.S. Bureau of Economic Analysis, *Survey of Current Business,* August 1998, table 2A, "Real Gross Domestic Product," pp. 151–152, and table 3, "Price Indexes and the Gross Domestic Product and Gross Domestic Purchases Implicit Price Deflators," p. 159; U.S. Bureau of the Census, "Resident Population Projections of the United States: Middle, Low, and High Series, 1996–2050," at the Census Bureau Website, http://www.census.gov/population/projections/nation/npaltsrs.txt, accessed September 28, 1998. Figures in constant (1997) dollars.

187 Number of enterprises in the United States: U.S. Department of Commerce, *1992 Enterprise Statistics,* December 1997, ES92–1, table 1, "Company Statistics: 1992," p. 7.

189 Items stocked by supermarkets: Randalls Food & Pharmacy, at the Randalls Website, http://www.randalls.com/peapod1.htm, accessed September 28, 1998.

189 Gain in life expectancy: *Historical Statistics,* series B 107–115, "Expectation of Life (in Years) at Birth, by Race and Sex: 1900 to 1970,"

p. 55, and series B 126–135, "Expectation of Life at Specified Ages, by Sex, for Massachusetts: 1850 to 1949–51," p. 56; *Statistical Abstract: 1996*, table 118, "Expectation of Life at Birth, 1970 to 1994, and Projections, 1995 to 2010," p. 88.

189 Shortening of the workweek: Jeremy Atack and Fred Bateman, "How Long Was the Average Workday in 1880?" *Journal of Economic History*, March 1992, pp. 129–160; Edward F. Denison, *Why Growth Rates Differ* (Washington, D.C.: Brookings Institution, 1967), p. 363; Theresa Dis Greis, *The Decline of Annual Hours Worked in the United States Since 1947*, Manpower and Human Resources Studies, no. 10, The Wharton School (Philadelphia: University of Pennsylvania Press, 1984); *Employment, Hours, and Earnings, United States, 1909–94*, vol. 1, pp. 3–4; data for later years can be found in *Employment and Earnings*; Angus Maddison, *Dynamic Forces in Capitalist Development* (New York: Oxford University Press, 1991), p. 270; ibid., *Economic Growth in the West*, p. 228; *Worldbook Encyclopedia*, 1993 edition, vol. 12, p. 11, s.v.

Epilogue

200 Americans' preferred decade, by age: "Which Good Old Days?" *American Demographics*, April 1996, p. 35.

Index

African Americans, 78–82
Americans' Use of Time Project, 58–59
Artificial intelligence, 166
Automobile industry
competition in, 48
employment in U.S., 124–125
U.S. producers, 93
Automobiles
computer techology applications in, 32
costs and prices in terms of work time, 42–44
current number of styles, 37
improvements over time in, 32, 35
ownership of, 10–11
production and material innovations, 47–48

Baird, John Logee, 162
Balance of payments
U.S. merchandise, services, and capital account, 99–101
Benefits, nonwage
rise in (1970s–1990s), 18
Bionics, 169
Biotechnology, 169
Brainpower
earnings and income related to, 83–84
of Information Age, 25, 171
Businesses
avoid protecting existing, 191
black-owned, 79
Hispanic-owned, 79
in service sector, 143
job creation and losses in small, 115

Calculators
declining prices of hand-held, 44

Capital accumulation, 175
Capital flows
foreign investment in United States, 99–100
outflows from United States, 100
to United States from Japan, 101
Capitalism
conditions for, 192
critics of, xviii, 50, 199–200
imperfections in, 201–202
supporters of, 157
triumph of, 186–190
winning over socialism, 190
Cellular phones, 28–29, 31
declining prices of, 45
China, 99
time to reach U.S. living standards, 106
Churn, the
as engine of economic growth, 115–126
as process, 158
payoff from, 137. *See also* Downsizing; Labor market; Productivity; Technology
Comparative advantage
countries with, 102
sources and enhancement of, 103
U.S. industries with, 104
Competition
blaming foreign, 101–102
in evolving auto industry, 48
in firms' offerings to consumers, 187
interaction with innovation, 187–88
Japanese, 91–92
role in rise of living standards, 157

Competitiveness
doubts about American, 91–99
of United States in trade, 99–106
Computers
applications in automobiles, 32
costs of computing power, 45–46
every-day uses for, 27–28
improvements over time in,
33–34
in auto production and vehicles,
48
offering of services by, 153
palm-size, 34
Computer software
applications, 31
creation of, 27
Consumer demand
influence on economy's churning
motion, 123
mechanisms of free market to
meet, 190–194
ranking of wants and needs,
180–184
Consumer Price Index (CPI)
as instrument to measure
inflation, 18–21
comparison of prices of goods
(1970 and current), 39
Consumers
as force in free enterprise
economy, 187–188
debt burden of, 13–14
preferences of, 179–184
utility function of, 184
Consumer spending
Engel's law, 149
for services, 11–12, 148–152
on cultural activities, 60–61
Consumption
as indicator of well-being, 4
at different levels of income,
182–184
comparison of U.S. and other
country households, 95–96
data of American, 95–96
evolution of, 180–184
of poor people, 14–17
post–World War II, 47
present-day, 21
1970s era compared with present-
day, 5–12

Cost of living, falling real, 40–46
Credit system
consumer debt, 13–14
U.S., 192–193

Downsizing
as conservation, 135
by corporations, 112
criticism of, 53, 136–137
effect on labor market, 126,
128
effects in firms of, 126–133
firm-related, 106–115
firms' reasons for, 130–135
of farm-related labor, 128. See
also Job losses
Earnings
factors influencing variation in,
81
lifetime, 82–87
of women working at home,
81–82. See also Income;
Wages
Economic growth
criticism of slow U.S., 106–108
with savings and investment, 191
Economic performance
Information Age as next phase
of, 24–25
of United States (1950–1990s),
96
Economy, Japan
growth rate (1960s), 107–106
Economy, U.S.
compared to other countries,
92–98
comparison of present-day with
1970s, 5–12
creation of new jobs in, 112–113
criticism of, 6
driving force of, 187
effect of imports on, 103–104
growth rate (1990s), 106
history of economic development,
189
imperfections in and performance
of, xv–xviii
increased productivity in, 48
job losses and layoffs, 112–113
mechanisms to maintain
successful, 190–194

Economy (*cont.*)
  myths related to, xiv–xv, 96, 99,
    195–196
  role in raising living standards,
    190
Edison, Thomas, 162
Education
  components of, 175
  for higher-paying jobs, 175–177
  for human capital, 175
  levels achieved by black and
    Hispanic workers, 79–81
  necessity of, 193
  school choice to improve quality
    of, 193
  women's economic gains related
    to, 80
Electronic mail
  everyday uses of, 27, 29
Emerson, Ralph Waldo, 157
Employment
  ebbs and flows of, 115–116
  EC policies to avert job loss,
    135–136
  effect of imports on, 104
  for workers losing jobs, 132
  in U.S. service sector
    (1960s–1980s), 141–143
  in U.S. transportation-related
    industries, 124–125
  sources in United States of
    opportunity for, 113
  total U.S. (1900–1997), 117, 120.
    See also Downsizing; Job
    creation; Job losses;
    Unemployment
Engel, Ernst, 149
Entertainment, new products, 29–30
Entrepreneurs
  in free-enterprise system, 137
  in service sector, 141–143
European Community (EC)
  averting job loss in labor markets
    of, 135–136
  economic performance in, 136
Exports, U.S. share, 94

Faggin, Federico, 162
Families
  incentives for two-income, 62–64
  incomes of two-income, 88

Fast-food industry, 147–148
Firms
  after downsizing, 126–133
  downsizing in United States,
    106–115
  effect of the economy's churning
    motion on, 121–127
  meeting needs of consumers,
    187–188
  U.S. publicly-traded, 93. *See also*
    Businesses
Foods
  costs and prices in terms of work
    time, 44
  post–World War II innovations,
    47
Free enterprise
  dynamic nature of, 191
  expectations created by, 201

Genomics, 169
Goods
  as part of services, 140–148
  costs of (1947–98), 149, 152t
Government
  effect of excess regulation by, 191
  role in free market economy, 189
  role in promoting free trade, 193
  role in retraining of unemployed,
    192
Gross Domestic Product (GDP),
    184–185

Happiness, xvi
Hispanics
  economic gains of, 78–82
Hoff, Ted, 162
Holography, 166
Hours of work. *See* Work time
Households
  appliances and conveniences, 10,
    25–30, 56, 95–96
  chores, 62
  consumption of U.S. compared to
    other countries, 95–96
  decrease in sizes of, 42
  financial contribution of working
    women, 64
  incentives for two-income, 62–64
  parents' work in two-parent,
    62–63

time devoted to chores of, 55–56
today's poor, 14–15
Housing
costs and prices in terms of work
time, 41–42
Human capital
creation of, 174
importance of, 193
in production process, 171
of Information Age, 170–171

Income
changes in lifetime earnings,
82–87
consumption at different levels of,
182–184
factors influencing variation in,
88
including fringe benefits, 18
in service sector, 148–156
real per capita rise in, 18–19. *See
also* Wages
Income distribution
economic reason for unequal,
87–89
factors influencing inequality of,
87–89
interpretation of statistics related
to, 70–72
lower ranks in, 82–83
Panel Survey of Income
Dynamics, 73–74
widening gap of, 88–89
Income per capita
dwindling U.S. LEAD, 107
in United States, 93–95
Industrial sector
displacement of some firms in
U.S., 121–123
job creation by new industries,
46–47
job losses in U.S., 114–115
job shifts related to new modes of
transportation,124–126
Inflation
adjustments in statistics for, 186
CPI as price index to measure,
18–21
flawed indexes of, 186
measured *versus* actual, 20–22,
186

Information
created, transformed, and moved
by modern tools, 170–173
demand for, 157
Information Age as next phase of
economic
development, 24–25
role of Internet in reducing costs
of, 45–46
via telemedicine, 31
Innovation
as catalyst for technologies,
28
as modern phenomenon, 25
conditions to encourage, 192
financing of, 49–50
in athletic equipment, 34–35
in medicine, 30–31, 169
interaction with competition,
187–188
tested in marketplace, 157–158
Institutionse in free market
economy, 192
Integration technology, 167
Intelligence
emotional (EQ), 174–175
intelligence quotient (IQ),
174–175
Internet, the
access to, 27
new jobs associated with, 117,
120t, 121
retail stores merchandizing on,
38–39
role in reducing costs of
information, 45–46
Inventions, 159
Investment
by Americans in money-earning
instruments, 13
in education, 175, 178
in human capital, 174
in United States by foreign
investors, 99–101

Jacquard, J. M., 162
Japan
competition in America from,
91–92
economic slump in, 92
foreign investment in, 101

Japan (*cont.*)
  investing in United States, 101
  lifetime employment system, 136
Job creation
  by new industries, 46–47
  in service sector, 146–147, 153
  replacement of old with new jobs,
    117–126
  sources in United States, 93–94,
    113–115
Job losses
  dealing with unemployment, 192
  fears related to, 65–66
  in sectors of U.S. economy, 14–15
  in United States (1990s), 112–113
  offset by new jobs with economic
    change, 124–126
  reality of, 112
  U.S. manufacturing sector, 129–133
  worker worries about, 198
Jobs
  avoid protecting existing, 191
  in service sector, 141–143
  workers with second and third, 58
  working at home, 66

Labor force
  characteristics of service sector,
    143, 145–146
  entitlements in EC member
    nations for, 136
  layoffs by U.S. firms (1990s),
    112–113
  new jobs for, 117–127
  ratio of women to men in, 80
Labor market
  EC averting job losses, 135–136
  effect of churning in the
    economy, 116–117, 120–127
  flexibility in today's, 66
  future skill-related demands, 121
  recycling in, 188. *See also*
    Downsizing; Employment; Job
    creation; Job losses
Leisure time
  choices related to income levels,
    183–184
  declining costs of activities in, 44
  entertainment, 61
  money allocated to leisure
    interests, 59

of workers (1973–98), 58
  time spent for, 59–61
  trend toward more, 54–59
Living standard
  American advantage in, 95–96
  comparison of income groups
    (1975–1998), 76
  current compared to twenty-five
    years ago, 21–22
  effect of economy's churning on,
    128, 133
  factors influencing rise in, 63,
    137, 157, 190, 192
  indicators of U.S., 4–15, 36–39,
    76–78
  myths related to, xiv, 4, 6, 53,
    195–196
  of poor people (1990s), 14–16
  reality of, xv
  rising in nineteenth-century
    United States, 123
  with new and improved products,
    32–39

Manufacturing sector
  effect in United States of imports
    on, 103–105
  output and employment in
    United States (1990s), 93
  wage levels in, 146–147
Market, the
  as basis for U.S. economy, xviii
  factors influencing growth of,
    158–165, 179–180
  role in America's success, 189
  testing of innovation, 157
Maslow's Hierarchy, 181
Materials science, 168
Mazor, Stan, 162
Medical technology advances,
  30–31, 169
Men
  holding more than one job, 58
  wages of women compared to, 64
Micromachines, 168
Microprocessor
  routine chores and repetitive
    tasks of, 170–173
Minorities, 78–82
Misery index, xviii
Mobility, downward, 75, 82–83

Mobility, upward
  as measure of living standard,
    75–76
  in current economy, 89
  of minorities and women, 78–82
  pattern in Panel Survey, 73–76
  pattern in Treasury study,
    77–78
  reality of, xv
  with change in lifetime earnings,
    84–85
Money
  changing value of, 39–40
  exchange rate between time and,
    40
  time as, 40, 179
  value of, 194
Moore's law, 33–34

Nanotechnology, 168
National Automated Highway
    Systems Consortium,
    168–169
National Income and Product
    Accounts, 184–185
Noise-reduction technology, 167
Nordhaus, William, 20

Occupations
  changes in (1900–1990s),
    117–127
  education for higher-paying jobs,
    175
  shift related to new forms of
    work, 124–125
  women's choices of, 81–82
Opportunity
  basic needs for finding, 85–87
  measurement of, 72–77
Optics, 166
Ownership
  of autos, 10–11
  of homes by poor people, 14
  of private property, 190–191
  rates of home, 8–9

Panel Survey of Income Dynamics,
    University of Michigan,
    72–77
Pharmaceutical industry, 30–31
Photonics, 166

Physical capital, past and future,
    171
Poverty
  decline in number of poor people
    (1949–1980s), 16–17
  median duration (1990s), 74
Poverty rate
  1970–1997, 14–16
  adjusted for inflation, 16
Prices
  comparison of (1970 and
    current), 39–51
  initial prices for new products,
    49–50
  maintenance of stable, 194
Production methods, old and
    modern, 36
Productivity
  after downsizing, 126–133
  as determinant of time's value,
    40–45
  factors in increased, 48
  gains in European Community,
    136
  increases with new technologies,
    48, 188–189
  myths related to, 64
  of U.S. industries and businesses,
    93
Products, consumer
  declining prices of, 44–46
  emerging technologies in,
    165–170
  improvements over time, 32–35
  initial investment to develop,
    49–50
  in modern autos, 32
  measuring value of, 184–185
  new products entering U.S.
    markets, 24, 39
  post–World War II innnovations,
    47
  predicted prices of future new,
    46–47
  rich people as purchasers of high-
    priced new, 48–50
  variety of models, colors, and
    styles, 36–39
Property rights, 190–191
Protection, trade, 101–102
Publishing industry, 38

Recognition technology, 167
Recreation, 30. *See also* Leisure time
Retail stores
    access on the Internet, 38–39
    space and specialization, 38
Retirement, 56–57
Ricardo, David, 102
Robinson, John, 59
Robotics, 167

Saving, 121–123
School choice, 193
Schumpeter, Joseph, 49, 116
Services
    consumer demand for, 153–156
    consumer spending for,
        148–152
    costs of (1947–1998), 149, 152t
    factors in rise in value of, 149,
        151
Service sector
    as percentage of U.S. economy,
        185
    balance of trade in services,
        99–106
    businesses in and components of,
        139–148
    consumer spending in, 148–149
    contributions to everyday life,
        148
    growth and diversity of, 143,
        145–146
    household, personal, and
        information services in,
        153–156
    output of and employment in,
        141–143
    wage levels in, 146–147. *See also*
        Fast-food industry
Sholes, Christopher Latham, 162
Slesnick, Daniel, 16
Smith, Dale, 32
Specialization
    comparative advantage in
        national, 102
    gains from, 63
    in auto industry, 47
Sports
    increased participation in
        (1970–1994), 59–60
    spectator, 60

Statistical measurement
    inaccuracies of official, 186
    of Gross Domestic Product (GDP),
        184–185
    of National Income and Product
        Accounts, 184–185
Stock market performance, U.S.
    (1990s), 93

Tariffs, 104, 106
Taxes, 191
Technology
    advances in modern medical,
        30–31, 169
    applications in modern
        production process, 31
    as fuel for the churn, 158
    cellular, 28–29
    effect on everyday life, 35
    everyday uses of computer
        technology, 27–28
    increased need for service with,
        153
    increase in productivity with,
        188–189
    maturing of emerging, 165–170
    Moore's law, 33–34
    myth and reality, 158–165
    performance of U.S., 93–94
    spillovers, 163
Telephone industry
    employment in (1970, 1996),
        128–129
    workers displaced (1920–98),
        159–160. *See also* Cellular
        phones
Television
    current number of models and
        channels, 37–38
    declining prices of, 44–45
    innovations with growth of cable,
        38–39
    predicted prices of high-
        definition, 46
Thoreau, Henry David, 40
Time
    costs and prices expressed in
        currency of, 40–41
    is money, 40, 179. *See also* Leisure
        time; Work time
    as scarce resource, 54

Trade
  advantages of open system of,
    102
  promotion of free trade, 193
  role in determining jobs
    available, 104
  United States as leader in
    international, 94
  U.S. tariffs, 104, 106. *See also*
    Balance of payments;
    Protection, trade
Transportation innovations,
  123–126
Treasury Department study of
  income, 76–78
Twain, Mark, xvii
Unemployment
  European Community, 136
  recommendation for dealing
    with, 192
  United States, 136
United States
  as Number One producer, 93
  comparative advantage for, 103
University of Michigan, Panel
  Survey on Income Dynamics,
  72–77

Van Buren, Martin, 133–134
Virtual reality, 167
Volunteer work, 61

Wages
  as barometer of living standards,
    4–5
  determined by productivity, 40
  in low-skilled occupations, 178
  in manufacturing sector, 146–147
  in service sector, 146–147
  myths and reality of, 17–22, 53
  nonmonetary benefits as percent
    of, 18

of women compared to men,
    64
  of workers with higher education
    degrees, 175–178
Welfare, consumer, 45
Women
  economic gains of, 78–82
  financial contribution of working,
    64
  holding more than one job, 58
  wages of men compared to, 64
  working at home, 81–82
  working outside home
    (1970–1995), 58, 62
Workers
  efficiency of American, 54–56,
    63–67
  human capital of, 170–178
  layoffs from U.S. companies,
    112–113
  wages and benefits as total
    compensation, 18
Workplace
  improved conditions in
    (1975–1998), 64–67
  increased number of women in,
    58, 62–64
  on-the-job leisure pursuits, 67
  working conditions, 67
Work time
  costs of household products in
    terms of, 42–43
  for household chores, 55–56,
    62–63
  leisure pursuits during, 67
  prices and costs expressed in,
    40–51
  second and third jobs, 58
  to buy consumer products, 46
  working less, 54–59
World Competitiveness Report, World
  Economic Forum, 94